Talking Problems

SUNY series in Communication Studies
Dudley D. Cahn, editor

Talking Problems

Studies of Discursive Construction

RICHARD BUTTNY

State University of New York Press

Published by
State University of New York Press, Albany

Printed in the United States of America

For information, address State University of New York Press,
90 State Street, Suite 700, Albany, N.Y., 12207

Production by Diane Ganeles
Marketing by Michael Campochiaro

Library of Congress Cataloging-in-Publication Data

Buttny, Richard.
Talking problems : studies of discursive construction / Richard Buttny.
p. cm. — (SUNY series in communication studies)
Includes bibliographical references and index.
ISBN 0-7914-5895-4 (alk. paper)
1. Discourse analysis. 2. Interpersonal communication. 3. Social interaction. 4. Oral communication. I. Title. II. Series.

P302.B88 2003
302—dc21

2002045259

10 9 8 7 6 5 4 3 2 1

For jrc

Contents

Acknowledgments ix

Introduction 1

Part I: Tellings in Talking Problems

1. Ascribing Problems and Positionings in Talking Student Teenage Parent 19
2. Clients' and Therapist's Joint Construction of the Clients' Problems 43
3. Therapeutic Humor in Retelling the Clients' Tellings 71

Part II: Reportings in Talking Problems

4. Reported Speech in Talking Race on Campus 95
5. Demanding Respect: The Uses of Reported Speech in Discursive Constructions of Interracial Contact, *with Princess L. Williams* 123
6. Discursive Constructions of Racial Boundaries and Self-Segregation on Campus 149
7. Conclusion 169

Appendix 183

Notes 187

References 191

Name Index 207

Subject Index 211

Acknowledgments

This book is an outgrowth of prior studies originally written as journal articles. Five of these chapters began as journal articles and were revised for this volume. Revising the articles for a book allowed me to remove inconsistencies and errors. Also, in revisiting the studies I was able to look at the connections among them and to examine the findings in a broader theoretical framework. Chapter 3 is a slightly revised version of "Clients' and therapist's joint constructions of the clients' problem," *Research on Language and Social Interaction, 29* (1996) and chapter 4 of "Therapeutic humor in retelling the clients' tellings," *Text, 21* (2001). Chapter 5 is a revision of "Reported speech in talking race on campus," *Human Communication Research, 23* (1997), chapter 6 of "Discursive constructions of racial boundaries and self-segregation on campus," *Journal of Language and Social Psychology, 18* (1999), and chapter 7 of "Demanding respect: The uses of reported speech in discursive constructions of interracial contact," *Discourse & Society, 11* (2000) (coauthored with Princess L. Williams).

Many folks have helped me along the way in preparing this book through conversations, data sessions, and responses to papers. The Bakhtinian notion that others' voices appear in your own writing is clearly evident in these pages. In particular I would like to acknowledge Bill Benoit and an anonymous reader for their comments on the complete manuscript. The series editor, Lee Cahn, was very encouraging and the production editor, Diane Ganeles, helped me pull it all together. Most of all, I am grateful for Jodi Cohen—my severest critic and caring supporter throughout—along with Daisy and Oscar, dear companions all.

Introduction

The idea for this book grew out of conducting a series of studies that dealt with talk about problems of various sorts—problems of being a teenage parent in high school, problems of interpersonal relationships during therapy, and problems of racism and interracial relations on a university campus. In each of these contexts, some critical evaluation gets articulated by participants such that certain actions, events, or states-of-affairs are taken as problems. These problem formulations open up a variety of responses, positionings, and remedies from participants. How such problems are told, oriented to, criticized, and accounted for—in short, talked about—will be the foci of these studies.

The use of "talking" in the title[1] is meant to highlight the turn to taking talk seriously as a way to understand diverse phenomena such as problems. Talk, and the related notions of conversation, language use, and communication, are important because of their formative functions in cocreating social realities. Talk is the primary site for human sociability. As Langenhove and Harré put it, "within conversations . . . the social world is created" (1999, p.15; also cf. Cronen, 1995). This "the formative function of talk" view takes issue with the structural notion that activities like talking problems are, well, just talk. Talk is said to be largely inconsequential due to larger, or underlying, realities that structure action. What really matters are social structures such as institutional realities, power, or socioeconomic status, or on a psychological level, underlying attitudes or cognitive schemata. On this traditional view, talk is merely at a micro level and is constrained by, or an epiphenomenon of, these more important social or psychological structures. At best, talk is a vehicle for communication, a conduit for conveying our cognitive contents (Reddy, 1979; Stewart, 1995; Edwards, 1997). However, when we consider problems at the local level, at how participants make sense of and communicate about their circumstances, talking problems matter to them in terms of responsibility, possible options, being understood, and the like. That is, persons formulate, orient to and act towards such states-of-affairs as problematic.

Another key word in the title is "problems." This is not to say that all of the talk in the data is about problems, but problems are a central feature. We will see that participants talk about the problems of being too young to be a parent and the difficulties of being a student and a parent, the problems of openness and trust in relationships as discussed in a therapy consultation, or the problems of everyday racism and race relations on campus. While each of these contexts may be said to involve problems, we will need to get down to the specific communicative practices and practical-moral realities thereby created.

Dictionary definitions of 'problem' offer some interesting leads. The *American Heritage Dictionary* (Morris, 1975) defines 'problem' as "A question or situation that presents uncertainty, perplexity, or difficulty." The *OED's* definition begins, "Literally, a thing thrown or put forward; hence, a question propounded for solution" (Simpson & Weiner, 1991). A problem can be said to be a formulation of a situation as a difficulty; it creates uncertainty or perplexity as to what to do next. How the problem gets articulated by participants will be crucial in understanding the situation. Problems are linguistic abstractions from actions or events, which come to constitute that state-of-affairs for certain actors. Also, problems call for solutions. Just as interlocutors can disagree as to the nature of the problems, so they can disagree as to what is to be done about it.

Communication research, and the social sciences generally, have a long legacy of focusing on social problems (Benson, 1985; Manicas, 1987). The approach taken here will not look at problems as theoretically driven "big issues" or in terms of policy, but rather as ordinary persons' concerns—how participants orient to, communicate about, and act towards events as problems (Maynard, 1988). Problems emerge from the flow of circumstances and get identified, defined, told, framed, and reframed in various ways (Brenneis, 1996). Problems can be told through various communicative actions such as narratives, claims, descriptions, accusations, complaints, and the like. Problem tellings range from in-depth narratives to cursory accounts, from open conflict to indirect allusions, from recounting past events to imagining future possibilities. Problems can be seen as having a kind of "natural history"—initially vague or unnoticed, becoming increasingly recognized, then discussed with others, possibly leading to conflict or even bringing in third parties as mediators (Emerson & Messinger, 1977). Who or what gets identified as "a problem" can have important social or material consequences (Tracy & Muller, 2001).

Any human activity has the possibility of being done poorly and so can be said to go wrong or fail in various ways. Going wrong or failing can disrupt the routine, taken-for-granted understandings of everyday life from which problems can arise (Garfinkel, 1967). What counts as a "problem" is itself a member's gloss. The notion of problems dovetails with related notions in the literature such as troubles, failure events, incidents, disputes, conflict, and so on. The notion of "troubles" gets developed by Jefferson's "troubles-telling sequence in ordinary conversation" (Jefferson, 1980, 1988; Jefferson & Lee, 1981). To give an overview of this sequence, the trouble is "approached" by various "initiating" moves or "premonitorings." The trouble gets "arrived" at by an "announcement" that projects a "response" from the recipient. The "delivery" of the troubles is done through an "exposition," such as by description of symptoms or events. Various "diagnoses, remedies, or reports of other experiences" may get "worked up" by participants. The troubles-talk is brought to possible "closing" by "optimistic projection," "an invoking of the status quo," or "a making light of the trouble." Finally an "exit" is achieved by a "closure" or "transition into other topics." This trouble-telling sequence is "elegant but weak" (Jefferson, 1988, p. 439) in that no actual empirical instances were found that contained all of these elements in this ordering. This trouble-telling sequence is useful, however, as a "template" for examining the varied ways of doing troubles talk.

Troubles-telling often converged with related activities such as (i) "building a case" in which a trouble constituted a misdeed, (ii) "negotiating a plan" in which a trouble constitutes an obstacle, or (iii) "dispute" in which a trouble constitutes a source of contention (Jefferson & Lee, 1981, p. 402). These three activities, so to speak, "contaminate" the troubles telling in the sense that different components and trajectories enter the interactional sequence. For instance with a "dispute," a troubles telling leads a recipient to offer advice which, in turn is disputed by the teller. So instead of troubles telling, with the focus on the teller and his/her experiences, we find with a dispute the focus is on "the problem and its properties" (Jefferson & Lee, 1981, pp. 41; 413; 416). This is a useful distinction between the troubled person and their tellings of what troubles them on the one hand, and the problem and its properties on the other. The studies of this volume mostly focus on the latter. The problem and its properties lead to talk such as formulations of the problem, blames, remedies, accounts, and the like.

Morality is inextricably bound up with social interaction. What counts as a problem implicates some sense of morality or protomorality (Bergmann, 1998). Problems and their implicated moral systems are seen by the speech activities of praise or blame, approval or disapproval, respect or disrespect. A people's morality or protomorality gets displayed through their discursive assessments, evaluations, or judgments of actions or persons.

Analytic Perspectives and Methods

> Social conduct and social relations are essentially accountable phenomena. They are constituted through our practices of reporting, describing, and reasoning—and therein lies the central role that language plays in conducting social reality. Any consideration of the accountability of social conduct brings directly into focus moral dimensions of language use: in the (interactional) circumstances in which we report our own or others' conduct, our descriptions are themselves accountable phenomena through which we recongnizably display an action's (im)propriety, (in)correctness, (un)suitability, (in)appropriateness, (in)justice, (dis)honesty, and so forth. Insofar as descriptions are unavoidably incomplete and selective, they are designed for specific and local interactional purposes. Hence they may, always and irretrievably, be understood as doing moral work—as providing a basis for evaluating the "rightness" or "wrongness" of whatever is being reported (Drew, 1998, p. 295).

This passage from a recent article by Paul Drew succinctly states some of the issues to be investigated here. Persons naturally make criticisms, complaints, or blames in portraying what happened and who is responsible. Persons can be held accountable for their actions. Here we want to further develop this notion of "the social accountability of communication" (Buttny, 1993). The analytic concern is in how participants talk about and account for actions, events, or states-of-affairs as problems, and in so doing jointly construct the problem's significance, magnitude, and solubility.

The content of the various problems participants discuss here—intimate relationships, teen parenthood, and race/racism—will be taken as joint constructions. The interest is in how participants' versions of events get heard and oriented to as problems, what interactionally unfolds as a consequence of this, how participants' position themselves, and what social realities are thereby created or recreated. The notion of the coconstructed character of problems will be a central issue here. In looking at talking problems the challenge is to uncover interesting aspects of the phenomena beyond just stating what the problems are about, the content of the talk. One way to do this is to consider *how* we engage in problem talk, the *practices* used to talk problems. Secondly, given that someone is often said to be responsible or accountable for problems, how do participants *position themselves*, or *others*, in the course of talking problems. How persons talk about problems and how they position themselves result in certain representations of the events getting told—the *discursive construction* of problems.

The analytic perspectives of discursive constructionism and conversation analysis will be drawn on to approach the social accountability of talking problems. A sketch of these perspectives is offered along with a statement of how they will be used as methods.

Discursive Constructionism

It is widely recognized that a person, an action, event, or state-of-affairs can be described in more than one way—as problematic or not, and with varying shades of culpability. An interesting feature of talking problems is the malleability of "the problem" by different interlocutors' versions of it. This malleability of the problem through talk is why we have adopted the perspective of discursive constructionism.

Problems are taken as "discursive constructions," meaning by this that problems get conjointly constructed through persons' evaluations and assessments in talk (Edwards, 1997; Potter, 1996). Problems have no independent existence apart from humans' versions and evaluations of them.

The particular version of the problem is always situated and offered to some particular recipients. In any situation there may be certain facts of the matter, conditions about which all would agree, such as the fact of being a student teenage parent. But that this fact gets taken as a problem by participants, to what degree, and with what consequences, is a matter that is interactionally achieved.

Persons can be said to have a "stake" (Potter, 1996) in their portrayal of events or in their own or others' positionings. In talking problems, a person may position him/herself in a desired manner in order to, for instance, look good, avoid responsibility, be liked, and so on. This preferred presentation of persons, actions, events, states-of-affairs, institutions, and the like involves rhetoric (Sanders, 1995; Billig, 1996; Tracy, 2002). Traditionally, rhetoric has examined political concerns on a more macrolevel, but rhetoric is found on the interactional level as well, particularly in dealing with problems. As Tracy (2002) puts it, "A rhetorical perspective assumes people talk in particular ways in order to accomplish desired identities (or avoid disvalued ones) . . . Communicators select one way of talking rather than another in order to present themselves and altercast others in particular ways" (pp. 26–27). Rhetoric provides a useful lens for the analysis of how events are portrayed and persons get positioned. For instance, in a court of law a defendant's description of what happened is not simply a neutral representation of events; obviously there are interests at stake that lead to certain rhetorical practices in retelling events. So rhetoric can be seen at work in the positionings that persons take up, their altercasting or positioning of others, and their version of events.

During talk-in-interaction, participants position themselves relative to each other. Positioning involves a person's stance towards him/herself, or towards the interlocutor(s), in the course of communication. As Langenhove and Harré (1999) define it, "A position in a conversation, then, is a metaphorical concept through reference to which a person's 'moral' or personal attributes as a speaker are compendiously collected. One can position oneself or be positioned as e.g., powerful or less, confident or apologetic, dominant or submissive, definitive or tentative, authorized or unauthorized" (p.17). These attributes of the person may be preexisting (e.g., as part of one's identity or reputation) or they may emerge through the encounter. These attributes can be used as a conversational resource to notice something about oneself or another—to avow the quality as one's own, to ascribe it to an interlocutor, or attribute it to a third party. These personal attributes in positioning become particularly visible in talking problems because they matter in how persons are seen in terms of reputation or social accountability.

Positioning is an extension of the notion of subject positioning from narrative theory (Davies & Harré, 1999). Within a narrative there is a range of possible subject positions that a character can take on that can be coherent within that narrative. So we can speak of "being positioned" by the narrative. Certain discourses make available certain positionings that persons can take up. For instance, the traditional discourses of gender offer men and women certain positionings in relation to each other that they can take up [Hollway, 1984 (cited in Langenhove & Harré, 1999, p. 16)].

Positioning is also an interactive construct; it involves how persons become characterized within a jointly produced narrative or conversation. One may be said "to position oneself," or "be positioned by others," in talk-in-interaction. Interactants can negotiate and change their positionings and reposition themselves.

Positioning has an affinity with Goffman's notion of "footing" in that each attempts to capture persons' locations with respect to each other. As Goffman puts it, "A change in footing implies a change in the alignment we take up to ourselves and others present as expressed in the way we manage the production and reception of an utterance" (1981, p. 128). Footing is perhaps most evident in changes of footing—for instance, changes of footing from serious to humorous, from involved to distant, and the like. While the notions of footing and positioning seem quite similar, we will use footing to capture a person's stance toward what is being said and use positioning to capture more person-level alignments. So, in a conversation one's footing may be in agreement or disagreement, involved or distant, serious or ironic, and so on. Positioning, on the other hand, involves avowed or ascribed characterizations of the person, e.g., as joyful or bereaved, as dutiful or unfortunate, as realistic or unrealistic, and so on (Bamberg, 1997; n.d.).

When positionings are seen as contradictory, that can create a problem for a person. In everyday life there are any number of contradictory positions that can be taken as problematic, for instance, a friend who betrays a best friend, an instructor who does not teach well, or in an intimate relationship, not being open with one's partner. These are "contradictory positions," not as a function of formal logic, but as a matter of our socio-logic. "Contradictory" in the sense of the conventional understandings of these positionings in society. One's actions may be seen to be inconsistent with one's positioning. Contradictory positions are conflicting discursive locations; their significance depends on how persons talk about, make sense of, and act toward such conflicting positions. Seeming contradictions, of course, can be explained away, made understandable and transformed as not problematic—they can be "reconciled or remedied." But, in general, ascribing contradictory positions of another person can work to raise or formulate a problem for that person.

This notion of the positioning of persons can be supplemented by a parallel development in ethnomethodology—the notion of membership categories (Hester & Eglin, 1997; Watson, 1997). Persons can be identified by any number of membership categories, e.g., parent, child, student, teacher, young, old, and so on. Given the indefinitely large list of categories available, we need to consider what it reflects when any particular category is selected and made relevant in conversation. For any given membership category, there will be any number of qualities or predicates to describe an individual within that membership category, e.g., for parent, predicates such as loving, involved, supportive, and the like are quite familiar.

Certain predicates of a particular category may be seen as conflicting, as we will see in the following chapter—being a parent and a teenager and a student. The point being that ascribing "conflicting category predicates" of another can work as a way to raise a problem (Watson, 1978; Hester, 1998). This notion of "conflicting category predicates" converges with the above-mentioned "contradictory positions." For our purposes the important question becomes, What do these conflicting category predicates make relevant as a response or implicate for action? (Watson, 1997; Psathas, 1999). That is, how do persons orient to conflicting category predicates, and what do they do in response?

Discursive constructionism highlights how speech activities such as tellings, narratives, positionings, and category selection result in persons' sense of the social reality of the problem. We are interested in, not only the content of the problem, but also in how problems get interactionally constructed. The following perspective and methodology of conversation analysis offers us tools to further examine the interactional aspects of problem construction.

Conversation Analysis

Conversation Analysis is an outgrowth of ethnomethodology (Maynard & Clayman, 1990). Each has a concern with structure or organization of persons' knowledge and action. Problems can be conceived as being socially organized or structured in talk (Sacks, 1992). To get at this organization, the project is to describe our practices for talking problems. Talk is conceived as unfolding temporally and sequentially. To examine talk is to examine social action and interaction; this is why the term has been coined, "talk-in-interaction" (Schegloff, 1980). The focus is on what interlocutors are doing in and through their utterances. In speaking one is doing things with words, performing actions, and thereby projecting or "sequentially implicating" (Schegloff, 1984) a certain range of responses from others. For instance, uttering a criticism may lead the recipient to deny, apologize, account, and the like. Should the recipient fail to respond in one of the range of relevant ways, this absence will be noticeable and accountable. Interlocutors display to one another an understanding or agreement, or lack thereof, with one another's utterances. What the recipient takes from prior turn and makes relevant in his/her response will display certain understandings and evaluations of the prior. Participants orient to each others' actions and understandings on an ongoing, moment-by-moment basis.

Conversation analysis conceives of talk as coconstructed or jointly produced through interlocutors' communicative practices. "Coconstructed" in the sense that, for instance, how a problem is told and interactionally unfolds depends on interlocutors' versions, reactions, and uptakes (Schegloff, 1982; Mandelbaum, 1993). The claim, "communication is coconstructed," is by now nearly axiomatic, not only in conversation analysis, but throughout communication studies and related disciplines. However, the particular ways this coconstruction is achieved through communicative practices in different contexts is often overlooked in empirical analysis.

Conversation analysis views context as empirically available in the talk-in-interaction. Instead of the traditional approach, where context gets invoked by the researcher as ethnographic background knowledge to further interpret the text, conversation analysis argues that context needs to be oriented to by the participants in order to be deemed relevant for them (Schegloff, 1991). Contextual features, such as institutions (e.g., courtroom talk, classroom discourse) or features of the persons involved (e.g., race-class-gender), need to be displayed, marked, or oriented to by the participants in some empirical way.

Summary

The social accountability in talking problems gets developed by drawing on the perspectives of conversation analysis and discursive constructionism. Through avowals, ascriptions, accounts, narratives, and other communicative practices, participants construct moral or social realities. The focus here will be on *communicative practices*, *positionings*, and *constructions—how problems get interactionally formed and oriented to,* and *how interlocutors position themselves in the course of such problem talk*. The different perspectives on teen parenthood, therapeutic discourse, and race relations will be covered in these respective chapters.

Methods

The following is a reconstruction of the methods used in the studies of the following chapters. The data is drawn from tape recordings of various communication contexts. Videotapes of a lunchtime conversation in high school and a school-family meeting are used in chapter 2. Videotapes of therapy consultations are used for chapters 3–4. Audiotapes of conversations on race matters are used in chapters 5–7. More specific discussion about how the tape recordings were gathered and other issues pertaining to the individual study are given in each chapter.

The tape recordings used in the studies were initially watched or listened to a number of times. From these repeated lookings and listenings a sense of what is going on on the recordings gradually began to arise. Transcripts were drawn up of the relevant sections of the tapes to aid the observations. The transcripts were made using a Jefferson-like format (see Appendix for transcription conventions). The transcripts were read numerous times along with observing the tapes.

From these observations, what the participants are doing, how they are orienting to each other, and how the interaction unfolds began to come into better focus. Descriptive claims as to what the participants are up to were provisionally put forward. These claims were further scrutinized and revised by further reexamining the transcripts and tape recordings. This way of working involves a tacking back and forth among the observations of the tapes and transcripts and analytic claims to check, refine, and better articulate and describe the actions and interactions.

Another aspect of the methods process involves seeing the data in terms of the analytic perspectives (such as the perspectives described above). Methods put the analytic perspective into practice. Observations are unavoidably theory-laden (Brown, 1977). But we are not prisoners of our perspective; sometimes the observations take us beyond our analytic notions, and we can extend, qualify, or correct our perspective. Our perspective should guide us, but not blind us. So this step involves adequate knowledge of the analytic perspective's vocabulary in order to apply it to the data. This step is often taken for granted or ignored in discussion of methods.

The following analytic questions were posed in observing the data, the tapes, and transcripts. Some data seem to reveal more to certain questions than to others. The following list should not be used in a mechanical-like fashion or necessarily in this order. Also, this list is not meant to be in an order. The questions should be considered as both a means of discovery into what is going on on the tapes and transcripts, and as a way to substantiate one's claims. As regards the latter, methods are seen here as a way to build an argument or make a case to support analytic claims about the data (Jackson, 1986; Jacobs, 1990). Following methods does not guarantee insight or sound knowledge claims, but offers a way to be systematic, so other analysts can see how you got there.

1. Having selected a phenomenon to study (e.g., reported speech, narrative, ascribing problems), describe its identifying characteristics or qualities. By what criteria do we know that this stretch of talk, these transcribed words on the page, count as the phenomenon in question?

2. Look at the phenomenon as part of an interactional sequence. Consider the circumstances or conditions that make the phenomenon relevant. Why this now? In what sequential environments does the phenomenon occur?

3. Consider what the phenomenon makes relevant. That is, what does it project or sequentially implicate as a response from recipients? (Step number two looks to the antecedents to the phenomenon, while this step focuses on the consequents of it).

4. Examine how participants' display an orientation to the phenomenon (Beach, 1990). How do recipients take the phenomenon, understand it, or evaluate it as displayed in their talk? This has been called "a next-turn proof procedure" (Hutchby & Wooffitt, 1998) in conversation analysis. When this is available in the data, it provides a powerful technique to examine how communicators orient to what each other is doing. Given that typically there is a range of possible next moves to a prior utterance, consider what the actual, particular move displays about the participants' understanding, positioning, or alignment.

5. Look to how is the phenomenon conjointly produced by participants. That is, instead of viewing the phenomenon as what an individual is doing, consider how participants mutually accomplish the doing of the phenomenon.

6. Is the phenomenon part of a larger discourse unit? For instance, reported speech is commonly located within a larger structure of a narrative or argument. Describe how the phenomenon fits within the larger structures. How does it function within this discourse unit?

7. Consider the rhetorical aspects of participants' versions of what happened. Look to how participants frame actions, events, or states-of-affairs in order to present their preferred version of discursive constructions of the social reality. How are these competing versions proffered by participants to be convincing?

8. Examine how participants position themselves, or are positioned by others, in the course of talk-in-interaction. Positioning involves the stance, location, or alignment that persons take up in relation to each other.

In the following chapters some of these questions will receive more attention than others in light of what the data offer.

Preview of Chapters

The various studies of talking problems will be arrayed into two sections and six chapters. Section one is comprised of three chapters, one on the difficulties of being a student teenage parent and the other two on problems in interpersonal relationships during therapy consultations. These studies are combined into this section because they all involve "tellings" in talking problems. Drawing on Shotter's (1981) distinction between "tellings" and "reportings," tellings involve first-person avowals of problems or second-person ascriptions of problems. First-person avowals as when "I" reveal, admit, or tell a problem. Second-person ascriptions as when one ascribes a problem of another, e.g., "You" did such-and-such. With tellings the participants are copresent, so the problem talk involves the pronouns "I" or "you."

Section two is comprised of three chapters on talk about racism and interracial relations. These conversations occur within one's own group. Much of the problem talk is about the racial other who is not copresent. This talk involves third-person "reportings," as in "he," "she," or "they" did (or did not do) such-and-such. These reportings are typically critical descriptions or evaluations of a racialized action, event, or state-of-affairs. These reportings come as much from firsthand experiences as from media stories or secondhand accounts. In reportings, the person(s) being described or criticized are not copresent to respond, defend themselves, or account.

Part I: Tellings in Talking Problems

CHAPTER 1, "ASCRIBING PROBLEMS AND POSITIONINGS IN TALKING STUDENT TEENAGE PARENT." This study examines two contexts in which a participant's positioning as a student teen parent becomes discussed. In the four peers conversation, being a father becomes contrasted with the person's age, leading to the ascription that he is too young to be a father. These conflicting aspects of the membership category, young father, are used to coconstruct problems. Such ascriptions of problems lead to various forms of responses in which the teen parent interactionally positions himself through concessions, narratives, and accounts. A second case study looks at a high school interview with a returning student mother and her family. The school's codirector uses a similar device of ascribing conflicting category predicates of the teen mother to articulate a potential problem. The grandmother's accounts are acknowledged, but not discussed, as solutions to the codirector's problem ascriptions. The possible institutional consequences of this problem ascription are presented by the codirector.

CHAPTER 2, "CLIENTS' AND THERAPIST'S JOINT CONSTRUCTION OF THE CLIENTS' PROBLEMS." This study examines how the rhetoric of therapeutic reframings gets interactionally achieved through the practices of telling clients about themselves and third-turn evaluations. The work of the therapist is contingent on the clients' narratives, responses, and positionings. Therapeutic retellings may draw on aspects of the clients' accounts; these retellings are designed as tentative, limited, and open to further revision from the clients. The therapist not only tells the clients about themselves, s/he also queries their responses to these tellings. Following the clients' problem-tellings, the therapist may attempt to reframe by: (a) giving minimal agreement and moving on to add a different account, (b) making relevant an aspect of something the client said but drawing different implications from it, or (c) using what the client has said as a conversational resource to formulate the therapeutic interpretation. One technique was for the therapist to position himself as aligned with the clients through confirming while simultaneously attempting to transform some aspects of the clients' version of the problem. The therapist engages the clients in coconstructing the problems and solutions.

CHAPTER 3, "THERAPEUTIC HUMOR IN RETELLING THE CLIENTS' TELLINGS." One of the principle activities of therapeutic discourse involves a "retelling the clients' tellings" (Holmgren, 1999). Telling the clients about themselves can be a delicate enterprise especially when such tellings differ from the clients' own tellings. One way to tell clients about themselves is to humorously exaggerate their condition. Humor seems to work to invoke a playful frame of clients' relational circumstances that disarms their resistance and creates an environment for presenting a contrasting interpretation. Humor seems to be a kind of fallback option for when the serious efforts of therapy are not working well. Humor arises in the sequential environments of repeated serious efforts at explaining a therapeutic version, of disagreements, or in pursing a response that is being withheld. The humor in therapy is not turn initial; it arises in response to some difficulty. Disagreements were the most common environment for using humor. Humor offers the therapist a way to reframe the ongoing interaction or the discursive position being advocated. While humor may be conceived of as a break from the serious activity of therapy, this is clearly not the case in many of the excerpts examined here. In broad strokes, the humor seems to work to disarm the clients' resistance while simultaneously offering an alternative vision of the relationship. The serious functions of humor can create a complication for the recipient in how to respond. There seems to be a duality in some humor in that one can orient to the humorous or the serious aspects of the utterance.

Part II: Reportings in Talking Problems

CHAPTER 4, "REPORTED SPEECH IN TALKING RACE ON CAMPUS." In talking race, university students sometimes report the speech of others, or themselves, to recreate what happened during an incident. Reported speech is used within narratives to vividly convey what was said, purportedly through the actor's own words, or as evidence to support general claims. The speaker is not merely reporting speech, but also assessing the problematic character of the actions performed through others' words. Reported speech is relevantly tied to assessment. Assessment reveals the reporting speaker's positioning towards the reported speech. The reported speech used in talking race presents the other as: ignorant, biased, racist, ridiculous, or honest. African Americans discursively portray Whites as unwilling to admit racism, as stereotyping, or as duplicitous in intergroup relations; while Whites frame African Americans as exaggerating racism or as overemphasizing their ethnicity. Representing others' actions through invoking their words is a way of criticizing, challenging, or resisting such troublesome racialized events.

CHAPTER 5, "DEMANDING RESPECT: THE USES OF REPORTED SPEECH IN DISCURSIVE CONSTRUCTIONS OF INTERRACIAL CONTACT." This investigation examines discursive uses of respect in talking about interracial contact. In discussing the documentary, *Racism 101*, the most frequently quoted portion by African-American and Latino participants was a segment on demanding respect from Whites. Our first study analyzes such discourse—reported speech—for what is made relevant from the original documentary segment. The participants' reported speech conveys little of the exact wording of the original, but does capture its spirit through using similar structural features: the repetition of 'respect,' a contrast between liking and respect, and addressing this to Whites. These uses of reported speech are participants' ways of performing the power of another's words in the sense of being able to articulate a compelling discursive position on an interracial problematic. The second study employs focus-group interviews to further explore the meanings of respect for African Americans. We examine narratives of disrespect during interracial contact in public places, such as during service encounters in stores. Participants' narratives told of being disrespected by being overly monitored, not receiving service, or being treated in a derogatory fashion, in short, the perception of being treated differently than Whites. Reported speech was used in these narratives to construct the White service worker's actions, how the narrator responded, what could have happened, or what in-group members say as an aggregate. Reported speech allows narrators to articulate the subtext to what is being said. Also, the evaluation of these incidents told of the emotional costs of being the recipient of disrespect.

CHAPTER 6, "DISCURSIVE CONSTRUCTIONS OF RACIAL BOUNDARIES AND SELF-SEGREGATION ON CAMPUS." This study examines North American college students' discursive constructions of identity, boundaries, and voluntary segregation on campus. Participants watched the documentary, *Racism 101*, at home with others and immediately afterwards tape recorded their discussion about the video and related race matters. None of the participants disagreed with the existence of separateness on campus, but offered different accounts and positions. Some criticized such self-segregation, while others justified it as understandable due to commonalties or differences. Still others were ambivalent or avowed conflicting accounts that seemed to reflect a dilemma, such as wanting more meaningful interracial contact but being unable to know how to achieve it. African Americans cited preserving group identity as a justification for boundaries. The findings fit with racial formation theory in that participants are partaking in different discourses so as to articulate, explore, or criticize different positions on interracial matters.

CHAPTER 7, "CONCLUSION." This final chapter is reflexive in that we reexamine our findings in terms of our approach of the social accountability of talking problems and the perspectives of discursive constructionism and conversation analysis. Also, we consider alternative interpretations of our data. In particular, we focus on issues of ethnicity, gender, and power. We end with some conjectures about change and the ownership of problems.

Part I

Tellings in Talking Problems

1

Ascribing Problems and Positionings in Talking Student Teenage Parent[1]

> (A) person understands themselves as historically continuous and unitary. The experiencing of contradictory positions as problematic, as something to be reconciled or remedied, stems from this general feature of the way being a person is done in our society (Davies & Harré, 1999, pp. 36–37).
>
> (T)o act rationally, those contradictions we are immediately aware of must beremedied, transcended, resolved or ignored (Davies & Harré, 1999, p. 49).

These two passages from Davies and Harré (1999) capture a phenomena to be examined here—the notion of "contradictory positions as problematic." Ascribing contradictory positions of another person can work to raise or formulate a problem for that person. Especially important for the present study is that one can position oneself, or one can be positioned by others, in jointly produced accounts. The focus here will be on *how problems get interactionally formulated by the actor and interlocutors,* and *how participants position themselves in relation to these problems.* To approach these questions, we examine the *conversational practices* interlocutors use in formulating, ascribing, and accounting for problems.

Student Teenage Parents

Within contemporary Western society, being a student teenage parent is a problematic position to be in. As a recent policy review puts it, "Teenage pregnancy and parenting are among the nation's greatest tragedies because of the burdens they impose on future generations . . . (A)n especially strong link has emerged between teenage parenthood, long-term welfare dependence, and poor outcomes for children" (Maynard, 1997, p. 89). Teenage parenthood is considered as a kind of "irrational behavior" in that teenagers do not intend to get pregnant and have families at an early age, and doing so conflicts with their own stated values (Maynard, 1997, p. 89–90). Other reviews of research make similar kinds of dire reports. "Teen mothers are less likely to complete high school than their classmates . . . Adolescent parenting results in a loss of human potential" (Card, 1999, pp. 257–258). The prospects for teenage parents do not seem promising.

While these trends present a portrait of major difficulties for the student teenage parent, our interest here is in how this positioning is taken at the local level. That is, how do participants in two different kinds of situations make sense of, orient to, and talk about being a student teenage parent?

Data

This study examines two conversations that involve discussion of being a student, teen parent. The two conversations are taken from Frederick Wiseman's documentary film, *High School II* (1994). The first is among four high school peers conversing at lunch break in which one of the participant's being a father becomes discussed. The second data segment is taken from a meeting among a returning high school student with her baby and her mother and brother meeting with the school's codirectors, a social worker, and the homeroom advisor. The two segments (12 minutes and 14 seconds, and 11 minutes and 8 seconds in length respectively) were adopted from the 3 hour and 40 minute documentary. A reviewer described Wiseman's approach to documentary, "There is no narration, no identification of characters. His camera simply settles in and eavesdrops" (James, July 6, 1994). Given this more naturalistic approach to filming, we adopt these segments as data, or talk-in-interaction.[2] Wiseman's documentaries have been used as source of data in other discourse studies (Buttny & Campbell, 1990; Mehan, 1990; Philipsen, 1990/91; Sanders, 1995; LaGrande & Milburn, in press).

Four Peers Conversation

Conflicting Category Predicates as Joint Achievement

In the following excerpt, four high school peers are having a conversation during a lunchtime break. The conversation touches on various topics, among them a story about leaving an infant alone in the back of a car, while the mother goes to work. While discussing this topic, one of the participants, BH, is asked about *his* child. Consider how BH's positioning, or membership category, as a parent becomes oriented to by participants.

Excerpt 1. Four peers.

(Note: pseudonyms are used to identify the participants.)

(Discussing leaving children alone in a car and BH's child's recent illness)

13 OW:	>How old is he?<
14 BH:	He's one (.) ↑how many months?
15	fourteen months, ↑something like that.
16 WH:	Fourteen that's
17 OW:	A month and two- a year and two m[onths
18 BH:	[A year
19	and two months, °something like that°
20 WH:	( )
21 OW:	( )
22 WH:	>How old are you BH<
23 BH:	I'm eighteen.
24	(1.1)
25 WH:	°Damn°
26 BH:	I'm eighteen and two months=no:::: h[hh
27 OW:	[hhhhhhh
28 BH:	I'm eighteen and (.) ↓I don't know
29	I'm about to be nineteen soon.
30	(1.9)
31 WH:	( ) being a father (dude)
32 BH:	°That's- that's one thing I::,° ↑[I never imagined=
33 NH:	[$And I remember you$
34 BH:	= myself be[ing a father

By way of background, this conversation shifts from discussing a news story (not shown in this excerpt) about a child being left in a car all day to WH's own child. This is the first point during the conversation in which BH's membership category as parent becomes mentioned. The topic of BH's child is not brought up by BH, but by an interlocutor, WH, by asking how the child is doing (not shown in this excerpt). BH tells about his child's recent illness, and then OW asks the child's age (line 13). A few moments later, WH asks BH how old he is (line 22). After BH tells his age, WH responds with "°Damn°" (lines 23–25). WH's, "°Damn°," can be heard as responsive to BH's age as a father, that is, to these "conflicting category predicates" (Hester, 1998) of BH being a father and being eighteen years old. In this sense, WH's "°Damn°," implicates a possible critical assessment or evaluation of BH. WH's assessment, "°Damn°," is mitigated somewhat by being momentarily withheld [the 1.1 second gap (line 24)] and being uttered somewhat quietly.

BH does not immediately address head-on the implicated assessment of WH's "°Damn°". Instead, he shifts footings and jokingly answers the question again about his age. BH uses a humorous child-like format by stating his age in years and months, which occasions laughter (lines 26–27). BH then restates his age, this time without irony, but corrected to almost nineteen (lines 28–29). This repetition of stating his age, corrected to almost nineteen, can be heard as responsive to WH's implicated assessment.

In response, WH explicitly raises the membership category of BH's "being a father" (line 31). The fact that BH is a father is already known by the participants. So WH's identifying BH as a father can be heard as "noticing" it (Schegloff, 1988) or drawing attention to it. WH's utterance, "(   ) being a father (dude)," can be heard as juxtaposed to BH's prior self-description, being almost nineteen (lines 29–31). This is more than a juxtaposition of descriptive facts; it underscores these contradictory positions or conflicting category predicates. Citing these conflicting category predicates is a way of formulating a problem.

BH's response (lines 32–34) displays that he takes these conflicting category predicates as raising a problem. While only a portion of WH's comment (line 31) is understandable from the videotape, BH's response goes along with WH's assessment. As BH avows, "I never imagined myself being a father" (lines 32–34), seemingly conceding to this problematic positioning of being a too-young father.

Before BH can further explain this avowal, NH comes in overlapping BH. BH and NH overlap for a moment, but BH drops out and lets NH continue before telling his side. Consider NH's story about BH (lines 35–41) and then BH's version of the story (lines 53–57).

Excerpt 2. Four peers

(Continuation of excerpt 1.)

32 BH: °That's- that's one thing I::,° ↑[I never imagined =

33 NH: [$And I remember you$

34 BH: = myself be[ing a father

35 NH: [$No I remember you, (.)

36 we used to hang out with Alvin? at his house

37 and he goes ↓hell:: no I'll never get a girl pregnant

38 and boom >he was the first one to get a girl pregnant

39 I remember that< (.) remember we used to be like

40 remember when BH used to say this.

41 ↓I'm like yep.$

42 BH: Always talk about people.

43 NH: We'd stay at Alvin's house . . .

((skip nine lines))

53 BH: I used to always talk about-

54 I used to see young girls having babies

55 I used to be like >damn< (.)

56 < what the hell they doin' man::. >

57 (.) and then it happened to me?

Looking at NH's brief narrative, he tells of a contrast between BH's words and actions (lines 37–38). NH uses direct speech attributed to BH, "he goes ↓hell:: no I'll never get a girl pregnant" (line 37). This reported speech is then immediately contrasted to the reported action of BH being the first to get a girl pregnant (line 38). Again we see an interlocutor juxtapose conflicting predicates about BH—in this case, between what he said and what he did.

BH goes along with NH's story, indeed, he adds to it (line 42). A moment later, BH tells his own story echoing NH's story (starting at line 53). BH also begins by contrasting what he said and what he did. BH's telling (lines 55–57) is structurally similar to NH's version (lines 37–38): each underscores the conflict between words and actions—that events went contrary to what he originally said. One important difference between these two versions lies in how BH's reported action positions himself as unwilling agent, "then it happened to me" (line 56). NH's formulation positions BH as a more active agent, "and boom >he was the first one to get a girl pregnant" (line 38). How events and agency are portrayed in narratives constitutes how actors are positioned in terms of accountability, e.g., as an active/passive agent, as (ir)responsible, as (un)fortunate, and the like.

Positioning Within the Narrative

In the following excerpt BH tells his story of becoming a father. Notice how he positions himself with respect to the pregnancy and the other people involved.

Excerpt 3. Four peers
(Continued from excerpt 2.)

58 BH:	But I- I didn't want to-
59	we didn't want to keep the baby ↓at first.
60	(1.5)
61	But then:: we had to keep it.=
62 WH:	=Why?
63 BH:	It was too la:te to do anything ↑about it.
64 OW:	How do you feel no[w
65 BH:	[When we told our parents::
66	↓she was already six months.
67 OW:	Six months. ↑Damn they didn't notice::?
68 BH:	No:: she ain't show:::
69 WH:	Girls they- don't be showin' man::
70 NH:	Especially she be wearing baggy clothes.
71 OW:	Yup:: (.) you get away with that.

72 BH: $Yep she got away with it 'til she was like six months $

73 then after that::[(.) every::body: was shocked::.

74 WH: [So- so how your parents take it

75 OW: Yeah. They got mad at y'all?

76 BH: My parents ↓didn't get mad,

77 ↑I mean they was ma:d yeah but

78 (1.3)

79 ↑what could they do about it?

80 OW: °That's true°

81 BH: But her- her parents was like

82 they're going to have to get married

83 (1.0)

84 WH: °Right°

85 BH: Not her parents but her gran:dmo:ther::. (.)

86 ↑so we did.

A striking feature of the way this narrative is told is through BH's use of a rhetoric of necessity—what he "had" to do. There are two aspects of necessity discourse at work in this narrative: the physical necessity of being pregnant and the practical necessity arising from that for practical action. Initially he contrasts what he wanted (corrected to "we" wanted) (lines 58–59), to what they "had" to do (line 61). BH explains the necessity of the situation, of having to have the baby, "It was too la:te to do anything ↑about it . . . ↓she was already six months" (lines 63–66). The practical implication of her being six months pregnant is that any choice in deciding to have the baby or not is removed as an option.

This resource of necessity is drawn on again a moment latter. In describing his parents' reactions, BH contrasts their being somewhat "mad" to the formulaic expression, "↑what could they do about it?" (lines 77–79). Again we see that the physical necessity implied here is presented as constraining actions. This physical necessity is also taken as making certain actions practically necessary—getting married. This is evident from the reported speech attributed to her parents, corrected to her grandmother, "they're going to have to get married" (line 82). And as he concludes, they followed this direction, "↑so we did" (line 86). His narrative of the physical necessity of the pregnancy is taken as creating an obligation, a practical necessity, which indeed they adhere to.

BH positions himself through the narrative as initially not wanting the pregnancy, but once it was too late to do anything, he went along it. The "it" he went along with is his obligations to family. Note the important positioning of family (his parents, her parents, and her grandmother) in determining what must be done (lines 76–86). On one level, this narrative can be heard as a "sad tale" in that BH has to do something that he does not want to do, but on another level, this can be taken as a story that puts obligation to family before individual wants. This narrative makes understandable the conflicting positions in which BH finds himself.

While BH's story makes understandable his having the child, a recipient's assessment can make relevant a different aspect of the story. This device of conflicting category predicates is seen again in the following excerpt, this time with a humorous uptake.

Excerpt 4. Four peers

(Continued from excerpt 3.)

[BH's narrative of why he got married and had the child]

87 NH: ( )

88WH: Where's the ring man?

89 BH: H[Hhhhhhh

90 OW: [Hahhhhhh

91 BH: It's being repaired.

92 WH: Yeah rig[ht

93 BH: [Being made to my own- my size

94NH: $That's what you told me last year man! come on!

95 I remember you told me last ye[ar.$

96 OW: [$( ) off$

97 NH: Take that shit off man (.) you down with O.P.P.

98 OW: Hhhhhh[h

99 BH: [Hhh[hhhhhhhh

100 NH [hhhhhhhh

Following BH's story of getting married and having the child, WH changes footings by asking, "Where's the ring man?" (line 88). The transcription of "Where's the ring man?" fails to adequately capture the noticeable prosodic shift to a kind of ironic tone. Other participants notice this shift as seen by their laughter. This can be heard as a teasing query, as noticing a kind of deviance. The tease turns on the conflicting category predicates of being married and not wearing a ring. Conventionally, of course, drawing attention to a married man not wearing a wedding ring can be heard as implicating a lack of serious commitment to marital fidelity.

BH's account (line 91, 93) is oriented to by the others as being facetious. Indeed the account gets explicitly dismissed through the use of a humorous frame. Both NH and OW use a smile voice in discounting the veracity of the account (lines 94–97), and NH facetiously attributes BH's involvement with a rap group (line 97). The participants then flood out into laughter (lines 99–100).

Repeated Problem Ascriptions and Positioning

The problematic positioning of being a too-young father becomes raised again by WH later in the conversation. The repetition of problem formulation can intensify that problem (Labov, 1984). Also, repetition implicates that prior accounts have not adequately answered or resolved the problem.

In the following excerpt, NH narrates how he heard about the pregnancy.

Excerpt 5. Four peers
(Continued from excerpt 4.)

101 NH: (I remember last year) ↓yo my girl's pregnant

102 I was like ↑<u>who</u>::

103 When he told me I was like

104 (0.7)

105 WH: Yo [( ) should be (.) I <u>flipped</u>

106 NH: [( )

107 NH: >I remember he told me outside<

108 wha::::::t:: you stu::pid:: about this:

109 (.)

110 BH: °That's something man. °

111 (2.9)

112 BH: At [first- I still can't believe that I'm a parent.

113 WH: [( )

114 WH: No 'cause you too young (dude) you eighteen

In his story NH tells of BH informing him about the pregnancy. NH reports his reaction to the news and what he said to BH, that he is being "stu::pid::" (line 108). While this brief story lacks situated details or reasons, it can be heard as a problem story in that it focuses on a complication that is not resolved (VanDijk, 1993). Also, the narrator's evaluation of BH's position is clearly critical (lines 107–108).

In response to this story about the news of the pregnancy, BH avows its impact with, "°That's something man. °" (line 110). This indexical expression, "That's something," becomes clarified somewhat by the admission of the difficulty in fully believing his new identity as a parent (line 112). That is, BH concedes to the problematic position of a not yet fully realized change in status. BH's response here is similar in format to his earlier response when his being an eighteen-year-old father initially came up (see excerpt 1, lines 31–34). In each, BH concedes to the interlocutor's assessment and expresses disbelief in being a father.

In response to BH's avowal of disbelief, WH reasserts the conflicting aspects of BH's membership category—being "too young" to be a father (line 114). In coming just after BH's concession, WH's ascription, "too young to be a father" (line 114), can be heard as an explanation for BH's avowal of disbelief. Also, WH's ascription of BH is a more explicit version of his prior problem ascription "( ) being a father (dude)" (excerpt 1, line 31). This ascription positions BH in a seemingly irresolvable problematic state.

Just as interlocutors can be critical as in ascribing problems, so can they be supportive in helping respond to problems. Interlocutors' supportive, challenging, or humorous remarks make relevant a range of responses that become part of how an account unfolds, gets told, and coconstructed. For instance, consider OW's response (lines 115–117) to WH's problem ascription (line 114).

Excerpt 6. Four peers

(Continuation of excerpt 5)

110 BH:	°That's something man.°
111	(2.9)
112 BH:	At [first- I still can't believe that I'm a parent.
113 WH:	[( )
114 WH:	No 'cause you too young (dude) you eighteen
115 OW:	How you feel about it now?
116	like how do you feel about your baby and everything
117	(.) since at first you didn't want to keep it and all.
118 BH:	I love: my kid:: and I'm- I'm proud that we uh you know
119	went through with it and we had the baby.
120	(1.8)
121	'cause: (.) I- >I don't know< it's hard to:
122	(1.4)
123	just::: (.) think about not having the baby around ↓so::.
124	(1.2)
125	((raise shoulders)) That's basically it =
126	= that's the reason- I don't know but
127	(1.6)
128	the ba::by: [is something.

As described above in the analysis of excerpt 5, WH makes explicit his ascription of the conflicting category predicates—being too young to be a father (line 114). WH's problem ascription here is not only rather explicit, but also repeated (cf. excerpt 1, line 31). The problem ascription projects an account, explanation, or response of some kind from BH. Before BH can respond, OW intercedes and asks him about his feelings about the baby (lines 115–117). These questions, in effect, allow BH to change footings and reposition himself from the implications of being a too-young father to his feelings about the baby. For the membership category, father, there is nothing problematic about a father's feelings about his child. Loving your child is part of the category-bound activities of being a father. In addressing OW's questions, BH's account positions himself more favorably—as loving the child and being "proud" that they "had the baby" (lines 118–128). Also, this change of footing allows BH a way to both avoid responding to WH's ascribed problem and to obliquely answer it.

Problem Ascription through Formulating the Point of Another's Story

Formulating the point of another's story can be used as a resource to ascribe problems of another. For instance, consider WH's ascription of BH's motives (lines 129–130).

Excerpt 7. Four peers
(Continuation of excerpt 6.)

128 BH: the ba::by: [is something.
129 WH: [>It's like if you could have done you would have<
130 but now that he's here (yo)
131 BH: Yeah but (1.4) a baby is a life you know so that's
132 WH: >Ain't like a doll<
133 BH: I know:: (1.3) it ain't like- (.) ↓I don't know it's weird
134 (1.2) having a kid and ↑then being there to see it be born.
135 that's ( ) ((narrative of being present at the birth))

As BH comes to a possible completion point, WH offers an account about BH's motives vis-à-vis the pregnancy and the child (lines 129–130). WH's account here formulates what is seemingly the point of BH's own prior narrative of why they had the baby (see excerpt 3). However, BH resists WH's formulation of his motives from that prior narrative. BH resists the ascription by adhering to a discourse consistent with the positioning of a father's love for his child, rather than conflicting predicates of a too-young father (line 131). BH's account resists WH's formulation by appealing to a higher principle. WH does not pursue the issue further; rather he responds to BH's account by a humorous remark seemingly making light of the issue (line 132).

Formulating the point of another's prior narrative can be used to articulate a problem for another. We see this practice again in the following excerpt, as an interlocutor formulates an upshot of BH's story (lines 1–2).

Excerpt 8. Four peers

((Narrative of being present at the birth))

01 WH: That shit must've changed your <u>life</u> completely
02 around ↓man, ↑right?
03 BH: ((nods head)) °I [can't believe it°
04 WH: [You still be hangin' out with your
05 friends °though°?
06 (1.3)
07 BH: Nah everything's changed=my whole life has changed
08 (1.4)
09 I don't act like it sometimes (.) when I'm in school
10 but outta school I gotta act like ((nods head))
11 OW: You gotta be more responsible
12 BH: <u>Yeah</u>:: I'm responsible and (I'm)
13 NH: Yeah you're still bummin' man h[hhhh
14 OW: [hhh[h
15 BH: [Everything changes
16 OW: At least- at least you are re[sponsible about because there's =
17 WH: [>How do you support your kid man<
18 OW: = a lot a guys out there that wouldn't care

WH formulates the upshot of BH's narrative of being at the birth of his child (not shown here), that BH's life must have "changed," to which BH concurs (lines 1–3). While the descriptive term, “changed,” can be taken as positive, neutral, or negative, as the talk ensues “changed” takes on more of a problematic hue. As BH explains why he does not hang out with his friends, he draws on WH’s prior term “changed” in avowing, “Nah everything’s changed=my whole life has changed” (line 7). In using another’s descriptive term, “changed,” BH can be heard as coconstructing his account to articulate his positioning.

Another coconstruction practice is seen, as BH is explaining this change and is seemingly searching for a word (line 10), and OW cocompletes the utterance with “more responsible” (line 11). BH emphatically agrees and uses her term in his avowal “I’m responsible” (line 12). Given BH’s acceptance of her term, a moment later OW adds, “at least you are responsible” in comparing him to other young fathers (line 16 and 18). Using another’s term in the course of explaining oneself shows a coconstruction practice in accounting.

In sum, we have seen the various problem formulation practices work to project a response from BH to confirm, deny, or account for these problems. BH responds in different ways—by avoiding the issue, by conceding and avowing the problem, by telling a narrative to explain it, and by justifying himself. Through these responses, BH positions himself in two main ways: by what he had to do given the physical necessity of the pregnancy and the practical necessity arising from this. A second kind of positioning BH avows is a father’s love for his child. Interestingly, this latter positioning taken on by BH arose in response to an interlocutor’s supportive questioning in an accounts slot. Changing footings to the positioning of a father’s love for his child allows BH to resist the problematic implications of his own prior, unwanted pregnancy story. Different kinds of positionings are ascribed and taken up as regards being a student teen parent.

School-Family Meeting

Consider another case of the discursive uses of student teen parenthood as problematic. This instance occurs in the course of a meeting in a high school. A high school student, newly a mother, returns to school after being away for the pregnancy. The meeting with the codirectors, her homeroom advisor, and a social worker along with her family members—mother, brother (also a high school student), and infant child. The school representatives are observably White and the family members are observably Latino.

Formulating the Student-Mother's Problem

In the following excerpt the codirector raises some of the problematic aspects of being a teen parent.

Excerpt 8. School-family meeting

(Participants: CD1 = codirector, CD2 = codirector 2, SW = social worker, HRT = home room teacher, MO = student mother, GM = grandmother, BRO = brother of the student mother).

(Discussion of whether participants wanted a boy or girl baby)

CD1: You turned out okay John
>Alright< so now:: the dilemma is,
there's a lot of issues
(1.4)
It's very hard (1.2) to go back to school
when you have >a little baby< ↑right
(1.5)
I mean there's a lot of complications in your life
>ya know< how much slee::p you're gonna ge::t::
how you're going to do the studying on the si::de
your own (.) friends::

The co-director moves the discussion from an amiable recollection of newborn babies and their gender to seemingly the point for the meeting—the student's potential difficulties in returning to school. She initiates this topic by identifying the student's situation as a "dilemma" (line 2). This is the initial point during the meeting in which the codirector turns to "the problem." The codirector articulates the problem by noting the difficulty or conflicting positions of being a student and having a "little baby" (lines 5–6). She proceeds by using the extreme case formulation, "a lot of complications in your life" (line 8) (Pomerantz, 1986; Edwards, 2000). This problem formulation then gets unpacked by the codirector listing the conflicting category predicates: problems with sleep, studying, friends (lines 8–11). In uttering this list of problems, she prosodically stretches the final word of each of the three complication statements (lines 9–11).

This word stretching works to emphasize and underscore the sense of these complications.

The codirector's ascriptions of the teen mother's positioning is recognized as a problem as seen by the grandmother's account (beginning at line 14).

Excerpt 9. School-family meeting

(Continuation of excerpt 8.)

11 CD1:	your own (.) friends:: and,
12	(1.2)
13	and: [all your
14 GM	[The ( ) baby is going to stay with (.) me
15	in the room in the bassinet
16	(1.3)
17	so she could sleep.
18 CD1	So she could sleep ([ )
19 GM	[Right (.) this way
20	when she comes out of school she'll go home,
21	do her homework,
22	then::: she'll be with the baby.
23	(1.7)
24 CD1	But she is trying to live two lives right?
25 GM	((rolls her eyes))

While the codirector's ascription of problems is seemingly addressed to the student mother, the grandmother intercedes and speaks for the family. The grandmother overlaps, as the codirector's listing of conflicting category predicates moves on to a fourth point (lines 11–14). The grandmother's account offers a kind of solution (lines 14–22) to the codirector's ascribed problem. In other words, the grandmother does not contest the codirector's problem formulation, but presents a candidate solution to it.

The codirector's response avoids addressing this candidate solution offered in the grandmother's account (line 24). Instead, after a

1.7 second gap, the codirector formulates her version of the problem, “But she is trying to live two lives right?” (line 24). That is, the codirector articulates the upshot of her prior list of conflicting category predicates, clearly hearable as contradictory positionings.

How is the codirector’s response to the grandmother’s remedy taken? In the next turn, the grandmother rolls her eyes (line 25). Such a nonverbal behavior could be interpreted as a display of exasperation with the codirector for not agreeing. Given the timing of this eye roll, it seems instead to be occasioned by the codirector’s prior tag question, “right?” (line 24). So the grandmother’s rolling of eyes seems to display agreement with codirector’s problem formulation. At any event, the grandmother says nothing further to the codirector’s lack of response to her account.

The codirector proceeds to further articulate the problem, again using this device of conflicting category predicates to formulate and justify her ascription.

Excerpt 10. School-family meeting

(Continued from excerpt 9.)

24 CD1 But she is trying to live two lives right?

25 GM ((rolls her eyes))

26 CD1 To be- how old are you?

27 (0.6)

28 MO Fifteen

29 CD1 To be a fifteen year old

30 (.)

31 and to be a <u>mother</u>?

32 (1.9)

33 So that’s complicated.

34 CD2 And a st↑udent.

35 CD1 And a student,

36 so she’s gonna be a ↑fifteen year: old::

37 (1.4)

38 with friendships and

39 (2.5)

40 and then she's a ↑daughter

41 and then she's a sis::ter

42 and then she's a mo:ther::

43 and (.) there's a lot of- and

In this excerpt the codirector formulates the teen mother's problem as "she is trying to live two lives" (line 24). As she specifies in support of this formulation, "To be a fifteen year old (.) and to be a *mother*?" (lines 29–31). The juxtaposition of these conflicting category predicates is oriented to as a problem (also as seen in excerpt 8). The codirector repeats her summation, "So that's complicated" (line 33); compare "I mean there's a lot of complications in your life" (excerpt 8, line 8).

The other codirector adds another conflicting predicate, "And a st↑udent." The codirector builds off of this by repeating it, repeating her age, and then listing her membership category predicates: friendships, daughter, sister, and mother (lines 35–43). Other than the teen mother's exact age, these category predicates were already known by the participants. The codirector's listing of these category predicates is a way of noticing them, drawing attention to them. Given that these predicates are heard as conflicting, works to formulate and underscore the problem.

Possible Institutional Consequences

Having ascribed these problems, the codirector moves on to some possible consequences for her schooling.

Excerpt 11. School-family meeting
(Continuation of excerpt 10.)

43 CD1 and (.) there's a lot of- and

44 (1.2)

45 and ↑you want to graduate .hh

46 MO ((nods head))

47 CD1 Are you determined to do °that°?

48 MO Yes ((nods head))

49	(1.2)
50 CD1	At the moment you're hoping to do it ↑here
51 MO	Yes ((nods heads))
52	(2.1)
53 CD1	Are you- the- >the reason I say that at all< is that
54	(0.8)
55	↑I would love: it to work out that way
56	(0.7)
57	>I really ↓wo[uld<
58 MO	[Yeah I want it[to
59 CD1	[Some other schools:::
60	where it's also possible to bring your child with you
61	to school have some ad↑van:tages.
62	(1.4)
63	So: just keep that in mind
64	>I mean< it's not a defeat if you decide at some point
65	that you want to be somewhere
66	(0.9)
67	where the (.) baby can come to school with you

First of all, the codirector asks the student mother if she wants to graduate (line 45). This query comes after the listing of contradictory positionings in formulating the problem (excerpt 10, lines 35–42). Also, this query comes instead of the prior, self-corrected, seeming summation statement, "there's a lot of-" (line 43). This uncompleted formulation is similar in structure to her earlier formulation, "there's a lot of complications in your life" (excerpt 8, line 8).

In any case, the codirector asking her if she wants to graduate can be heard to implicate a potential problem given that graduation is a conventional goal of the membership category, student. To put this another way, the codirector would not be asking her if she wanted to graduate if there was not some fairly strong likelihood of this not occurring. This implication of problems graduating is further heightened by the codirector's follow-up queries (lines 47 and 50). The codirector's third-turn response "Are you determined to do °that°?" (line 47) suggests some possible difficulty in achieving graduation, that it will take extra determination. Following the student's affirmative answer to this query, the codirector responds with, "At the moment you're hoping to do it ↑here" (line 50). This inference-rich query, again throws into some doubt the student's prior answer. In this query the codirector's choice of descriptive terms seems particularly revealing: the student is ascribed as "at the moment . . . hoping" to graduate, rather than, say, realistically expecting to graduate. Also, graduating "here"—the student's current school—may be difficult, in contrast to an implied somewhere else.

After these three strongly implicative queries (lines 45, 47, 50), the codirector makes explicit what she is getting at (lines 53–61). The codirector explains the option that another school, where the student mother can bring her baby with her, may be better suited for her. In short, the codirector raises the idea of the student mother going to another school as a possible solution to some of the problems that she has raised.

As the codirector discusses the possible institutional consequences arising from these ascribed problems, the grandmother recognizes this as seen by her account beginning with, "That's no problem" (lines 70–72).

Excerpt 12. School-family meeting
(Continuation of excerpt 11.)

64 CD1 >I mean< it's not a de<u>feat</u> if you decide at some point

65 that you want to be somewhere

66 (0.9)

67 where the (.) baby can come to school with you

68 (1.4)

69 ca[use

70 GM [That's no problem because I can take care of him.

71 (0.9)

72 I don't work ↑so:

73 CD1 ((nods head)) (4.1)

74 CD1 It's important to know that that option

75 exi[sts, there are some nice schools =

76 SW [(°Mm hum°)

77 CD1 = that we know of (.) where >that's possible<

The grandmother's account here is responsive to the institutional implications of the possibilities raised by the codirector. Like the grandmother's first account (discussed above), this one too has the character of a remedy to the problem. Also parallel to the first account, the codirector acknowledges the grandmother's account through a head nod (line 73) but avoids addressing it explicitly as such. Instead, the codirector reiterates her candidate solution for a possible future problem.

In excerpts 9 and 12 we see this three-part sequence: (1) the codirector's problem ascription, (2) the grandmother's remedial accounts to which (3) the codirector acknowledges but does not address and instead formulates her version of the problem. This practice of acknowledging but not addressing an account allows the codirector to, so to speak, "stay on message." That is, the codirector avoids getting into the particulars of the grandmother's solution, while restating the school's sense of future possibilities (lines 74–77).

The codirector cannot simply give her version of the problem and leave it at that; she needs to elaborate on it, make it understandable and convincing to the family.

Excerpt 13. School-family meeting
(Continuation of excerpt 12.)

74 CD1 It's important to know that that option

75 exi[sts, there are some nice schools =

76 SW [(°Mm hum°)

77 CD1 = that we know of (.) where >that's possible<

78 (1.2)

79 an:::d (1.0) and if at any point (.) you feel like it

80 or she just feels like?

81 (1.2)

82 she appreciates your (.) doing it

83	but she would like >to have her with her<
84	that's always- that's possible
85	(3.0)
86	°you need to know that's possible°
87	>Alright so there's< that's (.) ↓one (.) issue,
88	then the second issue is:: the complicated
89	social (.) dilemma in s↑chool (.) between
90	(1.2)
91	you and ah ((looks towards SW))
92	(1.9)
93 SW	Johnnie
94 CD1	Johnnie

In this excerpt the codirector, along with the social worker, offers an "option" for a future possible problem. As an institutional representative with specialized knowledge, the codirector can advise the family on what can be done within the schools. The codirector envisions a future problem in which the student mother wants her baby with her at school (lines 79–84). So the codirector offers this unsolicited advice to the problems she has raised and ascribed. In so doing, the codirector positions herself as a kind of counselor for these problems within school and beyond.

The codirector then moves to close down this topic by, "°you need to know that's possible°" (line 86), and open up a "second issue" on her agenda (lines 87–94). As we saw above, the codirector initiates discussion of the "dilemma" or problem. Here we see her closing it down and shifting to "the second issue" or "dilemma" (lines 88–89). In initiating and closing down such problem talk, the codirector displays her authority in running the meeting.

Discussion

The four peers conversation and the school-family meeting data, while quite different communication genres, are comparable in the focus on the problematic aspects of being a student teen parent. It may be a fact that one of the participants is a student teen parent, but how this gets made relevant, oriented to, and assessed is something that participants negotiate and jointly construct.

Looking again at the epigrams of this chapter our data do support the proposition of "contradictory positions as problematic," e.g., "too young to be a father," and "a fifteen year old mother" (Davies & Harré, 1999). In both transcripts these contradictory positions, or conflicting category predicates, arise from another's ascription. In the school-family meeting transcript, the codirector is much more explicit in problem ascription than that seen in the four-peers data. This explicitness may reflect the fact that the problem is already known to the participants, it is apparently the reason for this meeting with the family. Raising the problem of being a student teen parent can be seen as getting down to the task at hand. In contrast, the problem of the four peers conversation emerges from the contingencies of the talk—from the news story of babies being left in cars, to BH's baby, to BH as a teen father.

The positioning an individual takes vis-à-vis a problem is not solely the product of that individual, but is coconstructed among interlocutors. Participants avow and ascribe various categorizations to position themselves or others, and thereby, coconstruct their positionings. In the four peers data, being a parent becomes contrasted by others with BH's age, implicating a problematic positioning. The conflicting aspects of the membership category, teenage parent, result in various forms of tellings such as narratives, accounts, and claims that attempt to contextualize and make understandable BH's social/moral positioning. BH, for the most part, goes along with others' problem ascriptions of him. He concedes to many of these problem ascriptions and avows the magnitude of the situation. On one occasion BH tells a problem story echoing NH's immediately prior problem story about him. On other occasions, an interlocutor, OW, does support work for BH. OW, by asking a question, or at another point, cocompleting an utterance, allows BH to respond and shift footings and position himself more favorably—as loving his child or as being responsible. The resulting coproduced account of events works to reposition BH: he is a teen parent, to be sure, but one who loves his child and is responsible for his family, rather than just an unwilling father/husband.

The grandmother's account for her daughter displays recognition of the problems being ascribed. The grandmother's account positions the family as able to collaboratively remedy her daughter's problems with school. The grandmother explains that she will care for the child to allow her daughter to attend to her schoolwork. What is striking about these excerpts is how the codirector acknowledges but avoids addressing the grandmother's accounts. Instead, the codirector continues to formulate and elaborate on her version of the (potential) problems. This pattern fits with Heritage's (1984) observation of how institutional representatives use the third-turn slot to evaluate the clients' response to their initial turns, and thereby, direct the direction of the talk. The institutionality of this talk is also displayed in the codirector's interactionally opening and closing down the problem talk. In addition, the codirector counsels the student mother and grandmother on the future problems and advises them on other options. A way counselors position themselves in talking about another's problem is to discuss "possibilities" (Peräklyä & Silverman, 1991).

While our main focus has been on the ascription of and accounts for problems, what can we surmise about the position of being a teen student parent? Clearly from what we have seen, being a teen student parent is a problem position as seen by interlocutors' responses. There seems to be a kind of ambivalence or tension for BH between the freedom and pleasures of adolescence and the responsibilities and caring of parenthood. The connections between each of the teen parents and their respective families are interesting. The grandmother's accounts show that she is prepared to take on a significant portion of the mothering responsibilities so her daughter could have time to be a student. The high school system seems attentive to the needs of student parents. BH tells of not wanting to have the child at first, but going along with his girlfriend's family's decision for them to get married and have the child. That is, his obligations to family supersede his individual wants. It is a position that the two teen parents may not have desired to be in, but it has changed their life.

2

Clients' and Therapist's Joint Construction of the Clients' Problems

> Then I proposed another construct, building further on the notion of complementarity. I did this by *describing/transforming* what they (the clients) defined as a *conflict* into a mechanism that served to *balance their relationship*. This description not only legitimized each of their personal styles; it also defined the reaction of each to the other's style as only natural ... By means of these rather practical recommendations, I reinforced my *proposal of an alternative description of their predicament* [italics added] (Sluzki, 1990, pp. 121–122).

These passages from a therapist's own account of his interventions capture a sense of the phenomena to be investigated in this chapter. The therapist offered an "alternative description" of the clients' problems, transforming what the clients defined as "conflict" into a "balance(d) relationship." A remarkable feature of therapeutic practice is that the therapist may not find the clients' tellings of their own relational troubles convincing and, instead, offer the clients an alternative version of their situation. Such alternative versions or reframings are, of course, central practices in therapy.[1] What I want to do here is take what therapists commonly gloss as "reframings" as interactive achievements through talk between clients and therapist. Instead of privileging the voice of the therapist, the investigation focuses on: *How therapist and clients interactionally coconstruct a version of the clients' problems during an initial therapy consultation.*

Problems in Therapy

Certain situations are designed for the discussion and resolution of problems, as with counseling or therapy. During initial interviews, clients need to say why they have come to therapy. Clients commonly tell problems, implicate blames, and offer accounts (Buttny, 1990; Buttny & Cohen, 1991; Buttny & Jensen, 1995). These speech activities may be accomplished by narratives of incidents (Wodak, 1981; Sarbin, 1986) or descriptions of recurring negative patterns in their relationship (Edwards, 1995). Such narratives and descriptions are not neutral reports, but instead involve members' tellings of how to hear these events, and thereby, implicate responsibility and blame (Labov & Fanshel, 1977). What is particularly interesting is what the therapist picks up on and makes relevant from the clients' problem tellings and accounts. That is, how the talk moves from clients' problem tellings into the therapist's version. Such conversational movement seems to be one of the most artful practices of therapy: the reframing, redefining, or retelling of "the problem" (Gale, 1991; Anderson & Goolishian, 1992; Chenail & Fortugno, 1995).

In the course of the clients presenting their problems, the therapist remains far from a silent listener to these problem tellings (at least in my materials). At various points the therapist stops the clients from going on at length detailing their troubles, complaints, and blamings. The therapist actively engages in how the clients' problems get told: what gets picked up on and made relevant for further discussion, and finally, what becomes the problems for therapy (Scheff, 1990).

Such therapeutic interaction has been characterized as the therapist "reformulating" the client's problems in a way that is suitable for further work in therapy (Davis, 1986). Therapists, as members of a specialized community of practice, do more than simply reproduce the clients' terms, accountings, and assessments of the problems. The therapist reformulates the client's problems into different terms—to a discourse consistent with the therapist's perspective. According to Davis (1986), the reformulation process involves three stages: the therapist's defining the problem, documenting the problem, and pursuing consent from the client. To define the problem, the therapist needs to select an aspect of the client's behavior from numerous possibilities presented in the troubles-telling relatively early in the initial interview. This aspect of the problem is then reformulated into the therapist's version of what is "really" the problem. Usually it is not enough for the therapist to present the therapeutic version of the problem one time to convince the client. The therapist's formulation needs to be reintroduced as the problem throughout the session. Indeed, Davis (1986, p. 65) observed that "more than half of the session is devoted to persuading the client" of the problem as defined by the therapist. To accomplish this, the therapeutic version is documented by interpretations and instances from the client's own tellings. The client's consent is needed to proceed with the therapist's reformulation of the problem. Although the therapist's reformulation may be resisted, it seems more difficult for clients to disagree than agree with the therapist. In brief, the therapist displays expertise by "discovering" the problem quickly and then presenting this problem reformulation without disrupting the therapeutic interaction (Davis, 1986, p. 70).

The work of the therapist is contingent on the clients' narratives, responses, and positionings. During the initial session, the therapist takes the clients' versions of their problems as a beginning point and attempts to reformulate their account into a version consistent with the vocabulary of therapy (Davis, 1986; Hak & De Boer, 1996; Ravotas & Berkenkotter, 1998). These speech activities need to be performed with a certain delicacy or "professional cautiousness" (Drew & Heritage, 1992). A potential problem therapists face is how to present their version of the clients' situation when this departs from the clients' own version, i.e., to give "a retelling of the clients' tellings" (Holmgren, 1999). Telling clients about themselves involves making ascriptions of the clients' circumstances, and/or offering recommendations. Therapeutic versions of the clients' problems are designed as tentative, limited, and open to further revision from the clients. The therapist may describe the clients' past or present state-of-affairs, or talk about "possibilities," or what may happen in the future (Peräkylä, 1993). Therapists commonly qualify or mitigate their descriptions of the clients in various ways, such as by expressing uncertainty, downgrading their epistemological status, or drawing on publicly available facts (Peräkylä & Silverman, 1991; Bergmann, 1992). So therapeutic discourse will be examined for the communicative practices in coconstructing problems and what to do about them.

To approach this issue of coconstruction between clients and therapist two research questions are examined:

1. How does the therapist offer the clients an alternative version of their situation?
2. How does the therapist draw on the clients' understanding or assessment of the therapist's version as a resource for bringing the focus back to the therapeutic position?

Data

Two therapy consultations are used as data for analysis. One session involves an unmarried couple and the other a family of five. The same therapist was involved in both cases. For the couple therapy consultation examined here, the therapist has independently written a commentary on his intervention strategies (Sluzki, 1990). The therapist, Carlos Sluzki, identified his perspective as a combination of interactional and constructivist views (Sluzki, 1990, 108). The therapist's perspective, however, is not used because my approach involves a more fine-grained analysis of therapeutic-client reframings, whereas Sluzki's project covered the entire videotaped consultation session. This study privileges neither the therapist's nor the clients' point of view, but takes therapeutic practices as a joint achievement—as interactionally coconstructed among clients and therapist.

Telling Clients About Themselves

Therapy is commonly thought of as a form of institutional talk organized as an interview format: the therapist asking questions and the clients answering. However, some therapists ask few direct questions,[2] but instead attempt to elicit information from the clients by "telling them something about themselves" (Bergmann, 1992). This therapeutic practice of "telling clients about themselves" works as a technique to prompt the recipients to volunteer information about themselves. Bergmann (1992) called this therapeutic practice "information-eliciting tellings."

In my data, the therapist tells the clients things about themselves, not solely to elicit information, but also to suggest, propose, or open up the clients to different ways of seeing their circumstances. As already mentioned, a remarkable feature of therapy is that the therapist may not find the clients' accounts of their own relational troubles convincing; the therapist may propose an alternative reading of the clients' situation. Given that clients come to the initial therapeutic interview with their troubles, accounts, and narratives, how does this shift occur from the clients' problem-tellings to the therapist's version? How the therapist interactionally initiates this sometimes delicate move of "telling the clients something about themselves" is the main focus of this first section.

Practices of telling clients about themselves involve: (i) making *ascriptions* of the clients' behavior, motives, or circumstances, and/or (ii) offering *recommendations* as to a future course of action.

In making ascriptions' of the clients, the therapist may: (i) describe the clients' past or present state-of-affairs, or (ii) talk about "possibilities" or what may happen in "the future" (Peräkylä, 1993). As regards (i), therapists commonly qualify or mitigate their descriptions of the clients in various ways, such as by expressing uncertainty, downgrading their epistemological status, or drawing on publicly available facts (Peräkylä & Silverman, 1991; Bergmann, 1992). For instance, in the following, the therapist expresses tentativeness or uncertainty in making an ascription through the use of the mitigator *maybe* in line 1, in describing the family's circumstances.

Excerpt 1. Family

Ther: Well maybe ( ) maybe what's happening is the kids are
jealous (.) and they are managing to eh managing to get in
between the two of them and occupy so much attention

Other techniques evident in excerpt 2 are downgrading the epistemological status of the therapist's claims by identifying them as "my own fantasy" (line 1). Also, we see the therapist drawing on the publicly available facts, "by the way you describe, (.) the situation" (line 6) and "I already know you an half an hour" (line 7). The latter also serves to downgrade the therapist's ascriptions.

Excerpt 2. Couple

Ther: Do you know what my own fantasy is of all
thi[s if I may share =
Jenny: [>Uh huh<
Ther: = it with you? [.hh is that (1.2) quite by the =
Jenny: [>Uh huh<
Ther: = contrary (1.1) by the way you describe, (.) the situation
and b- ↑I already know you an half an hour [UHM UHM =
Clients: [hhhhhhhh
Ther: = that (1.6) my fantasy is that you
express whatever (1.5) sensible-sensitive emotion . . .

By drawing on these downgrading techniques, the therapist can tell clients about themselves, while simultaneously presenting these tellings as limited or open to revision.

The second way therapists form their ascriptions of clients is by discussing possibilities. Such "possibilities" may be articulated by the use of utterances with "irrealis verbs" (Gaik, 1992) of what *might*, *could*, *may* happen, for example, see lines 4 and 11–13 of (3) for the use of *may*.

Excerpt 3. Couple

Ther: >Okay< ah there is certain risk [(.) again that =
Jenny: [>Uh huh<
Ther: = if you- you use big words: (.) and ah (3.4) you
may end up getting into this endless quest (.) and
there is another risk and it is that if you are the advocate-
advocate of therapy (.) and you want in to therapy
and you are the advocate of therapy uhm and
but mainly of finishing therapy and being able to go on you
are already caught in a (grueling) struggle with therapy (.)
the struggle of I want more and I am content or I want
less: [so it reproduces a bit what may be ah: =
Jenny: [Uh huh
Ther: = ahm a stylistic issue in your.: (.) couple

Talk of future possibilities can also be formed by ascriptions of the clients using a conditional or hypothetical form (Peräkylä, 1993), for instance: "if you-you use big wor:ds: . . . you may end up getting into this endless quest" (lines 3–4). Telling clients about themselves using a conditional syntax implicates that the clients can avoid these negative consequences by refraining from doing the behavior referenced in the antecedent clause. By ascribing "future possible worlds," the therapist is able to raise delicate matters about the clients as well as to suggest alternative ways of seeing their problem, for example, as merely differences in style (line 13).

Therapeutic ascriptions of future possibilities are harder for clients to disconfirm than ascriptions about past or present states of affairs. Talk about possibilities is more difficult for clients to reject just because they are "possibilities" or speculations—contrary-to-fact conditionals. In the following, we see the therapist discussing a possible "risk" (lines 1–4) in their relationship and then attempting to support this by an ascription of their relational history, that "individual therapy created some problems" (lines 7–9). Both Larry and Jenny move to disagree with this past ascription of their relationship (lines 16–22).

Excerpt 4. Couple

Ther: Uhm: (2.2) .h the only risk is that you:: (.) each one may end
up being an advocate of (.) his or her own st- mode
(2.5)
Ther: Ah::: (0.6) and that may:: (3.6) >create some problems<
pt ah (.) indeed therapy create some problems, yeah?
Jenny: Um huh
Ther: And ah ↑so individual therapy:: ↑if I understand correctly
individual therapy created some problems in the couple
that you are trying to solve (.)↑ and reasonably so by means
of ah of ah: ah::: (0.9) bringing Larry into (.) ah: couple
therapy in which case ah both of you can tune up a bit
(0.8)
Jenny: Uh huh
Ther: Uhm
(1.3)
Larry: I don't think that individual therapy created problems
be[tween us
Jenny: [>It didn't< Yeah, it didn't create the problems but it
just made me more aware: (.) of problems

(1.3)

Jenny: The problems were already there (.) so they weren't

crea[ted they weren't created by the individual therapy but

Ther: [( )

Ther: What kind of problems were there?

So although the therapist designs ascriptions of the clients with cautiousness, sometimes they are challenged. This is the only instance in the two sessions, however, in which the clients mutually disagree with the therapist's ascriptions. But even when the therapist gets an ascription wrong, he is able to use that marked correction as an interactional resource to engage the clients in further problem tellings.

Interactional Resources

In addition to the therapist telling clients about themselves by using these recipient design techniques of professional cautiousness, we also need to look at the related issue of the interactional resources the therapist may draw upon. Given that the therapist's version differs in some way from that of the clients, how does the therapist respond to the clients' version? One way is for the therapist to initially build on or confirm what the clients have said, and then move into the therapeutic formulation. However, we will see that it is not always possible for the therapist to find something to agree with in the clients' versions, especially when the clients disagree among themselves. So we need to consider the alignment the therapist takes in relation to the clients' prior positions.

A valuable lead in this regard is Maynard's (1991a, 1991b, 1992) work in a language clinic concerning clinicians' delivery of bad diagnostic news to the parents of developmentally disabled children. Instead of directly giving the diagnosis, the clinician may initially solicit the parents' views on their child as a way to lead into the delivery of diagnostic news. Maynard called this latter approach a "perspective display series": (1) clinician's opinion query, (2) clients' reply, and (3) clinician's report and assessment (Maynard, 1991b, 167). If the parents' views are "close" to the clinical findings, then the clinician can "confirm" some aspect of the parents' version, "reformulate" it into a medical perspective, and give a further "technical elaboration" (Maynard, 1991a, pp. 468–469).

However, if the parents' views are "distant" from the diagnosis, then the clinician needs to work on "reducing the disparity" between the parents' views and the clinical diagnosis. Here I want to apply Maynard's observation of how the clinician (or therapist) confirms, or not, some aspect of the client's views as a way to lead into the therapeutic telling.

In the following transcript, the therapist confirms Jenny's avowal (lines 4, 7) while also making a recommendation.

Excerpt 5. Couple

Jenny: ...and uhm (.) I don't feel uncomfortable about it >at all<
(0.9)
Jenny: I just think it's something ne:[w
Ther: [Yeah in addition to
that [I
Jenny: [>it's something new <
Ther: I concur very much with you in the fact that precisely because
you have been exposed to several things in recent week[s .h =
Jenny: [Uh huh
Ther: = ah you should be:: skeptical to start with and >you know< to
move slowly
Jenny: Uh huh
Ther: Very important to go very slowly

The therapist moves into his version by "adding to" and "concur(ring)" with Jenny's version. Although the therapist's version, or recommendation, connects or aligns with Jenny's, it simultaneously attempts to redirect the implications of her statements, from Jenny being comfortable with therapy to the therapist's suggestion to "move slowly" in therapy. So here we see the therapeutic practice of confirming or agreeing in some sense with the client's version, but drawing a different upshot or implication from it.

Therapists may position themselves as aligned with clients while simultaneously moving to transform some of their views. This therapeutic practice is also evident in the following transcript though in a somewhat different way. The therapist confirms the client's version through positive assessments (lines 9, 11) of what she is doing. In addition, the therapist "draws inferences" from what the client is saying. Such inferences are displayed in the therapist's ascriptions (lines 18, 19, 21) of the client as a way to reframe the direction of the talk. The therapist picks up on an aspect of Jenny's accounts and makes relevant her participation in therapy as a sign of her commitment to her relationship.

Excerpt 6. Couple

Jenny: Yeah I think- I mean in the past I've- I've ah (0.9) been
a lot (0.5) less open with my feelings and I've repressed
a lot of my own feelings but I've been in therapy now for
awhile and a[h::
Ther: [For awhile? =
Jenny: = Yeah
Ther. How long?
Jenny: For about a year and a half
Ther. That's sweet of you! =
Jenny: = Hhh[h
Ther. [No it's ( ) it's great you know what
you know what frequently happens with
people in ther- individual therapy
Jenny: Uh huh=
Ther: = they end up doing:: their own stuff and ah they
leave ah their partners in another point in the planet
Jenny: Uh huh ha [ha ( )
Ther. [And ah so you're trying to:: to to bring
him up to a [point to ah: =
Jenny: [>uh huh<
Ther. = mode (.) [and a style that you have developed through =

Jenny: [Right

Ther. = therapy that's very very sweet of you, >°very nice°<

This transcript begins with Jenny justifying her prior implicit criticism of Larry for being "closed." The therapist's queries make relevant her involvement in therapy, which the therapist favorably assesses (lines 9, 11). The therapist explains by contrasting the problematic of individual therapy—growing apart—to an ascription of Jenny's motives of trying to involve Larry in therapy (lines 18, 19, 21, 23). This moves the talk away from Jenny's initial justificatory accounts to a favorable portrayal of her motives for being in therapy vis-à-vis her relational partner, Larry. Also, by making ascriptions of Jenny's motives as wanting to involve Larry in therapy as a sign of her love, the therapist can be seen–by a different analytic perspective—as "altercasting" (Malone, 1995), leading the clients toward a certain relational alignment consistent with the therapeutic portrait.

One of the most distinctive features of therapy is the character of the inferences the therapist draws from what clients say. The therapist at certain moments may be said to "hear beneath the surface" of clients' talk. The therapist displays expertise through such practices as drawing inferences and telling clients something about themselves that seemingly goes beyond what they have revealed in talk. The ability to make explicit an implicit subtext perhaps most dramatically demonstrates the therapist's professional competence.

Therapists can move to present their version of the clients' situation by explicitly confirming and adding to what the clients have already said (as in excerpts 5–6). However, the clients' positions may be distant from the therapist's own, such that the therapist may not find anything to confirm or build on from what the clients have said (also see Maynard, 1991b). Further, in sequential environments in which clients are disagreeing and disputing with each other, the therapist may tell the clients about themselves as a way to shift focus or topics. An instance of this is seen in excerpt 7. The clients disagree over whether Jenny overreacts to relational problems. The therapist responds, not by addressing the propositional content of the clients' dispute, but by commenting on the dispute itself—as "an old discussion" (line 26).

Excerpt 7. Couple

Larry: . . . and I think the balance between us is (0.5) is uh: about

right hhh[hh

3 Ther: [Um huh

4 Jenny: °Well: I don't know°

5 (0.6)

6 Ther: Yeah:

7 Jenny: I'm not so sure that I- I (.) overdo it though

8 (0.4)

9 >Because I talk to < other people: (.) ya know about problems

10 and they seem to have .hhh similar reaction

((skip nine lines))

20 Jenny: So: (0.8) the way he views: (0.6) uhm my: (0.6) over

21 reaction or the way somebody else would look at it

22 they might think that I'm even under reacting to

23 certain problems so it's again very subjective.

24 Ther: Uh hmm

25 (0.5)

26 Ther: Ah:: in addition to that this is an old discussion

In excerpt 7 the therapist makes an ascription about the clients in the sequential environment of the couple's dispute with each other. The therapist avoids entering into the dispute, but instead attempts to refocus the discussion. Notice how the therapist moves from Jenny's version by immediately responding with an acknowledgment token, "Uh hmm" (line 24) and then "adding to" (line 26) what the clients are saying—the ascription of their dispute as being "an old discussion." This sequential movement of acknowledgment token (or minimal agreement) combined with an adding to what is being said allows the therapist to form the response as structurally "preferred" (Sacks, 1987), even though the implication of the propositional content of this turn is to tacitly object to and shift the discussion.

Labeling a dispute "an old discussion" can be heard as to attempt to "transform" or "reframe" it, the implication being to cease the discussion because it is "old."[3] Further, this gloss, "old discussion," implicates that it is not just something that has happened once, but is a recurring interactional pattern, what Edwards (1994, 1995) called a "script formulation."

The following transcript offers another instance of clients openly disagreeing with each other, but here the therapist neither confirms nor acknowledges the clients' views, but instead moves to tentatively propose a new way to portray the clients' circumstances, from whether there will be "hollering," to the issue of the children occupying too much of the parents' attention.

Excerpt 8. Family

Mother: I think we'll just be a normal family I don't know
ya know ([ )
Father: [Well no you're you're not going to
stop all the hollering (.) somewheres along the line
you're going to run into a problem where you are going
to lose your temper and you are going to (.) holler
(1.3)
Father: Er- no one no one stops this completely I don't think
Ther: Well maybe (.) maybe what's happening
is the kids are jealous (.) and they are managing to eh
managing to get in between the two of them and occupy
so much attention and time that it takes uhm eh:: a
vacation for the two of you to be able to talk in peace
(.) without interference and without this noisy crowd

Notice how the therapist moves from the father's concern about the mother's "hollering" to the ascription of the children coming between the parents. Instead of explicitly responding to the father's concern, the therapist tentatively proposes another interpretation, "well maybe ( ) maybe what's happening is . . ." (lines 9ff.). In support of his ascription, the therapist draws on a prior discussion about hollering and alludes to the mother's earlier narrative of a peaceful vacation the parents took without the children. The therapist thus preserves some of the events from the family's earlier tellings, but reconfigures them into this present interpretation about clients. So here the practice of telling the clients about themselves gets achieved by the therapist drawing on various prior clients' descriptions or tellings and then using these materials to construct a different way to see their situation.

By way of summary, in this first section we have seen the therapist use various practices to move from the clients' accounts to the therapist's tellings. The therapist's ascriptions or recommendations are designed to display professional cautiousness: by forming utterances with qualifiers, by citing the therapist's circumscribed knowledge of the clients, and by discussing future possibilities. The therapist may also form problems with an if-then conditional syntax. The therapist draws on various interactional resources in doing tellings, such as by positioning himself as aligned or in agreement with the clients' accounts, but proceeding to draw a different upshot or implication from the clients' version. The therapist may add to what the clients have just said, but in so doing attempt to transform aspects of the clients' position or to comment on the clients' form of communication, for example, as "old discussion," to implicate that it should be transformed. In other cases, the therapist need not address the clients' assertions but instead offer alternative proposals.

These therapeutic practices do not guarantee that the clients will be convinced by the therapist's version. We need to examine the clients' responses to therapeutic tellings, and how the therapist treats their responses.

Clients' Responses to Therapist's Tellings as a Resource For Therapeutic Persuasion

In telling clients about themselves, the therapist cannot simply decree the validity of the therapeutic telling of the clients' problems. Therapy, of course, involves the art of persuasion, of opening the clients up to a different way to see their situation. Clients are not passive recipients of therapy; they may resist the therapist's articulation or take it in a different way; they may withdraw, remain silent, or continue to maintain their own point of view. So the therapist needs to know the clients' alignment or positioning vis-à-vis the therapeutic reading of their situation.

Therapeutic Tellings Project Clients' Responses

Client responses are sequentially implicated by the therapist's ascriptions or recommendations. Telling others something about themselves—whether as an ascription or recommendation—makes relevant a response from the recipient either to accept it or to put the record straight (Bilmes, 1985). The therapist's tellings open up a slot for the clients' responses to that telling. In other words, we have the adjacency pair formats:

1. therapist's ascription of other → clients' confirm/disconfirm
2. therapist's recommendation → clients' accept/reject.

Although this basic adjacency pair structure does occur, sometimes the therapist's ascription/recommendation is followed by a postpositioned query by the therapist that pursues the clients' responses. The therapist not only tells clients something about themselves, but asks them if it makes sense. The therapist attempts to involve the clients in addressing the therapeutic position by forming it as provisional, tentative, or subject to their confirmation (as seen also in the earlier discussion of professional cautiousness). Because the therapist's view of the clients typically differs in significant ways from their own views, the therapist needs client responses to work on coconstructing the alternative account. The postpositioned queries work as a prompt to engage the clients with the therapist's alternative.

For instance, in the following transcript, the therapist (lines 1–2) offers a differing version of the clients' situation from each of their own versions (the clients' accounts are not reproduced here). The therapist then pursues their assessment of this ascription (lines 5–6).

Excerpt 9. Couple

Ther: And that is a factor that inhibits you (.) .hh but
that is my own fantasy educated guess let's say
Jenny: >Uh huh<
Larry: [(.)
Ther: [Does it fit ( ) does it fit at all with your experience
of uh: ah:: [(.)
Jenny: [That's partially true because I assimilate
his emotions with my emotion

Here I simply want to note the therapist's ascription and pursuit of the clients' assessment. This transcript is the most explicit or direct case of the therapist's pursuit of the clients' response to his interpretation. In the other instances of therapeutic tellings, the therapist uses post-positioned queries in the form of various particles, such as "yeah," "Uhm," "Hmm," and the like (see arrows in excerpts 10–11). These serve to prompt the clients' responses to the therapeutic telling.

Excerpt 10. Couple

Ther: There is one rule of thumb that you can apply for this
situation (1.9) uhm: and it is that eh if you want to meet
his needs:? you have to listen? to whatever he expresses
emotion and do nothing about it, and on the contrary
ah and for you when you hear her expressing of emotions
you have to act (1.8) ah:: amplifying rather than damping
((three lines omitted)) so you can experience his emotion
less and you can experience she is ah: overemotional
(2.0)
Ther: → Hmm
Jenny: °Uh huh°
Larry: She does complain that I minimize (1.5) problems

Here, after the therapist's ascription and recommendation, there is a two-second gap, at which point the therapist's query, "Hmm," gets an acknowledgment token from Jenny before Larry's assessment response.

In excerpt 11, after the therapeutic ascription (lines 1–2), Jenny fills the brief gap (0.8 seconds) with "Uh huh," to which the therapist queries (line 5) whether Jenny agrees or is offering an acknowledgment token. Then after a noticeable silence, the therapist (line 7) proposes that Jenny critically evaluates his ascription and uses another postpositioned query (line 8). This ascription at line 7 indicates that Jenny's verbal response is called for and is noticeably absent.[4]

Excerpt 11. Couple

1	Ther:	. . . so it reproduces a bit what may be ah: ahm
2		a stylistic issue in your.: (.) couple
3		(0.8)
4	Jenny:	Uh huh
5	Ther: →	Yeah?
6		(1.6)
7	Ther:	You don't like what I'm saying
8	→	yeah?

These postpositioned queries allow the therapist to both tell the clients something about themselves as well as to solicit their involvement and response. So the therapist's turn can be seen as doing a telling and a questioning. Each of these utterance types projects a response, though the query seems to be more sequentially implicative for the clients.

Should the clients' responses reject or display reluctance to accept the therapeutic version, the therapist will not simply leave it at that; instead, the therapist may use the clients' responses as a resource to do more work in presenting the therapeutic version. Therapists may pursue their version of the problem even in the face of the clients' resistance (Labov & Fanshel, 1977).

Therapist's Third Turn

Given that the clients' responses occur in the slot following the therapeutic telling, the therapist can take *the clients' utterances as displaying understanding or assessment of what the therapist has just said*. As such, these client responses provide a valuable interactional resource in that the therapist can, in turn, move to correct, assess, or elaborate on the clients' alignment with the therapeutic position. That is, the therapist can employ a "third turn" (Heritage, 1984) to interactionally connect the client's positioning (as displayed in the second turn) to the therapist's tellings. So instead of the earlier-mentioned two-part structure, this should be seen as a three-part sequence involving at least three turns:

1. therapist's ascription or recommendation;
2. clients' response or evaluation
3. therapist's evaluation of the client's response

What makes the third turn sequentially connected is that it is responsive to the client's second-turn understanding/alignment and it makes relevant some aspect of the therapeutic telling in the first turn.

Excerpts 12 and 13 provide contrastive cases of the clients' responses to the therapist's recommendation and then the therapist's third-turn evaluation. In (12), the therapist makes ascriptions and a recommendation to the clients (lines 1–17) that each needs to adjust to the other's style more—Larry to "amplify" his affect toward Jenny, and Jenny to tone hers down with Larry. Jenny responds by accepting this proposal and formulates her understanding of it (lines 18–21) and, in turn, receives a hedged confirmation from the therapist in the third turn (lines 22, 24).

Excerpt 12. Couple

Ther: And my point is:: that eh (.) if you want to interact
more successfully and happily ah (1.0) you have to be
a little more like the other when you are with the other
when you are with your<u>self</u>, hhhh but when you are with
her? unless you amplify a bit whatever she brings about
she feels that she's throwing fire and getting ((vocalization))
nothing and in turn when you are- when you are
opening up with whatever thing? what for you is an
intense emotion is for you ((vocalization to minimize))
so you: also:: ah::: eh the technique quote unquote of
ah getting his emotion should be really by means
of (2.1) just listening and not reacting= it's easy to say
I'm an outsider I'm not involved in in an intense
relationship like the two of you are and therefore I can
say (   ) (1.3) uhm: but ah: (.) that's uhm (.) would

be my view and an important way of doing something
for:: the other >and therefore for yourself heh<
Jenny: We can certainly try it? It's sort of like role reversal
for a while =
Ther: = Ah:[:
Jenny: [In a sense ( )
Ther. ↑If you want.
Jenny: Uh hum hhhhh
Ther. °If you want° ah:

In excerpt 13 [a continuation of (12]), Larry formulates his own understanding of the therapist's recommendation (lines 25–28), in marked contrast to Jenny's. Larry's formulation here occasions a second third-turn slot for the therapist, this time to assess, correct, and elaborate on Larry's understanding (lines 30–37).

Excerpt 13. Couple
(Continuation of 12.)

Larry: (.) those are the words but I think (.) that what
he's really asking is that (.) .h we don't interact with
each other because of fear for the- be<u>cau</u>se of the
other we should be ourselves °more°
(1.9)
Ther: Uhm (1.5) up to a point
but it happens that on the contrary what I'm saying is
you can do- as much of it as you want when you are
interacting with the other however unless you talk
a bit in the language of the other you:: ah:: you: get
into a: into a big misunderstanding and for you to talk
in the language of her means to receive her emotions (.)
ah:: amplifying them a bit

In this second third-turn slot, the therapist, after a delayed initial qualified agreement (line 30), corrects Larry's understanding by presenting the gist of what he had said in his prior recommendation and further explaining (lines 31–37). So the therapist makes relevant Larry's misunderstanding in the course of evaluating Larry's response to the therapeutic position. The therapist explains and elaborates on his prior recommendation that they adjust to and communicate more like their partner.

In both excerpts (12) and (13), the clients' response includes a formulation of the therapist's prior recommendation. These formulations open up a slot for an evaluation from the therapist (Heritage & Watson, 1979). But not all client responses include a formulation of the therapist's first-part utterances. Still the client's responses can be taken by the therapist as a display of understanding of the therapeutic point. For instance in the following, Jenny's response (line 6) displays a misunderstanding of the therapist's recommendation (lines 1–2, 4), as evidenced by the therapist's overlapping correction (lines 7–8) and elaboration of the therapeutic view (lines 10–11).

Excerpt 14. Couple

Ther. Ah you should be:: skeptical to start with and > you
know < to move slowly
Jenny: Uh huh
Ther. Very important to go very slowly
(1.6)
Jenny: You sense that he's more ah[:
Ther [No in the contact
right no[w
Jenny: [>Uh huh<
Ther. ( ) that I experience you very ((gestures as guarded))
°and I experience° ((gestures as expressive))

Therapeutic talk has the potential of being "mystifying" or "oblique" (Peyrot, 1987) to clients, so this third turn seems to be an especially important site, in that it allows the therapist not only to assess or correct, but also to explain, clarify, or elaborate given the clients' uptake of the therapeutic position. In the following case, the client seemingly misses the point (lines 16, 18–19) of the therapist's prior ascription (1–14), so the therapist uses the third turn (17, 20–24) to make explicit his earlier point and further explain.

Excerpt 15. Family

Ther: Well maybe (   ) maybe what's happening is the
kids are jealous (.) and they are managing to eh managing
to get in between the two of them and occupy so
much attention and time that it takes uhm eh:: a vacation
for the two of you to be able to talk in peace (   )
without interference and without this noisy crowd
(2.5)
Ther: Uhm (.) and if that's the case (   ) if that happens to
be the case it seems then ah your own sense of responsibility
and love as parents have ah ah:: allowed for a situation
to happen that increases distance or a lack of a::
connectedness between the two of you as a couple uhm
and uhm in which case the kids (   ) would be helping
contribute to (   ) as a couple
(6.7)
Mother: They all like attention (.) and a whole lot of it
Ther: Yes but they are they are kids ([   )
Mother: [And they
vie with one another for that attention=
Ther: = It's about the two of you as a couple (.) as ah uhm::
(.) couple as a (unit) couple and that sometimes being
a mother and being a father occupies so much of one's attention
then (   ) the connection the two of you have

or may have or have had
(2.9)
Ther: And ah so:: if I was taking it from your own comment
of ah crying ah crying at the beginning of because of
the strain of the situation ( ) and then after a while crying
of the situation ( ) because that brings about seems
to bring about (.) ah:: the separation of the two of you

What the therapist proposes as the children coming between the parents and putting strain on their relationship (lines 1–14), the mother responds with an ascription of her children wanting "attention" (lines 16, 18–19). The noticeable gap of nearly seven seconds (line 15) between the therapist's and mother's turn suggests something is amiss. In the therapist's third turn he comes back to his initial ascription that the problem is really about the parents as a couple and the children separating them.

As a way to explain his point, the therapist documents his interpretation as based on what the client herself had previously said, "I was taking it from your own comment of ah crying" (lines 26–27). So again the third-turn slot is used by the therapist to correct the client's understanding and, further, to clarify and elaborate on the prior therapeutic ascription. Of course, this third turn does not guarantee that the clients will be convinced, but it does provide an opportunity for the therapist to address the clients' take on the therapeutic version.

Whether the therapist initiates an elaboration or correction in the third-turn slot is contingent on what happens in the clients' second-turn responses to the initial ascription. In the following, we see the therapist making an ascription about future possibilities of Jenny not wanting "to change too much" (lines 3, 7, 10–14), with which Larry immediately concurs (line 16). A discussion and disagreement between Jenny and Larry then unfold over the length of time Jenny wants to be in therapy (lines 27–46). The therapist intercedes by bringing the discussion back to his initial ascription over the length of time in therapy (47, 49–57). So although the therapist's intervention here is not literally a third turn, because the clients take nine turns after his initial ascription, nonetheless it serves the similar functions of bringing the discussion back to the therapeutic view in light of the clients' positioning, and of further elaborating and explaining.

Excerpt 16. Couple

1	Ther.	Do you follow me
2	Jenny:	= Yeah =
3	Ther	= The ri:.sk =
4		(.)
5	Jenny:	> °Um huh° <
6		(.)
7	Ther.	= of any change (.) is (.) that you may leave therapy
8		(.)
9	Jenny:	Um huh
10	Ther.	And if therapy in itself is a ritual (4.7) uhm: (.)
11		then it doesn't make sense for you (.) to do: to
12		change too much? in the direction >whatever direction
13		it may be because you would have to leave therapy
14		and therapy itself is a very important ritual< (.)
15		a token of appreciation for each other and of love
16	Larry:	That assessment is one that I- I mean (.) the real
17		purpose of therapy is to get out of therapy (.) as
18		soon as possible
		((skip six lines))
24		it's a paradox but that's one of the problems with
25		therapy is that you're drawn in and held in to the
26		ritual not (.) to the goals- not attaining the goals
27	Jenny:	But- but only until you can do it on your own I mean
28		it's almost like you- you acquire the awareness
29		in therapy (.) so you are able to handle your own
30		problems (.) you know it's almost like you- you learn
31		something in therapy and then you take it home and

you work on it =
Larry: = I know what the teaching is =
Jenny: = Yeah but I'm just saying it's- it's so that you can:
do it yourself (afterward[s)
Larry: [But of course
([ ) OBVIOUSly
Jenny: [I mean then then once you can do it yourself
why do you need therapy anymore?
Larry: Well that's the point why do some people stay in
therapy for ten years? (.) why [do some people
Jenny: [Well to that extent
th[en ( ) it's really dangerous
Larry: [Why do some people leave after a year? I think
it's the therapist that ah is good or bad based on
whether they can get you out the door
Ther: >Okay< ah there is certain risk (.)[again that if =
Jenny: [>Uh huh<
Ther. = you- you use big words: (.) and ah (3.4)
you may end up getting into this endless quest (.)
and there is another risk and it is that if you are
the advocate- advocate of therapy (.) and you want
in to therapy and you are the advocate of therapy uhm
but mainly of finishing therapy and being able to
go on you are already caught in a (grueling) struggle
with therapy (.) the struggle of I want more and I am
content or I want less

Notice that the therapist's intervention is a marked reference to his initial ascription by the repeated use of the same word "risk" (line

47, cf. line 3), which is emphasized by the micro pause immediately afterward. Also, the therapist calls attention to its being repeated by adding the indexical term "again" (line 47).

The therapist intervenes in the sequential environment of the couple's dispute about the length of Jenny's involvement in therapy. To initially gloss the therapist's moves here, he first addresses Jenny about the risk of lengthy therapy (lines 47, 49–50). The therapist then attempts to shift the discussion from the level of individual blames and accounts to framing the issue as "the couple" as an interpersonal system. To achieve this the therapist formulates the gist of both Jenny's position ("you want in to therapy," lines 52–53) and Larry's position ("finishing therapy and being able to go on," lines 54–55) and then draws the upshot of this opposition as a "struggle with therapy" (lines 55–57). By drawing on the gist of the clients' respective positions, the therapist can connect the clients' own accounts to the therapist's version.

Conclusion

Therapy has been characterized as involving both the discourses of medicine and of morality (Bergmann, 1992). We may add to this characterization the art of rhetoric—for in and through words the therapist attempts to persuade clients of different ways to see their problems. Seeing therapy as rhetorical has, of course, already been discussed (McNamee & Gergen, 1992). What is less understood—and to what this analysis attempts to contribute—is how the rhetoric of therapeutic reframings gets interactionally achieved through the practices of telling clients about themselves and third-turn evaluations.

Therapeutic reframings may be seen as a consequence of the therapist's conversational control (Scheff, 1968). "Conversational control" is a gloss on various practices that get played out in context. Conversational control may be empirically displayed through various interactional asymmetries between clients and therapist: For instance, the therapist initiates, whereas clients are responsive; the therapist asks questions, whereas clients give answers (Mellinger, 1995); the therapist controls the opening and closing of topics (Peräkylä & Silverman, 1991); clients tell their own problems, whereas the therapist tells the clients of their problems; the therapist "orchestrates" (Aronsson & Cederborg, 1994) the direction and focus of the talk by requesting, disattending (Jones & Beach, 1995), cutting the clients short, and repeating or elaborating on the therapeutic position. The therapist's third-turn evaluation slot can bring the discussion back to the therapeutic proposal. Conversational control gets achieved through the therapist's professional competencies and expertise, and the clients' interest and deference toward these (Peräkylä & Silverman, 1991).

Whereas these interactional asymmetries may work to provide some conversational control for the interview, at the same time we see the therapist's efforts to *involve* the clients in considering and addressing the therapeutic position. The work of the therapist is contingent on the clients' narratives, responses, and positionings. As we have seen, therapeutic tellings may draw on aspects of the clients' accounts; also these tellings are designed as tentative, limited, and open to further revision from the clients. Indeed, not only does the therapist tell clients about themselves, he also queries their responses to these tellings. The therapist wants to engage the clients in interactionally coconstructing the problem and solutions (Edwards, 1995).

One obvious way to involve clients is to ask them their views of the problems as a prelude to offering the therapeutic version. This resonates with Maynard's (1991a, 1991b, 1992) analysis of the perspective display series (discussed earlier). However, a major a priori difference between the interaction in the language clinic that Maynard studied and the present therapy context comes from the epistemological character of the "diagnosis." In therapy (such as the kind studied here), unlike the language clinic, there are no independent tests that can be performed to ascertain the problem. Therapists have no recourse to some medical technology or tests on which to base their diagnosis.[5] Indeed this therapist, Sluzki (1990), did not use the medical-laden term *diagnosis*.

In the one case (transcript [10]) in which the client, Jenny, withholds a response to the therapist's version and prompt, the therapist, instead of continuing, pursues a response by an ascription of disagreement and a further prompt. Such pursuit of a client response contrasts with Heath's (1992) observation of medical interviews: When patients withhold responses to the physician's diagnosis, the physician does not pursue a response from the patient. This contrast may reflect the distinction between doing therapy and doing medical examinations. The therapist needs to be much more of a rhetor to convince the clients of the therapeutic version.

In my data, the perspective display series is not empirically found. What is found is other interactional dynamics described by Maynard: the therapist looking to confirm some aspect of the client's accounts, moving to formulate them in a way consistent with the therapeutic version, and further elaborating on the therapeutic perspective. Both the clinician and therapist need to involve the clients, but in therapy, the problem and solutions are discursively formed through the clients' and therapist's talk. As we have seen, following the clients' problem-tellings, the therapist may attempt to reframe by: (i) giving a minimal agreement and moving on to add a differing account, (ii) making relevant an aspect of something the client said but drawing different implications from it, or (iii) using what the client has said as a conversational resource to formulate the therapeutic interpretation. One technique was for the therapist to position himself as aligned with the clients through the preferred responses of confirming while simultaneously attempting to transform some aspects of the clients' version of the problem. Of course, the therapist may not find anything to align or agree with in the clients' accounts, particularly in the sequential environment of their disputes.

In telling clients about themselves the therapist not only means to "prompt" the clients to respond (Bergmann, 1992), but also to convince the clients of this alternative version. Clients' responses provide a valuable resource in that the therapist can take these responses as a display of understanding and assess the clients' alignment in relation to the proffered reframing. In other words, the therapist can use a third turn (if need be) to explain, correct, or elaborate on the therapeutic version. The third part of this sequence, the therapist's evaluation, captures Davis's (1986) observation of the repetition the therapist employs in presenting the therapist's version. But crucially, such repetition is recipient designed to the clients' understandings and positionings as displayed in their second-part responses.

This third-turn slot of an expert evaluating the answer of a client is also found in the classroom setting (McHoul, 1978). Here we have the familiar sequence of the teacher's question giving rise to a student's answer followed by the teacher's evaluation. Indeed, the teacher's third-turn assessment, challenge, or further questioning is what characterizes the interaction as pedagogical (Heritage, 1984). Although there are obvious differences between the classroom and therapy contexts, to a certain extent the therapist's third turn serves a similar educational function: The therapist may correct, defend, explain, or elaborate on the therapeutic view. Part of persuading the clients is to open them up—to educate them—as to the plausibility or reasonableness of the therapeutic alternative.

In some sense, once clients present their problem to the therapist, it is no longer theirs. Problems are not simply the clients' subjective sentiments or inner cognitions, but become an object for examination through talk (Coulter, 1979). Problems can be scrutinized, questioned, and even challenged, in short, they are open to public criteria as to how they are to be described and ultimately evaluated. Clients are not the final authority for their own avowals or affect; clients who profess irrational fears or unwarranted alignments can be challenged or overruled by others for holding these positions. So therapeutic reframings of the clients' problems can be seen as the therapist offering a new language game for discussing the clients' situation. Similar to how Wittgenstein (1953) handled metaphysical problems in philosophy, some relational problems can be seen as problems of language: Change the language game that is played and how the problem is described, and the problem becomes, not solved, but dissolved.

3

Therapeutic Humor in Retelling the Clients' Tellings

In looking at the couple therapy materials used for chapter 2, I was struck by the artful use of humor by the therapist and clients. In that study, humor was examined only in passing, yet I had the suspicion that humor was doing more work than simply a time-out from the principal activity of therapy. So here the work of humor in therapy will be the primary focus. How does humor fit with the serious business of therapy?

Humor in Therapy

The usefulness of humor in therapy has long been recognized (Fry & Salameh, 1987; Strean, 1994). "(S)erious messages can be communicated by speech play and speech play is an important aspect of psychotherapy" (Ferrara, 1994, p. 144). Humor can facilitate introducing awkward topics because it signals the unreality of the issue and allows interactants to allude to the difficulty (Mulkay, 1988). The serious functions of humor allow a speaker to say things that may be unacceptable if stated seriously. "Irony is simultaneously assertion and denial: a way of mentioning the unmentionable" (Clift, 1999, p. 544). Humor can facilitate reframing the interaction or aligning interactants (Goffman, 1974; Gale, 1991; Norrick, 1993). For instance, humor may allow client and therapist to have fun together with the symptom (Frankl, 1967 [cited in Richman, 1996]). Humor is seen as involving a certain risk due to the unpredictability of response (Richman, 1996), but also as potentially leading to insight into "a half-known, feared, or suspected state of affairs" (Pierce, 1994, p. 109).

Various categories of therapist humor have been distinguished in the literature, for instance: "surprise," "exaggeration," "absurdity," "the human condition," "incongruity," "confrontation/affirmation humor," "word play," "metaphorical mirth," "impersonation," "relativizing," "the tragic-comic twist," and "bodily humor" (Salameh, 1987, p. 213–216). These categories, or related ones, have been used for coding or content analysis of the therapist's statements (Falk & Hill, 1992). Given our interest in the therapist-client coconstruction of problems through humor, categories that code only the therapist's statements will prove inadequate. Coding or content analysis is problematical for capturing the intricacies of talk-in-interaction (Beach, 1990).

We start by searching for instances of humor in this consultation. Having located a corpus of cases, we look at what makes the movement into humor relevant, what the humor projects, and how recipients respond to it. The project is to see how humor is designed and oriented to by participants, and how it works in therapeutic interaction. More specifically, we investigate the following research questions:

1. What resources do participants draw upon to move from the serious into humor?
2. What sequential environment(s) make for humor?
3. What does humor project or make relevant as a response from recipients?

Humor in Therapy Talk

Resources for Doing Humor

Most of the humor in this consultation is initiated by the therapist; of the fifteen instances of humor, all but three are therapist initiated. The therapist's humor appears to be designed for doing various therapeutic moves, most notably making ascriptions or recommendations about the clients. This is consistent with the already mentioned point from chapter 2 that one of the primary activities of therapy involves "a retelling of the clients' tellings" (Holmgren, 1999; also cf. Davis, 1986). The therapist's interpretation may differ in certain important respects from what each of the clients have said about their relationship. The therapist presents the couple with an alternative way to see their actions or relationship. In the present case, the couple's differences, rather than being problematical, are actually complimentary. This is contrary to Jenny's telling in which

Larry's inexpressiveness and inability to communicate are presented as the problem (Sluzki, 1990; Buttny, 1990). The therapist offers a different version of their relationship. Retelling the clients' tellings is a delicate activity, especially so when these retellings involve problems, critical descriptions, or alternative versions. As will be seen, the therapist skillfully uses humor in the service of telling the clients about themselves.

Consider the following excerpt in which the therapist moves from serious into humor. To frame his talk as humorous in this excerpt, he draws on three kinds of resources—the first of which is *metaphorical exaggeration* (beginning at line 45).

Excerpt 1. Couple

Jenny: So you're saying it's
complementation[( )
Ther: [> Up to a point < it sounds like you are
one of those fanatics that ah ju[mp into any: boat pkeek:: =
Jenny: [hh
Ther: = with all her soul and you ((deep heavy sound)) you h[a =
??: [heh
Ther: = you say hey wait- wait a min[ute lady, uh huh (.) no: =
Jenny: [hhh heh heh↑
Ther: = reality testing please (.) one two: thr[ee
Larry: [>That's righ[t< HA HA hah
Jenny: [heh heh heh heh
Ther: And uhm:: (.) you would be like a ba↑lloon↓ shooting into
any pla:ce (.) $drif[ting hh if it weren't for the weight =
??: [hah he
Ther: = and you would be$ ((deep heavy sound)) down here
(on flatland if it weren't for the balloon)

The therapist here playfully exaggerates the clients' relational positioning by using the figurative language of metaphors or analogies.

Jenny is described by the hyperbolic metaphor as being a "fanatic that jumps into any boat" (lines 44–45) or by the analogy of "a balloon shooting into any place drifting" (lines 54–55). In their relationship, she is balanced by Larry's cautiousness (line 49; 51) or "weight" (line 55; 57). These exaggerated images, under the guise of humor, allow the therapist to propose a differing vision of the clients' relational patterns than their own versions. It is not the figurative imagery as such that is humorous for the participants, but how that imagery exaggerates the purported interactional patterns of the couple's relationship.

A second resource to signal humor is the therapist's use of *nonlinguistic vocalizations*, e.g., "pkeek::" (line 45) and "((deep heavy sound))" (lines 47, 57). The use of "pkeek::" playfully depicts the verbal imagery "jump into any boat" (line 45). The next nonlingual vocalization, what is glossed as "((deep heavy sound))"[1] (line 47), is used without a co-occurring verbal image. This "((deep heavy sound))" not only substitutes for a verbal description, it also indexically performs the therapist's ascription of Larry. The second use of "((deep heavy sound))" (line 57) comes just before the description, "down here on flatland" (lines 57–8). These nonlingual sounds can serve as onomatopoeia. When accompanied by verbal descriptions, they work to emphasize, illustrate, or perform what is being verbally asserted. These nonlinguistic vocalizations work in conjunction with the metaphorical exaggeration to key the talk from serious into humor.

A third kind of resource the therapist draws on for humorous effect is imputing words to what Larry might or would say (lines 49–51), so-called *hypothetical quotes* (Mayes, 1990; cf. Goffman, 1974, p. 535). Larry's hypothetical response to Jenny epitomizes Larry as balancing Jenny. This fictitious quote is a way of extending or illustrating the exaggerated, metaphorical image of Larry. Interestingly, this hypothetical quote occasions the most laughter in excerpt 1 (see lines 49–53). Since he is the one being playfully quoted, Larry, in particular, shows his appreciation through a mock confirmation and laughter (line 52).

So we see the therapist drawing on three kinds of resources to be humorous: metaphorical exaggeration, nonlingual vocalization, and hypothetical quotes. This movement into humor, however, is not a break from the business of therapy. Under the guise of humor the therapist can continue to make ascriptions of the clients in a less threatening way.

We see that the therapist makes use of these resources again, as he draws on exaggerated imagery and nonlinguistic vocalizations in the course of making a recommendation.

Excerpt 2. Couple

112 Ther: [Because if it happens that either
113 you convince him that he should be like you?
114 or that you convince her that she should be like you?
115 you are going to either find two ba↑llons:: ah[:: drifting in the wind] =
116 Jenny: [Hehehehh heh]
117 Ther: = or [two eh rocks eh BBruuck ((i.e., crashing sound)) at the bottom =
118 Jenny: [heh heh heh heh heh
119 Ther: = of the lake? [huh? and ah::: [(0.9) up to a point =
120 Jenny: [hehh [>Uh huh<
121 Ther: = the differentness between the two of you (0.7)
122 is something that would be worth while respecting, (0.5)
123 ↑in spi::te of the fact that in the sur:face .hh it looks a bit like
124 ah::: (.) conflict.

As the therapist raises the counterfactual condition of each convincing the other of how to be, he invokes both the prior metaphors of balloons and rocks and the accompanying nonlingual vocalizations to describe their relationship. These metaphors (balloons and rocks [line 115, 117]) and vocalizations (BBr*uuck* ((i.e., crashing sound)) [line 117]) again are used to explain his "complimentarity" interpretation of their relationship.

The therapist not only returns to these metaphors, he *extends* them as "two ba↑lloons ah:: drifting in the wind or two eh rocks BBr*uuck* ((i.e., crashing sound)) at the bottom of the lake?" (lines 115–119). The repeated use of these devices still occasions laughter from the clients. Indeed, the *repetition* of the humorous bits seems to be a ready resource for being humorous. Repetition allows for a shortened version of the utterance.

Later in the session the therapist draws again on these resources of exaggerated figurative imagery and nonlingual vocalizations to tell the couple his view in contrast to their views.

Excerpt 3. Couple

Ther: . . . my fantasy is that you express whatever (1.5)
sensible- sensitive emotion of- (.) not anger but: some tender part
and you who are very hungry for (.) that kind of exchange
((swallowing sound))
(0.7)
Jenny: Devour it hhh
Ther: Get into to it and start to ah::m:: feed it
(1.4)
water [it ah:: want more and more all the same
Jenny: [>Uh [huh< hhh
Larry: [heh heh

Here again we see the therapist's use of hyperbolic metaphors and nonlingual vocalizations for humorous effect in presenting his version that differs from those of the clients. In offering his "fantasy" of Jenny, the therapist vocalizes a sound like swallowing (line 129). This nonword vocalization gets sequentially positioned after the metaphor of being "very hungry" (lines 128–129) and depicts her hunger for emotional exchange. Jenny formulates the therapist's sounds as "devour it" and then laughs (line 131).

The therapist continues with this "ravenously hungry" imagery as a technique to convey his alternative vision of the couple's patterns. Notice that it is not merely the therapist using this "hungry" metaphor, but that he exaggerates it—initially with the swallowing vocalization and then with a list of descriptors (lines 132–134), which also occasions the clients' laughter. By the third part of his listing, "water it," it becomes apparent that the therapist is being facetious in his description of Jenny, and it is at this point that she, then Larry, begin to laugh (lines 134–136). Again, while what the therapist says may be facetious, his point appears to be quite serious—it is at once playful and makes a therapeutic point.

As already mentioned, the activity of retelling the clients' tellings is a potentially delicate activity. Recipients may disagree or not like the ascriptions made of them. This is what appears to be happening in excerpt 4. To manage the emerging misalignment, the therapist draws on a facetious humor.

Excerpt 4. Couple

Ther: You don't like what I'm saying >yeah?< =
Jenny: = No: I- I'm thinking about it [uhm
Ther: [>I don't know if you
don't like what I say or is it the way you tilt your glasses
and then- I don't- [( ) understand one way or another<
Jenny: [hh[h: .h heh[heh hh
Larry: [haha [hahh
Jenny: $No:$ >I'm jus-< I'm trying to assimilate (.) everything
you said I'm trying to think about- . . .

The humor in this excerpt occurs as the therapist comments on the way Jenny tilts her glasses (lines 21–23). This comment is obviously facetious, since Jenny is not even wearing glasses. The humor seems to play on something like, "I'm reading your nonverbals." The humor assuages the disagreement between Jenny and the therapist. The therapist's move to humor comes in response to Jenny's denial (line 20) that she dislikes the therapist's prior ascription. The therapist exploits his own prior turn (line 19) by mockingly reiterating it as an alternative explanation to the tilt-your-glasses comment (line 22). The transcription of lines 21–23 fails to adequately capture the shift in the therapist's prosody to a quickened staccato, which seems to underscore the facetiousness of "the way you tilt your glasses" ascription (line 22). In other words, the prosodic shift co-occurs with the shift from serious to humor.

It does not appear obvious that the therapist is being humorous, or at least, the clients do not immediately laugh or display recognition to the therapist's "tilt-your-glasses" line, though a moment later both Jenny and Larry laugh. The clients' lack of an immediate response to the therapist's facetiousness in the above excerpt provokes the question of how speech is recognizable as humor. The humor in the first three excerpts seems fairly obvious and is oriented to by the recipients' laughter or appreciative comments. However, there are cases in which the speaker is intending to be humorous, but the recipients do not recognize it or display recognition, or cases in which a recipient takes something as humorous, which was not intended as such. For our purposes, humor is taken as a commonsense category in which at least one participant displays it or orients to it in some way. Misalignments or misunderstandings over humor are themselves interesting phenomena (as will be shown below). Our main concern here is how humor is used and oriented to by participants.

How members orient to what is being said, as serious or as humorous, is a fundamental issue in any interaction and clearly will influence how they respond. An interesting instance of this arises in the different responses to the therapist's comment, "Don't spit on your blessings" (line 80).

Excerpt 5. Couple

Ther: . . . but I insist that that makes it uh: (1.4) ah::: (0.7)
for the reason or the balance of the couple °huh?°
Jenny: Uh huh
Ther: So:::
(0.8)
Larry: Th[ere's some-
Jenny: [You're sayin[g:
Ther: [Don't spit on your blessings
(0.8)
Larry: Th[at's right, there's some point you can always =
Jenny: [hg[gh:: hhhhhhhhhhhhhhhhhhh
Ther: [HAh hah hah hah hah hah
Larry = want better >I mean< no matter at what point you are
(0.8) I think we always should want better? but if:: you can't-
you don't have the ability to be happy with what you have . . .

It is not at all obvious that the therapist's comment, "Don't spit on your blessings" (line 80), is meant to be humorous. This figurative speech or proverb can be heard as justifying the therapist's prior assessment about their complimentarity as a couple (lines 73–74) (Drew & Holt, 1998). Also, there is nothing unusual or marked in the therapist's delivery of this comment.

There is no immediate response to it from the clients as seen by the gap (line 81). Larry, then, responds by concurring with it and offering a second assessment (lines 82, 85–87). Jenny, however, immediately comes in with laughter (line 83), overlapping Larry, and then the therapist also joins in the laughter (line 84). Larry does not break for this laughter, but continues through with his serious point, while the therapist, then Jenny, cease laughing. So while Jenny and the therapist join in mutual laughter, Larry's not joining in makes for a momentary misalignment. This momentary disjuncture among the participants underscores the notion that humor is an interactional accomplishment. Humor sequentially implicates others to join in, or at least, show appreciation (Jefferson, 1979). For play to continue beyond the initial utterance, recipients need to partake in it (Hopper, 1995).

An interesting, unresolvable ambiguity with "Don't spit on your blessings" (line 80) is whether or not it is meant to be humorous. If not, then Jenny's laughter can be heard as a way to resist the therapist's position.

As already mentioned, the majority of instances of humor in the consultation are initiated by the therapist. One of the few cases of client-initiated humor is seen below. Both Larry and Jenny collaborate in moving into humor. Larry's muffled laughter gets articulated by Jenny's teasing question about the therapist's language (lines 12–19).

Excerpt 6. Couple

6 Ther: ... and for you to talk in the language of her means to
7 receive her emotions (.) ah:: amplifying them a bit
8 and for you to receive his emotions damping them.
9 Jenny: Uh hum
10 Ther: Er that's all and in that sense you are modulating the
11 channels
12 Larry: hh[h
13 Ther: [$You are$ uhm:: (1.0) eh connecting eh (1.1)
14 between- where the other one is at.

Jenny: Uh [huh
Ther: [>uh huh?<
(1.5)
Jenny: Do you have a degree in engineering you ↑sound
ju(h)st li(h)ke him? h[ehheh
Ther: [I do huh?[hhhh
Jenny: [$Ye[ah$ heh heh heh
Larry: [hah hah hah hah
Jenny: See he's into amplification and damp(h)ening an(h)d hh
( ) it's true ah

Jenny initiates humor through her "degree in engineering" question (line 18). She changes footings addressing the therapist's lexical choices, rather than his substantive observation. Jenny's humor exploits the therapist's previous turns in which he uses some engineering vocabulary (lines 7–11). In making light of the therapist's language, Jenny may be heard as teasing (Drew, 1987). Similar to the therapist's humor, Jenny draws on exaggerated imagery in being funny, and also, makes a facetious ascription of the therapist.

Jenny's humor can be heard as returning to the object of Larry's earlier laugh (line 12) following the therapist's description, "modulating the channels." Larry's laughter here allows us to raise the question of unintended humor. It is doubtful whether the therapist was trying to be funny with his imagery, "you are modulating the channels" (lines 10–11). The therapist's smile voice (line 13) overlaps and displays recognition of Larry's laughter, but he disattends to it by continuing with his therapeutic recommendation. Jenny's teasing remark, "degree in engineering" (line 18), aligns with Larry's prior laughter.

Jenny's initiation of humor occurs in the slot after the therapist's prompting as to his prior recommendation (lines 13–18). There is a 1.5 second gap following the therapist's prompt (line 16) before Jenny switches into humor. In reply to Jenny's teasing and laughter, the therapist offers a mock response, "I do huh?," combined with laughter to play along (line 20). Jenny offers a quick conformation to the therapist, as she and Larry overlap in laughter (lines 21–22). The humor gets extended as Jenny builds on the original image by offering an account of Larry's engineering vocabulary interspersed with laughter particles (lines 23–24).

Sequential Environments for Movement into Humor

Given the fact that the majority of the talk in this therapy consultation is serious, at what points do the participants move into humor? In other words, in what "sequential environments" is humor used? Consider the following excerpt that occurs just before excerpt 1.

Excerpt 7. Couple

29 Jenny Uhm:: what you're saying is that this might represent

30 what's actually going on in the relationship

31 > ya know this sort of < [me pulling =

32 Ther: [( )

33 Jenny: = in one direction and him pulling in another direction

34 wanting something else a[nd ( )

35 Ther: [But that may be a description

36 of the:: complimentarity of the relationship t[he fact that =

37 Jenny: [>Uh huh<

38 Ther: = eh:: ah:::: for a person to be able to dr:ag: requires another

39 person to be able to pull >for another person to pull requires

40 another person to drag in order to< go: in a certain (.) ah

41 balanced eh: speed and intensit[y (because it's)

42 Jenny: [So you're saying it's

43 complementation[( )

44 Ther: [>Up to a point< it sounds like you are

45 one of those fanatics . . . ((see excerpt 1))

Consider the sequential environment in which the therapist moves into humor. In this excerpt, Jenny formulates what the therapist has said (lines 29–34) (the therapist's utterances are not shown here). Formulations project a confirmation-disconfirmation response from the recipient (Heritage & Watson, 1979; Watson, 1995). The therapist does confirm her formulation with, "But that may be a description of the complimentarity of the relationship" (lines 35–36) along with further explanation (lines 38–41). Jenny, then, offers a second formulation, the gist of what the therapist is saying (lines 42–43). Given that a serious therapeutic interpretation has already been offered twice (the first version is not reproduced in this excerpt), the therapist responds to Jenny's gist with a qualified confirmation, "Up to a point," and then shifts footing into humor (lines 44–45 and see excerpt 1, lines 44–58). Humor is drawn on in the course of his third attempt at presenting his therapeutic position. So having to *repeat* or *elaborate* on a viewpoint seems to be a ready sequential environment for the movement into humor.

Another environment for humor appears when there is some *disagreement* or *misalignment* between participants. This environment of disagreement, or more precisely withholding agreement, is apparent in the following excerpt.

Excerpt 8. Couple

Ther: . . . or I $ wan(h)t I wa(h)nt less:,$ [so it reproduces =
Jenny: [Um hm
Ther: = a bit what may be ah:: (.) uhm: (.)
a stylistic? issue::: in your:: (.) couple.
(O.8)
Jenny: °Uh huh°
Ther: Yeah?
(1.6)
Ther: You don't like what I'm saying >yeah?<
Jenny: = No: I- I'm thinking about it [uhm
Ther: [> I don't know if you
don't like what I say or is it the way you tilt your glasses . . .

Here the therapist offers his interpretation (only a portion of which is shown [lines 11–14]) that Jenny and Larry have different styles. After

Jenny gives an acknowledgement token (line 16), the therapist pursues how they take his interpretation with the query "Yeah?" (line 17). Given the noticeable absence of a reply at line 18, the therapist ascribes disagreement to Jenny (line 19). Following her denial, the therapist moves to the "tilt your glasses" humor (cf. analysis of excerpt 4).

Another instance of drawing on humor in the environment of emerging disagreement is seen in the following.

Excerpt 9. Couple

105 Ther: At the same time[this complimentarity that we were discussing =
106 Jenny: [>Yeah<
107 Ther: is a useful one
108 Jenny: Uh huh
109 Ther: For the balance of the relationship, you shouldn't change it too: ↑much
110 (1.6)
111 Jenny: We:l[l:?
112 Ther: [Because if it happens that either
113 you convince him that he should be like you?
114 or that you convince her that she should be like you?
115 you are going to either find two ba↑lloons:: . . .
((excerpt 2)).

The therapist's use of humor here occurs in the course of a serious explanation and is designed to counter Jenny's reservations by further elaborating his viewpoint. In a serious manner, the therapist refers back to his "complimentarity" interpretation and recommends that their relationship not be changed "too much" (lines 105–109). Jenny's reply, "We:ll:" (line 111), implicates possible disagreement or resistance, to which the therapist responds by returning to his prior metaphoric imagery of balloons and rocks (see excerpt 2).

In excerpts 8 and 9, the therapist draws on humor to manage an emerging, possible disagreement with one of the clients. The therapist also uses humor in the sequential environment of disagreement between the clients. For instance, the humor found in excerpt 10 (below) comes after Larry and Jenny have each offered conflicting accounts (only the final portion of Jenny's account is reproduced (lines 114–115)). The therapist comes in to offer his "fantasy" (line 117) of their situation and uses ironic humor (line 122) in the course of moving into telling the therapist's view.

Excerpt 10. Couple

Jenny: ...he's saying (0.3) oh she's not interested anyway

or she has enough of her own problems these are .hh[h

Ther: [Do you

know what my own fantasy is of all thi[s if I may share =

Jenny: [>Uh huh<

Ther: = it with you? [.hh is that (1.2) quite by the =

Jenny: [>Uh huh<

Ther: = contrary (1.1) by the way you describe, (.) the situation

and b- ↑I already know you an half an hour

Jenny: haa[h:: haah:

Ther. [$UHM UHM$

(1.8)

Ther: Tha::t (1.6) my fantasy is that you express whatever (1.5)

sensible- sensitive emotion of- ((see excerpt 3))

The therapist intervenes, following Larry and Jenny's conflicting accounts, with what he calls his "fantasy" of the couple's situation. In making ascriptions of clients, therapists commonly use a "professional cautiousness" (Drew & Heritage, 1992) by qualifying or mitigating their descriptions, such as by expressing uncertainty or invoking limited knowledge of them (Peräkylä & Silverman, 1991; Bergmann, 1992). This notion of professional cautiousness has been conceived of as a serious activity, but here the therapist does this qualifying or professing limited knowledge by the ironic preface, "↑I already know you an half an hour," which occasions laughter from Jenny (lines 122–123). As he continues with his "fantasy," or vision of the couple, he uses the further humor resources described in excerpt 3 (see above).

By way of summary, we have seen the therapist change footings from serious into humor in the sequential environments of repeatedly offering a therapeutic interpretation, of emerging disagreement or misalignment with a client or between clients, and in being professionally cautious. In the next section we turn to how participants respond to humor in therapy.

Responding to Humor

Typical responses to humor involve laughter or additional humor, but we will see that humor occasions a variety of other kinds of responses. What does humor sequentially implicate from recipients, and what do they make relevant from it?

Given that humorous utterances involve claims that are not meant to be taken literally, how is the recipient to respond? Looking at the responses to the "tilt-your-glasses" segment (see below), we see that Jenny, then Larry, laugh, thereby displaying recognition of the therapist's playful move (lines 21–25).

Excerpt 11. Couple

Ther: You don't like what I'm saying > °yeah?° < =
Jenny: = No: I- I'm thinking about it [uhm
Ther: [> I don't know if you
don't like what I say or is it the way you tilt your glasses
and then I don't- [( ) understand one way or another <
Jenny: [h[hh
Larry: [hh
Jenny: $ No: $ > I'm jus- < I'm trying to assimilate (.) everything
you said I'm trying to think about-
(1.2)
Uhm:: what you're saying is that this might represent
what's actually going on in the relationship
> ya know this sort of < [me pulling =
Ther: [( )
Jenny: = in one direction and him pulling in another direction
wanting something else and ( )

Following the laughter in response to the "tilt your glasses" segment, Jenny reasserts her accounted for denial of not liking what the therapist is saying (line 26). Her turn-initial, "No," is uttered with a smile voice (line 26). A smile voice is hard to analytically describe though easy to recognize in real time. To offer a gloss, a smile voice involves a markedly higher pitch and an intonational contour comparable to laughing during speaking but without any laughter tokens. By contrast, her turn-initial "No:" at line 20 is unmarked and hearable as serious. Her smile voice on "No" (line 26) displays a continuing recognition of the therapist's humor, though as the subsequent account shows, she moves into a serious mode. She cuts this account short (lines 26–27), and after a pause (line 28), formulates the therapist's earlier interpretation (lines 29–34).

The therapist's humor in excerpt 11 seems to function to *disarm Jenny's resistance* and *reengage her in considering his interpretation*. This latter point is evident from Jenny's formulation of the therapist's view (lines 29–34). Jenny's laughter plays along with the "tilt-your-glasses" humor, while her accounted for denial responds to the "You don't like what I'm saying." So she is responding to both the humorous and serious relevancies of the therapist's prior comments.

Turning to another case of responses to humor, recall in excerpt 1 the therapist uses the playful devices of metaphors, vocalizations, and hypothetical quotes. Jenny responds, not only with laughter, but also by formulating the upshot of the therapist's interpretation, "↑So he's a- he's a $ stable anchoring force in my li[fe (   ) $" (see below, lines 59–60).

Excerpt 12. Couple

54 Ther: And uhm:: (.) you would be like a ba↑lloon↓ shooting into
55 any pla:ce (.) $drif[ting hh if it weren't for the weight =
56 ??: [hah he
57 Ther: = and you would be$ ((deep heavy sound)) down here
58 (on flatland if it we[ren't for the balloon)
59 Jenny: [$(So he's a- he's a stable anchoring force
60 in my li[fe (   ) $
61 Ther: [↑I have the impression that ↓tha:t's
62 the way it looks a bit now↑

63 (1.8)

64 Jenny: .hh ↑Yeah (.) actually tha:t's: quite true in many ways . . .

In her formulation, Jenny extends the therapist's metaphor of Larry as a weight, to Larry as a "stable anchoring force" (lines 59–60). The propositional content of her response formulates the therapist's interpretation, while the prosody of her response with a smile voice displays recognition of the humorous mode. Her smile voice in uttering, "stable anchoring force in my life," evokes a continuing playfulness. Also using a smile voice to formulate the therapist's point can be heard as implicating a skepticism about it. So Jenny's response (lines 59–60) can be heard as continuing the humor occasioned by the therapist's metaphors while simultaneously displaying a serious recognition of the therapist's view.

In the prior two excerpts, Jenny responds to the therapist's humor by offering a formulation of what the therapist is saying. *Her formulation in response to humor displays recognition that the therapist's humor is not just play, but has a therapeutic point that her formulation attempts to articulate.*

Jenny's response (excerpt 12, lines 59–60), in turn, projects competing relevancies—the continued playfulness displayed through the smile voice, or the seriousness of her formulation. The therapist replies with a qualified confirmation of Jenny's formulation in a serious way (lines 61–62). It is striking here how the therapist shifts footing into a serious mode; his rise-fall prosody markedly departs from his prior humor (lines 54–58) as he confirms the content of Jenny's formulation. Jenny's reply (line 64), now also serious, concurs with the therapist's impression. The broader point here is that the movement out of or into humor is achieved by participants aligning or not with each other's footings.

As already mentioned, most of the humor in this session is initiated by the therapist. The therapist's humor seems embedded within a larger serious turn. The consequence of this embedded humor within a larger turn is that recipients' laughter or brief comments occur only in passing. Therapist-initiated humor does not lead to an extended humor sequence or a humor round. But the few instances of client-initiated humor have a rather different trajectory—some develop into an extended humor sequence. For instance, in excerpt 13, Jenny switches footings into humor (line 33) in the sequential environment of a disagreement between her and Larry. The humor of her remark gets developed by all the participants into a humor round (lines 33–63).[2]

Excerpt 13. Couple

Larry: . . . I'm not afra::id to show emotion I- [I
Jenny: [But
>you< you are °with me:, I think°
(0.4) you don't do it as much with ↑me:
as you do it with other people? .hh
(4.3)
Larry: Right, so it's not fear:, it might ↑be lack of tru:st
(1.1) °but it's not fear°.
Ther: Um hum (.) .hhh ah lack of trust means ah:: (0.9)
the ways in: which: (0.5) you ah::: (2.4) ah:: worry
(0.8) she may be handling those feelings:
Larry: Ye:s: (.) very goo[d
Jenny: [Uh huh > uh huh < =
Ther: = Yeah?
Jenny: Just like with his mother
(1.2)
Ther: H[ehhhhhhh ((whisper voice)) How psychoanalytic! =
Jenny: [HHhh heh: hhh heh hhhh
Larry: [hah hah hah hhhhhhh $That's right (.) that's right$
Ther: = they shoot you wit[h interpretation[s =
Jenny: [hh [hh
Ther: = one after the other ((whisper voice))
Larry: Or general categories
Ther: HA[HA ha ha ha ha
Jenny: [Hhh[hhhhh
Larry: [Anal compulsive neurotic
Ther: ((claps hands)) G[awd you are fan::tas:::t[ic! you learn:: =

Jenny: [Hhh [hh[hhhh
Larry: [hh
Ther: = you almost have graduated huh?
Larry: Hah hah[hhh
Jenny: [Hhh ↑Close he he hhh
Ther: Gawd, how nice,
Jenny: Hhh
Ther: Uhm
(3.3)
Ther: pt okay uhm?
(3.5)
Ther: Leaving aside your $mother for a momen[t$
Larry: [Heh hhh
Jenny: [hhhhh
Ther: uhm:: where were w[e?
Jenny: [( )
Ther: °where[what?° (1.2) you can't ( ) ha hhh =
Jenny: [heh[hehh heh heh heh heh hh
Larry: [hhhhhhhhh
Ther: = Uhm:?

This excerpt begins with the couple disagreeing over whether Larry is fearful or lacks trust (lines 19–26); the therapist intervenes and rephrases "lack of trust" (lines 27–29). Larry immediately concurs with this rephrasing. The therapist pursues more of a response from the clients (line 32), when Jenny comments, "Just like with his mother" (line 33). There is not an immediate response, as seen in the 1.2-second gap, which may reflect the ambiguity of the remark. Jenny's utterance here could be heard as a criticism, adding another issue (e.g., "his mother") to the conflict. From viewing the videotape, however, Jenny smiles as she utters, "Just like with his mother," and smiles more broadly upon competition during the 1.2 second gap. The smile may be taken as a cue by recipients for how to take, "Just like with his mother." The smile here works as a "key," in Goffman's (1974) terms, to attempt to transform the talk from serious into humor.

The therapist's response of laughter (line 35) ratifies "Just like with his mother" as humorous. The clients, then, immediately join in, overlapping with laughter (lines 36–37). The therapist immediately adds, "How psychoanalytic!" (line 35), uttered a whisper voice, sotto voce. The therapist's assessment here is clearly facetious—a kind of mock praise or tease. The therapist's comment here obliquely refers to a prior exchange (not shown) in which he cautions Jenny about the dangers of spending too much time in therapy. Humor may exhibit the well-known quality of being double-edged, what Mulkay (1988) calls "the duality of humor," in combining the serious and the unserious. The therapist's reply, "How psychoanalytic!," seems to exhibit this double-edged character. Indeed, it artfully matches the double-edged quality of "Just like with his mother."

The therapist continues with this mock praise of Jenny and psychoanalysis uttered in a whisper voice (line 38–40). Larry joins in developing this mock line by adding some well-known psychoanalytic terms (lines 41 and 44). Jenny sustains the playfulness of the mock praise by laughing in overlap with the therapist (lines 42–43) and going along with his teasing comment that she has almost graduated (lines 48–50).

The humor sequence abates following the therapist's ironic capping assessment, "Gawd, how nice" (line 51) and Jenny's brief laughter. The therapist initiates transition back to the business at hand, and the clients do not continue with the humor (lines 53–56). However, the therapist rekindles the humor by the ironic comment, "Leaving aside your $ mother for a momen[t $" (line 57), uttered with a smile voice. The clients readily join in continuing the sequence with overlapping laughter. The therapist initiates this round of humor by alluding to Jenny's initial remark. As the therapist attempts to get back on track, Jenny says something indecipherable (line 61), which the therapist plays along with, (line 62) generating more overlapping laughter (lines 62–64). This excerpt exhibits the longest humor sequence in the session. Jointly producing this extended humor sequence allows the participants to align, unlike the immediately preceding misalignment over the competing fear-versus-mistrust attribution.

Discussion

Humor seems to be a kind of fallback option for the therapist when the serious efforts of therapy are not working well. We saw that humor arises in the sequential environments of repeated serious efforts at explaining a therapeutic version, of disagreements, in pursing a response which is being withheld or in being cautious. The therapist's humor arises in response to some interactional difficulty. When participants withheld agreement with a therapeutic interpretation, or when they conflicted with each other, one response was to draw on humor. Disagreements were the most common environment for using humor. Humor offers the therapist a way to attempt to reframe the ongoing interaction or the discursive position being advocated. For instance, under the guise of hyperbole the therapist can continue to articulate his interpretation, albeit within a humorous frame. Even client-initiated humor, such as Jenny's "Just like with his mother" (excerpt 13, line 33), allows for a brief "time-out" from explicit disagreement between her and Larry. So, humor in therapy functions as a lubricant to grease the conflicting edges of therapeutic contact.

Humor has been conceived of as a break in frame from the primary, serious activity at hand (Goffman, 1974). But in the above transcripts therapeutic work goes on in and through much of the humor. This is most obvious in the therapist-initiated humor, but even in client-initiated humor some of the therapist's playful responses embody therapeutic moves. For instance, the therapist facetiously ascribes "psychoanalytic" to Jenny in the course of a humor (excerpt 13, lines 35–48). This ascription, said in jest, seems to allude to the issue of Jenny's over-involvement in therapy. Humor, instead of being a complete break from the business of therapy, allows for therapeutic moves under a different guise.

To do humor various resources can be drawn on, as we have seen in this therapy session: hyperbole, metaphors, hypothetical quotes, repetition or extension of prior humor, facetiousness, irony, nonlingual vocalizations, and prosodic features, e.g., smile voice, whisper voice, mocking voice. These resources are not unique to therapy, they may be found as well in ordinary conversational contexts (Mondada, 1998). While these resources may be general devices, in the present transcripts they are used in making therapeutic moves, e.g., exaggerating an image to offer an alternative construction of the relationship, making ascriptions of the clients, disarming a client's disagreement, or illustrating an image.

There are various kinds of responses to the humor used in therapy. While humor is an invitation to laugh or play, the largely serious activity of therapy can implicate competing relevancies. The serious functions of humor can create a complication for the recipient in how to respond. There seems to be a "duality" in some humor in that one can orient to the humorous or the serious aspects of the utterance (Drew, 1987; Mulkay, 1988). When the therapist uses humor to offer his interpretation, the clients can attend to the humorous or serious aspects. On the one hand, there is a sequential implication to show appreciation for the humor through laughter or further humor, but on the other hand, to assess the therapist's interpretation through a confirming or disconfirming response. This latter point of assessing the therapist's interpretation becomes especially salient to the extent that the therapist's humor is evaluative (Clift, 1999, p. 546).

The sequential movement into or out of humor is a joint accomplishment. Recipients need to ratify a prior utterance as humor by signs of appreciation or adding to the humor. For the humor frame to be sustained, participants must partake in it.

The majority of instances of humor in this consultation are initiated by the therapist. The few cases of client-initiated humor appear in the mid- to end portions of the session. This asymmetry in initiating humor may reflect the clients' orientation to the therapist as expert by their refraining from disrupting the largely serious activity of therapy (Buttny, 1990). To move from the serious business of therapy into humor reflects a certain presumption on the part of the initiator. Initiating humor and laughter can have a disruptive effect that clients may want to avoid.

We began this investigation by noting that one of the therapist's main speech activities involves a retelling of the clients' tellings. Making ascriptions of others can be a delicate enterprise, especially when the ascriptions differ from the clients' own avowals. A common way to make delicate ascriptions of another is to allude to them such as with metaphor (Ferrara, 1994). Allusions allow the recipient to infer the message without the speaker explicitly uttering it. A seemingly opposite strategy is to humorously exaggerate the clients' condition such that the ascription seems facetious, but at the same time, obliquely articulating a truth. This kind of humor seems to work to invoke a playful frame of clients' relational circumstance, which disarms the clients' resistance and creates an environment for presenting the therapist's contrasting interpretation.

Part II

Reportings in Talking Problems

4

Reported Speech in Talking Race on Campus

> I was very proud of the fact that Black students decided to stand up. Martin Luther King said, you know that a man can't ride your back unless it is bent. And that was one of the things we spoke about at the rally—was that it was time for us to stand up, so that nobody would ride our backs on campus anymore (Student, *Racism 101*).

> People were saying everything was an isolated incident, an isolated incident, but you started to see isolated incidents at the University of Michigan. You started to see isolated incidents at the University of Massachusetts. You started to see isolated incidents at Mount Holyoke and so forth. So now we have thousands of isolated incidents that were going on (Student, *Racism 101*).

> A lot of what you begin to see now are a lot of White students saying, Enough. I'm sick of hearing about racism. We dealt with that six months ago. And so I think, in reality, things are even worse. Things possibly are worse now than they were six or seven months ago (Student, *Racism 101*).

A variety of discourse formats are used in talking race: people tell racial narratives (e.g., stories of racism or interracial conflict), assert general propositions (e.g., "things will never change"), give examples from their own direct experience or from readings or the media, or provide explanations (e.g., "people prefer to hang out with their own kind"). A rich source of materials for analysis is how some speakers quote the words of others, or themselves, so-called "reported speech." Prior discourse analyses of race and racism have concentrated mostly on narratives and accounts, but have overlooked this phenomena of reported speech. The practice of reporting another's speech is seen in the epigrams. "Martin Luther King," "people," and "a lot of White students" respectively are used as sources for quotes. These quotes draw on another's words while simultaneously shaping them for the reporting speaker's own purposes. This "double-voiced" quality (Volosinov, 1973) is what makes reported speech such an intriguing site for analysis of talking race.

This investigation will examine *reported speech as a conversational practice* and *how it serves to discursively construct realities about race*. Under "practice," the different forms reported speech can take are examined, how reported speech is connected to assessments, and how reported speech interactionally functions in context. Under "discursive construction of realities," participants' ways of representing racialized incidents and events is examined through the use of reported speech. The notion of "race," and the particular racial categories, "White" or "African American," are taken as sociohistorical constructions, rather than fixed, physiological designations (Hacker, 1992, ch.1; Miles, 1989; Sanjek, 1994). The concept of race reflects sociohistorical and political conditions, not a scientific grouping of peoples. 'African American,' 'Latino,' and 'White,' are used because these seem to reflect the current preferred usage among these respective peoples.

Reported Speech

> The transmission and assessment of the speech of others, the discourse of another, is one of the most widespread and fundamental topics of human speech. In all areas of life and ideological activity, our speech is filled to overflowing with other people's words, which are transmitted with highly varied degrees of accuracy and impartiality. The more intensive, differentiated and highly developed the social life of a speaking collective, the greater is the importance attaching . . . to another's word, another's utterance, since another's word will be the subject of passionate communication, an object of interpretation, discussion, evaluation, rebuttal, support, further development and so on (Bakhtin, 1981: 337).

Using the utterances of others seems to offer rich material for understanding how members construct a "portrait" of the other (Basso, 1979). The notion, "portrait of the other," is meant to capture how out-group members are presented though reported speech. As Basso found in his study of Western Apache jokes about Whites, most of the portraits of out-group members are ridiculous or critical. This finding can be broadened beyond humor and jokes to other discourse types such as reported speech.

Reported speech is commonly thought of as direct or indirect speech (Coulmas, 1986; Li, 1986). Direct speech purportedly reproduces the words of the original source, while indirect speech conveys the prepositional content but not the source's words. Direct quotes allow for the performative aspects of the original speech, since the reporting speaker can draw upon the original language as well as the prosodic and stylistic dimensions of those words (Bauman, 1986).

Various distinctions have been made in the literature about reported speech (adopted from Sternberg (1982: 109–110):

1. The reporting speaker may quote another person or quote him/herself.
2. The quote may be of what was verbally said or of what was thought, what may be called "reported thought."
3. The quote may be verbal or nonverbal, where the latter includes bodily movements and vocal qualities, such as intonation or regional/ethnic accent or dialect.
4. The quote can report the words of a single person or of a dialogue between two or more persons.
5. The quote can be of what was actually said or be fictional, that is, contrary-to-fact—what "should" or "could" have been said or what "will" be said.
6. The quote can be overtly marked by a reporting clause, shift in intonation, or in writing by quotation marks; or it can be unmarked.
7. The quote can be continuous or interspersed with the reporting speaker's commentary.

Strictly speaking the notion of reported speech is a misnomer, not only because of the issue of the reproduction or accuracy of the material quoted, but more basically, because the previously uttered words are now being used in a different context (Sternberg, 1982). As Tannen (1989) observes, reported speech is really "constructed" speech in that the quoted prior text serves the purposes of the current speaker in the present context, such as to "involve" the hearer in the present speech event. Reported speech is "recontextualized" in the reporting context (Suchman, 1993).

In the course of talking race, participants at times quote the speech of others or of themselves. While we commonly think of quoting to invoke the words of an authority (as, for example, Martin Luther King is commonly quoted), reported speech can be put to multiple uses. It can be used to discredit the original source ("People were saying everything was an isolated incident"), or to summarize the attitudes of others ("a lot of White students (are) saying, 'Enough. I'm sick of hearing about racism. . .'"). Reported speech can serve various functions: to dramatize a point, to give evidence for a position, to epitomize a condition, and so on.

Reported speech commonly, though not exclusively, occurs in narratives. Much of our actions about which we tell stories are things done with words, so what I, or another, has said becomes the resources we can draw on in narratives. Reported speech seems reserved for capturing the most crucial or interesting parts of the narrative. This may be because reported speech, especially direct quotes, come closest to presenting what was said, and thereby, done. The reported speech conveys the "what was said," but some context for the reported speech is necessary to indicate "what actions were done" along with their social significance. Reported speech fits into these speech activities as a form of "evidence" and as a way to hold another "responsible" (Hill & Irvine, 1993). Quoting another's words can convey an air of "objectivity" about what happened in that the recipient can "see for themselves" what another said and did (Holt, 1996).

Reported speech can be characterized as a "double-voiced discourse" reflecting both the original speaker and the present speaker (Bakhtin, 1981). "Double voiced" in that the present speaker appropriates the quoted discourse for his/her own purposes in the present context. In reporting speech, one is doing more than merely reporting—one is also, at least implicitly, commenting on that reported speech (Bakhtin, 1981; 1986). To comment on prior speech is to assess it or evaluate it, and thereby, to discursively position oneself and others (Davies & Harré, 1999).

Reported speech can take various forms. To illustrate, in the following excerpt, C reports the speech of a White student by summarizing it (lines 4–6) and then directly reports her own speech in response (lines 7–8).

Excerpt 1. Three African Americans

3 C: I mean me and another White student talk about this,

4 he say he can look around the room and pick which Blacks are

here because of academics and which Blacks are here because of
affirmative action by what they say in class
and I was like you can't say that but you can say
the same thing about some of these White students here

Reported speech can not only summarize what an individual said (as in lines 4–6), but also summarize the speech of an aggregate, e.g., "I've heard a lot of White people say the same thing about Black people." Perhaps the most interesting way to summarize a group is through a quote of the prototypical group member to epitomize the group's characteristic utterances (arrow):

Excerpt 2. Four Latinos

The way the White students reacted was like
→ well I didn't put it out.

So, we have the main types: (i) direct reported speech; and (ii) summary reported speech. The latter, summary speech, can be divided into three subtypes: (a) of an individual; (b) an aggregate; or (c) a prototypical group member (Payne, n.d.). In addition, a third main type, (iii) hypothetical quotes (Irvine, 1996; Mayes, 1990), involve speech which 'could,' 'would,' or 'may' be said (lines 22–23):

Excerpt 3. Two Whites

B: but if someone comes up to me and says
I'm White and proud to be White and everyone should be proud to be White
I'm like who the hell is this freak get outta my face ya know

Since such quotes are fictitious, strictly speaking, they are not reported speech. But hypothetical quotes bear enough family resemblance to be considered alongside reported speech.

These various forms of reported speech work within larger discursive structures, such as narratives (to vividly convey problematic actions through what was said) or within claim-evidence sequences (as a form of evidence to support claims about racial matters). Through such conversational practices, the speaker is not merely reporting speech, but also assessing speech—the character of the actions recreated through the quotes. Reported speech is relevantly tied to assessment. Assessment reveals the reporting speaker's positioning towards the quoted words. Recreating others' actions through quoting their words is a way of criticizing or resisting troublesome events, or if a positive assessment, through valorizing or supporting such actions. Quoting others' utterances is a way to hold them socially accountable (Buttny, 1993) because through their own words, or summary thereof, the action in question gets "recreated" through talk. Invoking others' words can yield conversational power in ascribing meanings to the reported event and building conversational alliances (Álvarez-Cáccamo, 1996).

Studies of Racism and Interracial Contact

University campuses, traditionally thought of as alternative places in society, as havens for free expression and respect for differences, have not escaped ethnic and racial friction. Campuses across the USA have witnessed uncivil exchanges and hate incidents, such as racist and anti-Semitic graffiti, notes, slurs, and ethnic name calling (Sidel, 1994). These conflicts heighten the sense of difference and group boundaries as reflected in so-called voluntary segregation in social life among many groups on campus (Asante & Al-Seen, 1984; Gitlin, 1992; Scott, 1992). Such tensions are fueled by a decline in enrollments among traditionally under-represented groups, and a resurgence of an activist conservative agenda that calls into question recently enacted progressive policies.

Simply bringing members of different ethnic groups together on campus does not ensure amiable relations. The intergroup contact hypothesis predicts that negative stereotypes and prejudice will abate, as historically segregated groups come into contact. However, the data do not support the hypothesis (Hewstone & Brown, 1986). The contact needs to be frequent and intimate enough to overturn prevailing stereotypes and the sense of difference. For without such "quality communication," the perception of difference increases intergroup distance (Tzeng et al., 1986). Such sense of distance may be heightened by misunderstandings resulting from diverging cultural communication styles (Kochman, 1981) or different interaction orders (Rawls, 2000), which make for "difficult dialogues" (Houston, 1994; Orbe, 1994). Low levels of "communication satisfaction" resulting from those few occasions of intergroup contact reinforce one of the most common communication strategies—avoidance (Hecht et al., 1989; Martin et al., 1994).

Talk about race typically occurs *within* what persons define as their own racial group (VanDijk, 1987). People acquire and learn to articulate their racial attitudes from a variety of sources (e.g., mass media, parents, schools, firsthand experiences), but one of the most important is how such viewpoints are interpreted within one's peer group discussions. Participants, especially Whites, would likely be more reticent or circumspect in talking race in cross-racial groups (Kochman, 1981; Martin, et al., 1994; Pinderhughes, 1989). Whites are aware of norms against "sounding prejudiced," so they design their talk to appear "reasoned" and their narratives to provide "evidence" for their positions (Billig et al., 1988; Wetherell & Potter, 1992). While some of the Whites' discourse on racial incidents was found to be critical of Black people, it is not unequivocally so (Van Dijk, 1987). Often Whites' discourse is structured as reasonable, it uses rationale argument, bases claims on firsthand or secondhand experience, and is qualified in various ways (Wetherell & Potter, 1992; Verkuytem, Jong & Masson, 1995; Dixon, Reicher, & Foster, 1997). Billig et al. (1988) characterize these conflicting discourses as an "ideological dilemma"—of Whites being critical of minorities on the one hand, but not wanting to appear prejudiced on the other.

Van Dijk (1987; 1993) found that Whites in talking race discuss a narrow range of topics focusing on sociocultural differences with the implicit message of the minority's inferiority. The stories told about race are generally argumentative, used to justify negative conclusions about Blacks, and express blame and resentment. Such narratives were often "complaint stories" focusing on a complication that lacks a resolution. While only a few Whites spoke in explicitly racist language, their speech style and rhetoric revealed a "double strategy" of positive self-presentation and a negative other-presentation along with a critical distance toward minorities.

In general, there seems to be this asymmetry of perception—African Americans report on the continuing problems of racism, while Whites deny seeing it or claim that it is exaggerated (Pinderhughes, 1989; Essed, 1991). Blauner (1989) explains this asymmetry of perception by examining how each group takes racism: many Whites conceive of racism as individual prejudice or discrimination, while African Americans tend to see it, not only as individual, but as the way institutions are structured to privilege Whites.

Essed (1988; 1991) examined the narratives or accounts of "everyday racism" experienced by Black women (cf. Louw-Potgieter, 1989). Essed derived a cognitive model reflecting the knowledge systems upon which these accounts of racism are based. This model involves five categories: the context (the characters, time, and place), the complication (acts that deviate from the norm), the evaluation (the narrator's identification of the acts in question as racist), argumentation (reasoning involving inference or comparisons for how the narrator infers that the acts are racist), and the decision (what the narrator does in response). The argumentation category was found to be especially salient because it involves the Black women's everyday reasoning for inferring racism based on deviations from norms as well as comparisons to one's own prior experiences, to other Blacks, or to Whites.

Racial formation theory attempts to capture both the processes whereby "racial categories are created, inhabited, transformed, and destroyed" (Omi & Winant, 1994, p. 55). "(P)rocesses of 'racial signification' are inherently discursive . . . Inevitably, many interpretations of race, many racial discourses, exist at any given time" (Winant, 1994, p. 24). The present investigation attempts to empirically develop this notion of the discursive features of race by looking primarily at college students' talk about race matters. That is, to closely examine how the participants themselves talk race and engage in the conversational practices of formulating and criticizing, responding to opposing viewpoints, and characterizing the other. In short, to describe the discursive constructions about race, racism, and interracial contact.

The present study attempts to extend Basso's (1979) notion of a portrait of the other by examining the reported speech of African Americans, Latinos, and Whites in talking race. In other words, how does quoting the words of another serve to discursively construct that person and his/her actions? The project is to describe discursive constructions about race, racism, and interracial contact. That is, to closely examine how the participants themselves, college students, talk race through participants' uses of reported speech. To my knowledge, no other study has looked at reported speech as a site for race matters. Other discourse analyzes (Essed, 1991; Van Dijk, 1987; Wetherell & Potter, 1992) use broader categories so that reported speech gets coded as doing other kinds of activities. The second goal of this investigation is to examine reported speech as a communicative practice: What forms does reported speech take? How does reported speech interactionally function in context? What does reported speech make relevant?

Procedures and Materials

Participants were given the documentary *Racism 101* to watch at home with at least one other person whom they considered to be a member of their own group. Volunteers were solicited from two undergraduate courses and requested to contact others (e.g., roommates, friends) with whom to watch and discuss the documentary. The group size for watching the documentary in the volunteer's residence ranged from two to five participants. After viewing the videotape, participants were requested via written instructions to discuss their reactions to *Racism 101* in an informal and natural way (the researcher was not present). Specifically, the instructions read, "After the video, please discuss on the audiotape your opinions about the quality and quantity of interracial communication on college campuses, such as U. For example, problems with interracial friendships, voluntary segregation, and so on." The participants were given a tape recorder and asked to record their discussions. Anonymity was assured.

Thirty-eight students participated in the study: twenty African Americans, twelve Whites, and six Latinos. These postviewing discussions ranged in length from fifteen minutes to over an hour, with a median length of approximately thirty minutes. The audiotapes were transcribed. Some participants used forms of vernacular English that are preserved in the transcripts.

Racism 101 investigates the state of race relations and racism on North American university campuses. The documentary begins by observing that it is some twenty-five years since Dr. King's "I Have a Dream Speech" of a colorblind society, but on many of America's university campuses there are a growing number of racist incidents and ethnic conflicts. One of the hopes of the civil rights movement of the 1960s was that through school desegregation, the next generation of Whites and African Americans could learn together, get to know one another, and achieve racial harmony. The documentary is organized around the theme, the continuing problems of race and racism at university campuses. For instance, the documentary reconstructs a racial brawl at the University of Massachusetts, the furor caused by racist jokes aired over a radio station at the University of Michigan, and the controversy arising from the journalistic practices of a conservative newspaper at Dartmouth College. These incidents galvanize an African-American student response through organized demonstrations and demands for redress from university administrations. Many Whites and other ethnic groups on campus give support to the African-American cause, but campuses are far from unified on these issues. The final portion of the documentary shifts to more everyday life on campus and shows interviews with a number of students in dormitories and in fraternities and sororities who express varying viewpoints on racial issues.

In listening to the audiotapes of the students talking race, various themes regarding race, racism, and interracial contact became readily apparent from the data. The notion of "theme" is taken broadly here as recurring topics that participants discussed. From these themes, reported speech emerged as the area for analytic investigation. Transcripts containing reported speech, and the surrounding sequential context, were excerpted for analysis.

Reported Speech in Talking Race

The following three themes emerged from the data: "everyday racism," "perception of stereotypes," and "intergroup distance." While these content themes are familiar, the analytical challenge is to *uncover the features of reported speech as conversational practices and the participants' discursive constructions in using reported speech*.

Everyday Racism on Campus

Throughout the transcripts one finds a number of student narratives of racist incidents or bigotry on campus. Reported speech appears within such narratives to tell the particular events of what the characters said and did—what happened. Quoting another, or oneself, is a way to convey the actions of the narrative. However, narrators do not simply "report" what was said, they also evaluate it. So, reported speech is relevantly tied to the speaker's evaluation. For instance, in the following , C tells of how "the same exact letter" (that constituted one of the racist incidents in *Racism 101)* was "thrown in . . . my dorm." C's narrative uses a summary quote of the White students' response to the racist event (line 8) in contrast to what they could or should have said (line 11).

Excerpt 4. Four Latino women

C: uhm that was something that really caught my attention
because in my undergraduate program as well as something that (compared) with
the jiggerboos and open hunting season on porchmonkeys and stuff like that
the same exact letter that was hung (.) was thrown in my building my dorm
and my friend was the RA and

it was the worst experience that I ever had in my life,
it was ridiculous the way the White students reacted
was like well I didn't put it out
and it became an individual thing
and it wasn't a matter of
someone of my race offended you and something should be done
and the students were taken out of the dorm ...

The reported speech here (line 8) animates C's presentation of the White students' response to the racist note. Their denial of responsibility gets articulated by a summary quote of the prototypical, White student response, "well I didn't put it out" (line 8). This reported speech allows C to quote the words, not of a single individual, but of her formulation of the aggregate of White students.

This reported speech is made relevant by C's prior assessment, "it was ridiculous the way the White students reacted" (line 7). This is not to say that other discourse forms could not have been used at line 8 instead of the reported speech—clearly we could imagine other coherent moves in this slot, such as counterfactual descriptions, e.g., "it was ridiculous the way the White students reacted, *they didn't do anything*" (italics indicate constructed). Given that this reported speech is in fact used here after C's assessment, the question should be, How is this demonstrably relevant for the participants? The reported speech allows C to "show," rather than simply "tell," how the White students were doing "being ridiculous" by using their very words. The reported speech works as a piece of evidence to support that prior assessment.

C's criticism is further developed by juxtaposing what the White students actually did—denied responsibility as "an individual thing" (line 9)—in contrast to a more appropriate group-level response, "someone of my race offended you and something should be done" (line 11). This response in fact did *not* occur, but C draws on the resource of hypothetical speech (Mayes, 1990) to show what *could* or *should* have been said. So here the quotation is used to do the complaint of contrasting what happened to what could/should have happened.

Perhaps the most striking difference apparent in these transcripts is that students of color see racism as a recurring feature of their lives on campus, while Whites do not mention such racism, and in some instances, claim that it is exaggerated. How do participants discursively treat such differences? In the following an African American narrates an instance of such divergence.

Excerpt 5. Two African-American males

1 M: we was talking about track and
2 he was telling me about one guy on the track team that was kicked off
3 because he said like racist you know like words ( )
4 and was saying like well he (does this stuff a lot)
5 and a lot of White people like himself doesn't like it
6 but for some reason he didn't see it as racist?
7 he just saw them as stupid
8 and you know I couldn't understand[yeah =
9 N: [( )
10 M: = see the person as stupid but not racist

The reported speech takes the form of a summary quote (lines 1–7) to narrate a puzzling occurrence of a White student's refusal to attribute racism of another White, but instead, calls him "stupid." M then expresses bewilderment at the White student's reluctance to see the event as racist. M's assessment is positioned immediately after the summary quote (lines 8 and 10). Again we see the narrator both reporting the speech of another and assessing it, though in this case the assessment is positioned after the reported speech. The assessment is relevant to clarify the teller's positioning vis-à-vis the reported speech; sequentially it may come prior, after, or embedded within the reported speech—as can be seen in transcripts excerpts 1, 2, and 3 respectively.

The White student is portrayed by M, not as a racist (like the White racist athlete), but as not being conscious of racism. The quoted White student is, in a sense, favorably represented—as not liking the White racist athlete and calling him "stupid." But, at the same time, the quoted White is portrayed as not going far enough, by refusing to label him what he really is in M's eyes, a racist. In both excerpt 4 and 5, the Whites are portrayed through quotations as lacking awareness of racism, though in excerpt 4 they are criticized for it, while in excerpt 5 the narrator is more reticent. The reported speech of the White students works as instances of fact construction (Potter, 1996)—of a White myopia to racism on campus.

An opposing viewpoint, expressed by some Whites, is that the charges of racism on campus are exaggerated. The following narrative by a White female reconstructs a past event in which African-American students are portrayed as making something out of nothing—a racist incident out of just a couple of drunken White guys. A summary quote is used to convey a gloss of what the White males said in contrast to what the African-American females made out of it (lines 7–8 and 18–19).

Excerpt 6. Two White females

A: these two guys White males were falling down drunk in the elevator and they
happened to get in the elevator with two African-American women who were I
think pledging a sorority at the time so they had on the African-American sorority
uniform and as part of the pledge period they weren't allowed to speak to anyone?
so apparently, these drunken idiots probably woulda harassed me

B: Hhhh

A: (   ) and it became a huge racial issue and (.)
because he commented on her clothing which I mean in some cases these days
turns into a sexual harassment issue if you know somebody

B: What'd he say

A: it was a year and a half ago?

B: um huh

A: but I mean these students were- I think they were suspended or something but it
seemed really silly to me:: that (.) at the time it just seemed like it was an issue
that shouldn't have- considering the context? I don't think it was blatantly racist

B: Right

A: I think it was somebody was stupid and drunk and I don't remember there were
any you know I suppose overt racist comments but things that she inferred about
them asking her about her uniform and saying something about her clothing:: and
that sort of thing so I mean but everything turns into an issue

In this story, A uses the contrastive evaluative terms, "blatantly racist" (line 15) and "stupid and drunk" (line 17). Interestingly, these contrastive labels are similar to those of excerpt 5, "racist" and "stupid." In both cases the African Americans involved see the events as racist, while the Whites identify it as merely stupid. These differences in perception are discursively articulated by the Whites through undermining the African Americans' charges in their accounts of what happened.

For instance in excerpt 6, A portrays the African-American women as exaggerating by claiming that a major incident, "a huge racial issue" (line 7), was made out of something minor as articulated in summary quote, "he commented on her clothing" (line 8). This ascription of exaggerating gets reiterated again with a similar summary quote, "things that she inferred about them asking her about her uniform and saying something about her clothing::" (18–19). These descriptive terms, used in juxtaposition to each other to gloss what was said and done, reflect the speaker's negative evaluation of the event. Such representations of the incident, of course, are not neutral or disinterested, but display the narrator's work to undermine the African Americans' charges.

A initially narrates the incident (lines 1–9), but her interlocutor, B, asks for more specifics, "What'd he say" (line 10). B's query here suggests that a direct quote, rather than a summary quote, can more adequately convey "what really happened" for a controversial event like a racist slur. A direct quote can represent (or construct) the specifics of what was said and done from the point of view from the participants in the reported situation. The summary quote, "he commented on her clothing," glosses the event by the narrator's choice of words rather than those of the characters involved. A cannot report what was actually said, as evidenced by her account (line 11), so she repeats the gist and consequences of the incident as well as her assessment of it (lines 13–20).

By way of summary of this section, these three narratives reconstruct symbolic acts of racism (e.g., written notes and verbal slurs) committed by Whites against African Americans. As seen in excerpt 4 and 5, the narrators see the incidents as racist and portray the Whites involved as failing to respond appropriately. The White narrator in Excerpt 6 portrays the African Americans as exaggerating the character of the incident, and further denies that it is racist.

In these three stories of alleged racism, we see that the reported speech fits within the narrative format to convey the *crucial acts* of what happened in the incident. Much of what we tell stories about is "things we do with words." More basically, reported speech, even as a summary quote, allows the narrator to reconstruct more specifics of the event, so the "crucial acts" of the story lend themselves to presentation via reported speech. The reported speech works to give voice to the actors in the events so as to critically portray their actions.

Perceptions of Stereotypes

Stereotyping is conventionally conceived of in the social sciences by cognitive, perceptual processes. But the awareness of stereotyping also can be discursively portrayed (Billig et al.,1988). African-American participants seemed especially aware of the White students' stereotypes and perceptions of them. Reported speech can be employed as a device to articulate such stereotypes. For instance:

Excerpt 7. Two African-American females

A: I really liked what one guy was saying
because it was really honest
one of the students he was saying- you know from a White perspective
I know it was really hard for him and he was being really honest
about how there is an element of surprise when[
B: [When a Black person says
someth[ing intelligent
A: [Something intelligent right?
and a lot of times I feel I felt that since freshman ye[ar:: =
B: [That's right
A: = you know they hang- I feel sometimes they hang on your every word

Here A reports the speech of a White student from the *Racism101* documentary by directly quoting his words, "an element of surprise. . . ." This phrase triggers B's recall such that she can cocomplete A's utterance. A uses this quote as a comparable instance to her own experiences on campus. Her experience of being seen by Whites in such a stereotypical way gets articulated by the extreme case formulation (Pomerantz, 1986), "they hang on your every word."

The reported speech from the documentary sequentially works as a *rationale* for the student's own problem telling about being treated as a stereotype. This sequential organization is similar to excerpt 4 in which the narrator quotes a portion of a racist note from the documentary as a prelude to her experience of a racist incident involving "the same exact letter" (excerpt 4, line 4) as seen in *Racism 101*. The troublesome reported speech from the video makes relevant the speaker's own troubles telling.

Even though the reported speech in excerpt 7 negatively stereotypes African Americans, A favorably portrays the White speaker in a prepositioned evaluation, "it was really honest," and in an embedded evaluation, "it was really hard for him and he was being really honest." So, we do not find an invariant out-group hostility and in-group allegiance in the participants' evaluations. Some portrayals are more complex; as seen here, and in excerpt 7, out-group members are both favorably and critically assessed.

Thus far we have seen that participants can resist the derogatory messages of the reported speech by critically evaluating it. The reporting speaker can *challenge* the veracity of the reported speech in various ways. In the following excerpt, C reports the speech of a White student (lines 4–6 and 9–10) and then directly quotes herself as rebutting it (lines 7–8 and 11).

Excerpt 8. Three African-American females

C: a lot of White students feel that if you're Black you are here
because of a scholarship or affirmative action.
I mean me and another White student talk about this,
he say he can look around the room and pick which Blacks are
here because of academics and which Blacks are here because of
affirmative action by what they say in class
and I was like you can't say that but you can say
the same thing some of these White students here
he was kind of like it's true for some of them but really it's mostly
affected by Blacks and every Black here is on a scholarship
and I was like Hhh I'm not! you know that type of situation and that's how they
feel that if you're Black and you're here at U it's because somebody gave you a

handout and you don't really deserve it so you're beneath them and if you don't
succeed it's your own fault and you was never really inclined to succeed you was
just here as a free ride you know and you're supposed to drop out

This reported speech of the White student (lines 4–6 and 9–10) illustrates C's initial general statement of the stereotype, "if you're Black you are here because of a scholarship or affirmative action."

The reported speech (lines 4–11) takes the form of a reported exchange between C and the White student. This exchange is structured in a four-part sequence: (i) a summary quote of the White student's perception of African Americans as products of affirmative action (lines 4–6), (ii) to which C directly quotes herself to deny the criticism because it also includes the White students (lines 7–8). (iii) The White student is quoted as responding with a stereotypical generalization (lines 9–10), and (iv) C quotes herself in rebutting the stereotype through a counterexample (line 11). This reported exchange format allows C to have the final word. C's evaluation gets articulated in her reply to the White student in the reported speech.

C uses this reported speech to epitomize Whites' stereotypes of African Americans on campus as a product of affirmative action. The reported speech becomes relevant as an example to support her prior claim about White students' attitudes (lines 1–2). The reported speech works within a narrative and as evidence in a claim-evidence sequence. Upon completion of this reported exchange, she returns to her general point about White students' perceptions of African Americans (lines 11–15).

The following excerpt contains another instance of a reported exchange in which the reporting speaker rebuts another's stereotype, though here an African American's stereotype of Whites. The exchange is structured in a similar way: an initial reported speech of another's stereotype (line 2) followed by a direct quote of the reporting speaker's rebuttal (lines 4–5, 7). (Background note for excerpt 9: B, who is White, was a manager of the U radio station and the person quoted is an African-American assistant manager at the station.)

Excerpt 9. Two White females

B: she refused to play a White artist of jazz because
she said that White people couldn't play jazz (.)
and to me that was racism right there and

4 I would say to her if you want us to play Black musicians
5 who are good at modern rock
6 which was our primary format
7 you damn well better well play White jazz artists
8 and what would happen is that alternative music meetings would be where all the
9 Black people went and modern mus- modern rock music would be where all the
10 White people went (.) and it really became a White against Black issue

The spoken quotations used in here work to convey the actions of the narrative. In both excerpts 8 and 9 an out-group member is ascribed as stereotyping through reported speech, and then the narrator directly quotes herself in refuting the stereotype. The teller's version of events not only can rebut the other, but can foreground or focus on the specifics of her response through direct speech.

The narrative format allows the teller to reconstruct the cast of characters, and what was said and done, and also to assess the political-moral significance of the event. The narrator does not let the narrative stand alone; B evaluates the reported speech of the African-American assistant manager as "racism" (excerpt 9, line 3). Again, reported speech makes relevant an assessment from the narrator.

Spoken quotation seems to be an especially potent device for challenging, not only the propositional content of the quote, but also the source. For instance, in the following we see an African-American speaker mimicking "sounding White" in doing reported speech (lines 4–5).

Excerpt 10. African-American male and female

1 M: it's weird because I feel that the weight of the world on my shoulders
2 I'm like damn I can't fail a class I can't not do a report on time
3 I can't do bad on a test you know
4 it's like they look at me and go like ((*mimic a stereotypical White voice*))
5 Gee them niggers they just must of gotten in on affirmative action
6 or something like that you know

Here M uses a summary quote of the prototypical White students' perception of him as the African American in class (line 5). Again, we see this theme of the African-American perception of the White stereotype of African Americans on campus as a product of affirmative action (cf. excerpt 8).

M voices this prototypical White stereotype through what Basso (1979. p. 45) calls a "distortion principle" in sounding White. This distortion of the quotation works as *a commentary on how to hear what is said*: specifically, to mock, ridicule, or parody and thereby undermine the content of what is being said and its prototypical author (Besnier, 1993; Goffman,1981; Macaulay, 1987). This mocking practice by African Americans has been identified as "marking" (Mitchell-Kernan, 1986). It "reports not only what was said but the way it was said, in order to offer *implicit comment* on the speaker's background, personality or intent . . . The meaning in the message of the marker is signaled and revealed by his(her) reproduction of such things as . . . most particularly, paralinguistic mimicry" (Mitchell-Kernan, 1986, p. 176, emphasis added). In short, the distorted voice or marked prosodic cues work to negatively evaluate the propositional content of the reported speech (Álvarez-Cáccamo, 1996).

Comparable to reported speech, speakers also can quote their own thoughts, what has been called, "reported thought." In excerpt 10 (lines 2–3), M quotes his thoughts to display the pressures of being the object of a stereotype. The reported thought also works as evidence for his prior proverbial claim, "the weight of the world is on my shoulders" (line 1).

We see this device of reported thought again in excerpt 11. M ridicules his White classmates' nonverbal behaviors and reports his own thoughts in response to being seen as "the Black guy in class."

Excerpt 11. African-American male and female

(a continuation of Excerpt 10)

7 F: So you never feel individualistic,

8 you also feel as if you're M the Black guy in class =

9 M: = Yeah exactly

10 F: So everything you do is because you're Black

11 M: Every time something regarding race comes up they go like whoosh and I'm in the

corner going like my Go(h)d why(h) you looking at me I'm not the only- I didn't
like die and say I wanted to be a spokesman for my race somewhere ya know if
there was an application I didn't put it in ya know (.) but they look at you like that
and unfortunately there's very little I can do about that, because I am the only
Black in almost all of my classes I'm the only Black person in there

Here M narrates the experience of being the only African American in a class and being looked at by Whites for "the Black point of view." Again, M "marks" the White nonverbal behavior by characterizing their heads turning as "whoosh" (line 11).

M uses reported thought in managing this dilemma in a humorous way, but also as something beyond his control. In both excerpt 10 and 11, the narrator, M, constructs the event of "how Whites see him" (or, generally, see African Americans in a predominately White institution) as something over which he has no control.

M adeptly uses humor and laughter particles to minimize the situation by playfully exaggerating it, e.g., the Whites all turning their heads to look at him by "whoosh" (line 11) and his denying wanting "to be a spokesman for my race" (lines 13–14). Exaggerating an event for humorous effect allows the speaker to capture a truth about it—to epitomize an experience.

By way of summary of this section, we saw that reported speech can discursively portray others' stereotypes, but perhaps the most interesting finding was how participants use reported speech to *resist* or *challenge* stereotypes. Throughout we have seen how reported speech makes relevant an assessment that allows the reporting speaker to criticize the stereotype (excerpt 7). We also saw a reported exchange format that shows the rebuttal of another's stereotype (excerpt 8 and 9). Thirdly, reported speech was used in mimicking or "marking" the out-group's stereotype. This form of reported speech seemed especially artful in ridiculing not only the propositional content but also the source of the stereotype (excerpt 10 and 11). This ridiculing evaluation of the White students' position is implicated through the speaker's exaggerated voice quality.

Intergroup Distance

A theme prevalent throughout the discussions is the virtual absence of social contact between Whites and African Americans outside of class. As one of the students in the documentary put it,

"This is a campus of segregation for the most part. And I'm not even going to say segregation in terms of unwanted segregation or unfair segregation; I think it's more segregation by choice in terms of the social area" (*Racism 101: Transcript*, p. 22). How do today's students make sense of such intergroup distance, so-called voluntary segregation?

Participants draw on the reported speech of out-group members as a way to explain, or criticize them, for this lack of social contact. For instance, excerpt 12 starts with an attribution of what "White people say" as a way to give evidence for White students' attitudes towards African Americans. This speaker uses a summary quote to explain the social distance as based on Whites' purported fear of approaching African Americans.

Excerpt 12. Three African-American females

A: a lot of White people- like in the video they were saying that they don't even like to talk to Black people because they're scared that they might say the wrong thing or do the wrong thing whatever it is

A generalizes, "a lot of White people," and then illustrates by citing the White speakers "in the video they were saying," to display how she knows (Pomerantz, 1984). Again we see reported speech used as a form of evidence in a claim-evidence sequence.

Whites are portrayed as not knowing how to act around African Americans. This supposed fear that White students have of saying or doing "the wrong thing" is challenged by A's postpositioned comment, "whatever it is." This comment may be heard to cast doubt or display skepticism about the prior summary quote.

Another case of being skeptical about the reported speech is seen in the following . Here A directly quotes a White student from the documentary (lines 2–3) and then proceeds, in collaboration with B, to ridicule and challenge this account.

Excerpt 13. Two African-American females

A: It killed me that one of the guys said (.) he said something like
where do you see Black people at you don't see them on
campus where do you meet them at
I felt like I was an alien you know
B: We be in the sewers

A Yeah we hide in the sewers somewhere
what do you mean where do you meet Black people the same place
you meet any other person you know

Here A directly quotes a White student's account and then moves on to question its sincerity. A jokingly comments on feeling positioned as "an alien" (line 4). B in turn playfully continues this line of ridicule by further exaggerating their foreign status on campus as being "in the sewers" to which A collaboratively confirms through repetition and extension (lines 5–6).

A continues by addressing the White student she just quoted by challenging or rebutting his account (lines 7–8). Here A changes "footings" from ridicule and exaggeration to talking back to the quoted White student by addressing him with "you" (lines 7–8). Even though this "talking back" to the White student uses a form of direct address, "you," it is recipient designed for her coconversationalist, B. In terms of discursive construction, it can be heard to portray a seeming disingenuousness or duplicity on the part of the Whites.

The White students, by way of contrast, do not charge African Americans with duplicity; instead some Whites criticize African Americans for being overly sensitive about racism (see excerpt 6) or overemphasizing their ethnicity. In the following, B presents a dilemma White students perceive in dealings with African Americans over whether or not to make race relevant.

Excerpt 14. Three White males

B: There's one thing I wanted to say ya know as far as when I came here and I think
one of the biggest problems that people have- that White people have relating to
Black people on campus is how to deal with the issue of race because on the one
hand- and the way I was raised was to ignore it you know you treat everybody the
same, you- you- you act as Martin Luther King said you treat somebody on the
content of their character and not on the color of their skin and that's how you
judge them but at the same time and I always grew up that way but that kinda
comes in conflict when you have people who takes the attitude you know
that I am a Black person ya know and that's part of who I am? and I want that
acknowledged?

A: Um hum
B: But at the same time if you acknowledge that then you're treating them differently
which ya know makes other people angry so what you have to do is get to know
people first and on an individual basis try to decide whether or not you'll discuss
race with them or- or how you'll deal with the point of race, whether you'll ignore
it or you'll make it part of the relationship or discussions er

In his explanation, B quotes Martin Luther King on the value of being colorblind (lines 5–7) and then contrasts this to the reported thought of ethnic African Americans to express their attitude (lines 9–10). This contrast between the M. L. King quote and the ethnic, African-American attitude can be heard as a criticism of the latter, given that Dr. King is widely regarded as the foremost leader in the civil rights movement. By invoking the words of King, B can use these to countervail against the formulation of the African-American ethnic position. Surprisingly, this is one of the few cases in which reported speech is used to invoke an authority; the prior involve utterances of reported speech to criticize or ridicule the reported speaker(s).

In the excerpts examined thus far, most of the reported speech presents critical portraits of out-group members. But there are some instances of in-group members being critically portrayed through their reported speech, e.g., as guilty of voluntary segregation. In excerpt 15, A uses a summary quote of other African Americans criticizing her contact with Whites (lines 3–4) as a way to explain the distance between African Americans and Whites.

Excerpt 15. Three African-American females

A: but it's just the surroundings and the environment and the people I hang with
they're for me- even when I do communicate with White people it's like
what are you doing talking with this White person what's wrong with you
you're becoming an oreo or whatever the term[inology is
B: [Oh yeah that happens to
me too but I mean it's weird because . . .

Here A is lamenting the current state of interracial relations on campus. She uses a summary quote of other African Americans' criticism of her (lines 3–4) to illustrate how group boundaries can be interactionally maintained through speech.

Another instance of reported speech used to articulate the seeming intractable problem of intergroup difference is seen in the following.

Excerpt 16. Whites: one male and three females

M: Along those same lines someone said to me- a Black girl said to me last year
that uhm she hangs out only with Black people because she chooses to
she gets along with Black people better than White people
and in general she doesn't like White people
an:d I've heard a lot of White people say the same thing about Black people
I think in general people hang out with other people who are like them
and who have things in common with them
and in general there's a basic background difference between Whites and Blacks
and I think people sense that and don't inter- hang out really

Here a White male summarizes a quote of what "a Black girl said" (lines 2–4) and then immediately conjoins this with a summary quote of what "a lot of White people say" (line 5). M uses this reported speech as evidence for his general claim about cultural "difference" to explain this lack of social contact. So in excerpts 1 and 16, we see the speaker offering folk-sociological explanations about the state of interracial relations and using reported speech as evidence for these.

Discussion

The main concern of this investigation has been to find out how students talk race by looking at their use of reported speech. These seemingly innocuous conversational practices of reported speech offer an interesting site for understanding participants' discursive constructions. Reporting another's, or one's own, speech works to reconstruct the particular actions of racialized events and one's assessment of them.

It is important to bear in mind that these conversations occurred after watching the documentary, *Racism 101*, and were occasioned by the researcher's request for participants' viewpoints. Given these cautions, the discussions did seem naturalistic and resonated with other situated contexts of talking race.

Turning to the issues involving reported speech as a conversational practice, we saw that it can take various forms—a direct quote, or a summary quote of an individual or of the group. Direct speech is a powerful way to hold another accountable, since it more fully reconstructs the particular speech acts of the event purportedly through the person's own words. Summary quotes present the teller's gloss on what happened. For instance in excerpt 6, after hearing A's summary quote of an alleged racist incident, the interlocutor asks for a direct quote, "What'd he say," as a way to better understand just what happened by "hearing" what was said. Another comparison of direct and summary quotes was seen in the "reported exchanges" (excerpts 8 and 9) in which the reporting speaker initially summarized what her antagonist, an out-group member, said but directly quoted herself in rebuttal. This asymmetry between a summary quote of the other and a direct quote of one's self has the consequence of underscoring what the teller said and did. Also, the out-group member's problematic actions are presented initially, followed by the teller's rebutting response.

Reported speech can summarize what an individual said, and even, what a group or aggregate said. Summary quotes of the group seem especially pertinent for participants to make group-level ascriptions in talking race, e.g., "I've heard a lot of White people say the same thing about Black people" (excerpt 16). Perhaps the most interesting way to summarize a group is through a quote of the prototypical group member. This resource allows the reporting speaker to *epitomize* the group through their characteristic utterances, e.g., "the way the White students reacted was like well I didn't put it out" (Excerpt 4), or a White person to quote, what he takes to be, the prototypic, ethnic African-American view, "I am a Black person ya know and that's part of who I am? and I want that acknowledged?" (Excerpt 14). So, the distinctions Payne (n.d.) draws of summary quotes seem useful for capturing the reported speech of an individual or an aggregate.

Reported speech as a conversational unit fits within larger discourse structures such as narratives and claim-evidence sequences. Within narratives, the reported speech conveys the actions of the story, since much of what we tell stories about is what we and others did with words. For instance, the whole narrative in excerpt 5 is told as a summary quote of a prior conversation. More commonly, the reported speech works to convey crucial actions within the narrative (excerpts 4 and 9). Reported speech, especially direct quotes or prototypical summary quotes, works to vividly portray or highlight the key actions of the narrative.

Another environment in which reported speech can be made relevant is where the speaker quotes a segment from the documentary and then proceeds to tell a story of a comparable incident from the speaker's own experience (excerpt 4 and 7). The reported speech from the documentary warrants the reporting speaker's own narrative.

Many studies have looked at reported speech within narratives, but in my data, reported speech was just as readily found in "claim-evidence sequences" (cf. Baynham [1996] for reported speech in non-narrative formats such as classroom talk). Reported speech is used to provide the evidence, in the form of a personal example or second-hand account in support of a claim. The claim-evidence format readily allows for making general assertions about interracial conditions.

These various forms that reported speech can take may be seen as *conversational resources*, which speakers can *make relevant for invoking voices in reconstructing events*. Clearly narratives could be told and claim-evidence sequences made without the use of reported speech. But given that reported speech is used, what is it doing, how does it function? As we have seen, reported speech works as a way of (1) providing *evidence* (Hill & Irvine, 1993). By quoting another's words, the teller is purportedly removing his/her own interpretation and "objectively" (Holt, 1996) reporting what another said. Also, invoking another's utterances is a way to (2) hold them *accountable* (Buttny, 1993) or *responsible*, since through the reported speaker's own words, or summary thereof, the reprehensible action gets recreated through talk. Most of the instances of reported speech quote out-group members in order to criticize or complain about some troublesome incidents, e.g., refusing to admit racism, stereotyping, and so on. Direct reported speech works to (3) *involve* recipients (Li, 1986; Tannen, 1989), since they are shown, rather than told, what happened through the reported actor's own words (Sternberg, 1982). Reported speech also allows reporting speakers to (4) *distance* themselves from the message (Macaulay, 1987), since they position themselves as merely the animator but not the source of what is being said (Goffman, 1981). In discussing contested topics such as race and racism, this distancing function of reported speech seems especially salient.

Reporting speech is not simply "reporting," it is also editorializing—making *evaluations* or *assessments*. Reported speech makes relevant, or is made relevant by, an assessment from the reporting speaker. This is the third main point about reported speech as a conversational practice, reported speech is *relevantly connected* to an assessment. The reported speech does not stand alone. In each and every case of reported speech we find an assessment of some sort. The connection between reported speech and its assessment gets accomplished in various ways: the assessment component can be prepositioned (Excerpt 4), postpositioned (Excerpt 5), or embedded within (excerpt 9) the reported speech. The interlocutor(s) present may produce assessments or second assessments (excerpt 7). Also, assessment may be done through the exaggerated prosody or voice quality of the reported speaker, i.e., as a way to undermine what is being said (excerpt 10). It is in this assessment slot that we see the participants' contesting, criticizing, or challenging the problematic interracial events reconstructed through the reported speech. This connection between reported speech and assessment fits the above passage from Bakhtin (1981). The assessment component tells interlocutors *how to interpret or frame the reported speech*; it *displays the reporting speaker's positioning toward the quote*. These assessments most explicitly reveal the students' discursive reasoning in talking race.

In looking at the content of the participants' reported speech and assessments we move to our second main issue, the discursive construction of interracial realities on campus. Given that most of the reported speech conveyed problematic incidents, the students' responses largely were to bemoan these and complain about the dire state of race relations, or to contest them through challenges, rebuttal, or humorous ridicule. One way that these incidents were contested was by *contrasting* opposing positions in order to implicitly undermine one of them: an incident as "racist" versus "stupid" (excerpt 5 and 6), what the Whites said versus what they should have said (excerpt 4), what a White said versus what the two African Americans made out of it (excerpt 6), or King's colorblind society versus the ethnic African-American attitude (excerpt 16). Another way to contest an undesirable event was *to ridicule it through humorous exaggeration*: "marking" (Mitchell-Kernan, 1986) or parodying (Macaulay, 1987) a White voice (excerpt 10), or all the White students' heads turning as "whoosh" (excerpt 11), or claiming to feel like an "alien" (excerpt 13).

This discursive reasoning in the reported speech sequences provides rich materials for examining the reporting speaker's "portrait of the other" (Basso, 1979). Given that the assessment of the reported speech is largely critical, it is not surprising that so are the portraits of the other. In general, the speech of others across racial lines is presented as: insensitive, ignorant, biased, racist, or ridiculous. As we have seen, African Americans portray Whites as unwilling to admit racism, as stereotyping, or as duplicitous in intergroup relations; while Whites portray African Americans as exaggerating racism or as overemphasizing their ethnicity.

While most of the cases of reported speech portray out-group members in a negative light, there were notable exceptions to this pattern. For instance, there were some positive portrayals of out-group members (e.g., "it was really honest" [Excerpt 7]), plus some critical portrayals of in-group members, particularly over voluntary segregation (Excerpt 15). The data does not convey a unitary discourse of in-group allegiance and out-group hostility. These data suggest a qualification to the intergroup perspective that postulates an in-group favoritism and out-group hostility (Tzeng, et al., 1986). Instead there are multiple discursive positions in which students participate and interactionally construct viewpoints through talking race. Indeed, racial attitudes are interactionally tried out, articulated, justified, contested, acquired, or altered through such within-group discussions.

5

Demanding Respect: The Uses of Reported Speech in Discursive Constructions of Interracial Contact

with Princess L. Williams

> Now if we all want to integrate 'cause we want to integrate we want to hold hands and everybody wants to love each other, that's fine. But that's not the basis of everything. And it's more rudimentary than, you know, let's all be friends and hold hands. It's about let's respect each other. I don't care if you like me, you don't have to like me, you know, I might not like you either. But as long as we respect each other. For instance, I'm a student, I respect you cause you're a student, and you're working hard, trying to do your thing, you respect me for the same reason, and that's all I can ask for. You don't have to like me. You can hate me all you want. Just respect me. (African-American college student from the documentary *Racism 101*; Lennon and Bagwell, 1988)

The idea for the present study about respect arose from the fact that this epigram was the most frequently quoted part from *Racism 101* by the African-American and Latino viewers. The activity of quoting a speaker—whether from a documentary or any kind of communication encounter is—reported speech. Reported speech is used here to investigate the notions of respect and disrespect in talking race.

Two studies are pursued on different aspects of the discursive constructions of interracial contact. The first examines the performative aspects in demanding respect through reported speech. A reason why one may report on another's speech is due to the eloquence or forcefulness of that speaker. Sometimes another person's words can articulate one's sentiments better than one can oneself, and thereby make those sentiments more intelligible. The prior utterances of another can be used as conversational resource for an individual's expression now. Some participants cited the quoted segment on respect as a way to formulate a kind of solution to the problematic aspects of interracial contact.

A second study was undertaken to further investigate the meanings of respect. We conducted focus-group interviews with African-American participants. From these interviews, narratives about incidents of disrespect emerged as our primary data. Most all of the narratives involved an African American being the recipient of an act(s) of disrespect embedded within interaction sequences with Whites. The majority of incidents occurred in public settings, such as stores, during service encounters. Examining narratives of disrespect and the voices drawn on to tell these stories allows us to become more aware of some of the troublesome features of interracial communication.

Respect

The discourse of respect is widely used in African-American speech communities (Anderson, 1990), for example, "(E)veryone would feel that you're equal, you're a person, treat you with respect", or "(I)t was a issue again of respect, it's you're not hearing me, you're not listening to me." Respect has been identified as an African-American norm for friendship (Collier, 1996; Hecht et al., 1993). Everyday moral assessments of respect/disrespect occur throughout the larger North American society in ordinary conversations as well as in mass media such as movies, popular music, and sports commentary. In our studies, the notion of respect seemed at once obvious to participants, yet eluded an adequate comprehensive definition. Respect seems to be such a protean notion that it resists a singular meaning; instead it is used in multiple ways as part of various discursive positionings.

Participants' uses of respect are the data for this investigation, but before turning to that, we want to consider how respect is employed as an analytic concept in the human sciences. The concept of respect has received some attention in social and political theory. Societal institutions need to give respect to all social groups as a necessary condition for establishing a 'decent society' (Margalit, 1996). Disrespect can affect a person's normative understanding of self and have negative consequences for the social value of individuals or groups (Honneth, 1992). In short, not receiving respect can be humiliating for individuals. The respect that different ethnic groups can be expected to receive can be seen as a political or economic resource, since it involves how one's rights are enforced (Miller, 1993). Respect is necessary for developing connections with strangers because it reduces an individual's anxiety and uncertainty (Gudykunst, 1995, p. 36).

On a social communication level, respect can be seen as a basic principle of human interaction. Harré (1980, p. 24) characterizes respect as "a socially marked relation, shown by deference" to others: it is 'more than an attitude and not necessarily linked to an emotion.' Respect, and its opposite, contempt, are public displays that are "shown and ritually symbolically marked in the course of particular activities of daily life" (Harré, 1980, p. 24). So respect is implicitly communicated through persons' actions.

Penman (1990) develops this notion of respect by connecting it to the concepts of face and facework strategies. Different facework strategies are arrayed along a respect-contempt continuum and can be used to enhance face through respect or depreciate face through contempt (Penman, 1990, p. 20). Receiving respect supports a recipient's face, while being disrespected can be a threat to one's face. Brown and Levinson (1987) distinguish the notion of face into positive face wants and negative face wants. Negative face involves the want that our actions be unimpeded by others, the avoidance of threat or embarrassment. Positive face involves the want that our actions be seen favorably by others, that others' evaluations enhance our sense of face.

This positive-negative face distinction is reflected in different studies of respect. Research among Samoans (Duranti, 1992), Mexicans (Garcia, 1996), or the Gonja of West Africa (Goody, 1972) show that respect can be conveyed to another through verbal forms as honorifics or formal address terms. Such language choice 'gives respect' to the recipient and enhances their positive face.

The second approach to respect is connected to negative face, as when an individual fails to receive sufficient politeness or adequate treatment from another. Much of the work on interracial contact falls into this camp. Consider an extreme statement from *An American Dilemma*: "(white opinion) asks for a general order according to which *all* Negroes are placed under *all* white people and excluded from not only white man's society but also from *the ordinary symbols of respect*" (emphasis added; Myrdal, 1944, p. 65). Even today African Americans report the problem of receiving respect in intergroup contexts (Bailey, 1997; 2000; Hacker, 1992). Most Whites are privileged in that they can take respect for granted throughout the larger society, while people of color have to earn or prove they are worthy of receiving respect from Whites (Omi and Winant, 1994; West, 1994). Essed (1991) coined the term 'everyday racism,' to capture the recurring sleights, abuses, and put-downs that people of color regularly experience (also cf. Pinderhughes, 1989). So in interracial contexts, disrespect can be seen as a way of glossing the experience of being the recipient of everyday racism. Even middle-class African Americans report incidents of discrimination in public places, which present a cumulative burden of dealing with such incidents (Feagin, 1991). Unlike the 'old-style racism' expressed in explicit ideologies, such as the quoted passage from Myrdal (1944), most contemporary symbols of disrespect involve subtle and ambiguous acts that can be readily denied as being racist (Billig et al., 1988; Miles, 1989; Van Dijk, 1993a; Wetherell & Potter, 1992).

Study 1

Rationale

The present study grew out of the investigation of reported speech in talking race (ch. 4). In this prior study, reported speech was seen to work to reconstruct racial incidents through invoking what others, or the teller, has said. Most of the instances of reported speech quote out-group members to criticize, complain, or challenge them for some problematic acts. Much of the reported speech from students of color tells of experiences of being the recipient of racist notes or comments, being stereotyped in various ways such as being the product of affirmative action, or having their behavior in class overly monitored by White students. In listening to students' reported speech in talking race, what also can be heard is what might be glossed as 'the power of the spoken word.' 'Power of the spoken word' in the sense that participants' talk criticizes, challenges, or gives evidence for racialized incidents through narrating problematic events or giving evidence for claims.

A separate study is warranted given the importance of respect as a discourse coupled with the fact that this 'respect segment' (quoted at the beginning of this article) was the most quoted portion from the documentary by African-American and Latino participants. The present investigation seeks to extend the work of the earlier study into understanding participants' discursive constructions on interracial contact through focusing on respect. In addition, we seek to better understand the conversational practice of reported speech. Reported speech allows us to draw on others' words of strength and resistance, and make them our own.

Study 1 examines (a) how the reported speech on respect presents the students' discursive constructions on interracial contact; and (b) how reported speech works as a conversational practice. The methods for doing this study are identical to those described in chapter 4.

Performative Aspects of Using Another's Words

As mentioned, the most quoted part of the documentary, *Racism 101*, by the African-American and Latino viewers involved a segment in which a student calls for the need for respect between Whites and African Americans. Consider the original documentary segment and then how it is reconstructed in and through the participants' reported speech. This is a retranscribed version of the epigram.

Excerpt 1. *Racism 101*: Transcript: 19–20

Now if we all want to integrate 'cause we want to integrate
we want to hold hands and everybody wants to love each other, that's fine.
But that's not the basis of everything. And it's more rudimentary than,
you know, let's all be friends and hold hands.
It's about let's respect each other.
I don't care if you like me,
you don't have to like me, you know,
I might not like you either.
But as long as we respect each other.
For instance, I'm a student, I respect you cause you're a student,
and you're workin' hard, tryin' to do your thing,
you respect me for the same reason, and that's all I can ask for.
You don't have to like me.
You can hate me all you want.
Just respect me.

While there are many observations that a discourse analyst could make about this passage, what we initially want to do is see what the participants have to say about it as reflected in their reported speech. What do the participants draw on and make relevant in quoting it? How does this voice from the documentary enter the participants' voices?

In the following excerpt, A directly quotes a portion from the documentary segment (beginning at line 5).

Excerpt 2. Two African-American females

A: Well another thing I wanted to talk about was the boycott of classes on MLK day
and that goes back to people- not only Blacks being more unified
but Blacks and Whites in an effort to just create a better environment
like one of the students said
You don't have to like me but you know we do have to respect [each other =
B: [Yeah
A: = especially being in a campus setting of such a close-knit community
you know it's very important for us to respect each other (.)
I may not like what you're saying
I may not like your views
you may not like my views [but it's important that we respect each other =
B: [That's right
A: = as he said as students you know
B: That's right
A: We don't necessarily have to be friends but I think to keep the peace
and just you know to maintain a stable environment
it's important for us to respect each other

In reporting speech, as indicated by the quote marker, 'like one of the students said' (line 4), A draws on the student's discourse from the documentary (beginning at line 5). The notion of 'respect' is paramount in this direct discourse. To gloss the discursive positioning A adopts from the documentary: liking me is not required, but respect is. Further, an affect display is hearable here—an assertiveness or defiance, a posture of not caring if you are liked by Whites, but demanding respect from them.

One of the interesting features of direct quotes, in contrast to summary quotes, is that the reporting speaker can draw on, not only the content, but also the expression of the original speech. So, how is this expressive demand for respect structured in the participant's reported speech, such that she can partake in the original's performative power?

Beginning with the issue of the accuracy of the reported speech, the only phrase which is identical to the original is "you don't have to like me" (line 5 in excerpt 2 and line 9 in excerpt 1). In this situated context of excerpt 2, the accuracy of the reported speech is less salient than A's capturing the spirit of the original documentary segment. Like the original, the performative aspects of this supposed direct quote gets accomplished by the repetition of "respect" and the contrasting of respect to "liking." Respect gets contrasted to being liked by Whites. This can be more fully described by considering some of the structural features of the two excerpts. The most striking similarity is the contrast of "liking" to "respect." Compare: "You don't have to like me. You can hate me all you want. Just respect me" (Excerpt 1, lines 13–15) to "You don't have to like me but you know we do have to respect each other" (Excerpt 2, line 5).

This contrast between liking and respect gets further articulated in each excerpt . Each segment begins with a call for respect, which then gets elaborated by a contrast sequence between liking and respect, and is resolved by a final demand for respect (compare Excerpt 1, lines 5–9 to Excerpt 2, lines 8–11). These liking-respect-contrast sequences from Excerpt 1 and 2 can be arrayed into their five parts and placed adjacent to each other to exhibit their structural similarities (see Table 1).

As noted, these sequences each begin with a call for 'respect' (1), which then gets elaborated or explained by the respect-not-liking sequence (2–5). These sequences work by the parallel structure of like and not-like across race (2–4), which then gets contrasted with the demand for 'respect' in the final part (5). The repetition of the various forms of not-liking (2–4) intensifies that defiant positioning. The call for respect placed in the final part of the sequence (5) serves as a resolution to the repeated relational problematic of not-liking.

The contrast sequence of liking and respect appears in three other cases of reported speech. Each segment is organized by an initial call for respect, which then gets elaborated on by negations of 'liking' in contrast to 'respect.' In the following excerpts, we see a four-part, liking-respect-contrast sequence in the reported speech in

Table 1

Excerpt 1, lines 5–9	*Excerpt 2, lines 8–11*
(1) It's about let's respect each other	(1) it's very important for us to respect each other
(2) I don't care if you like me,	(2) I may not like what you're saying
(3) you don't have to like me,	(3) I may not like your views
(4) I might not like you either.	(4) you may not like my views
(5) But as long as we respect each other	(5) but it's important that we respect each other

excerpt 3, a three-part sequence in excerpt 4, and in excerpt 5 we see two, four-part contrast sequences.

Excerpt 3. Two African-American females

A:	You know what though? I think the guy in the movie that made	
	the comment about ( ) <u>respect</u>	←1st part
	now tha:t- may be one solution,	
	you don't have to like me =	←2nd part
	= I don't have to like you	←3rd part
	but pleas[e:: if we could respect each other for what we do =	←4th part

Excerpt 4. Two African-American males and one female

M:	And I was sayin it's all about respect	←1st part
	yo [u don't have to like what I d[o:: =	←2nd part
F:	[Exactly [exactly	
M:=	you jus have to respect what I do	←3rd part

Excerpt 5. Four Latino females

A:	I think it goes beyon:d: (.) the issue of color ( )	
	it's a matter of respect	←Ist part

I may not like ( ) the way you wear your hair	←2nd part
it's parted in the middle, you dress like a hippie	
I don't like it I don't have to like it (.)	←3rd part
I should just respect you as another individual.	←4th part
and it's a matter of respect,	←1st part
you may not like what I stand for	←2nd part
you may not like Fidel Castro?	←3rd part
but you must understand that it's a matter of respect,	←4th part

What seems to make the original documentary segment memorable, and thereby quotable, is the idea of cross-racial respect elaborated by the parallelism between respect and liking.

The transition into reported speech may be marked by a quotive frame as seen in excerpt 3, "think the guy in the movie that made the comment about ( ) *respect*" (lines 1–2) (also see Excerpt 2, line 4 and 13). But in excerpts 4 and 5, the speakers do not attribute the liking-respect-contrast segment as being from the documentary. Nonetheless their articulation of the notion of respect exhibits a structural similarity to the liking-respect-contrast sequence from the documentary segment. Given that all the participants have just watched the documentary, the speaker's change of footings into a quotive frame can be taken for granted rather than explicitly marked as a quote. Or, as Bakhtin (1986) points out, we often adopt others' words as our own without attribution (also see Becker, 1994). In either case, the importance of reported speech as a conversational practice, whether marked or not, is that it allows us to draw on another's words and use them for our own purposes.

The line between what are purportedly another's words and what are our words at times can be ambiguous. For instance, in excerpt 5 we can see the elements of the like-respect-contrast structure even though the speaker adds to this some particular relational contentions over a person's dress and hair (lines 3–4) and Fidel Castro (line 9). The reported speech blends into the speaker's own views.

Recipient Design and the Addressee Doing Reported Speech

As we have seen, in doing this reported speech participants draw on the performative aspects of the repetition of respect and use the liking-respect-contrast sequence. A third structural feature of this reported speech is framing the addressee as White people. The demand for respect, and the contrast with liking, is not presented as an abstract idea, but is addressed to Whites—even though Whites are not present. Addressing Whites constitutes part of the performative power of these speech events.

Returning to the documentary segment, excerpt 1, consider who is being addressed by the indexical term, "you," in lines 6–8 and 10–14. In this segment, an African-American student is being interviewed; we do not see or hear the interviewer or know his/her racial identity. One possibility is that the interviewer is White and the African-American student is addressing her/him. The other possibility is that the addressee is Whites in general. Strictly speaking we do not know. Given our interest in reported speech, what matters is what the participants do with this discourse, how the participants shape it in reporting it.

Looking again at Excerpt 2, as A switches footings and moves into reported speech, she uses the address term "you," and its variants, "your" and "you're" (lines 5, 9–11). In addition to the second-person address term, "you," she also employs the first-person plural, "we" and "us" (lines 5, 8, 11, 15, 17).

Excerpt 2. Two African-American females
(Note: "you," "we," and "us" are in bold type)

A: like one of the students said
You don't have to like me but you know **we** do have to respect [each other =
B: [Yeah
A = especially being in a campus setting of such a close-knit community
you know it's very important for **us** to respect each other (.)
I may not like what **you're** saying
I may not like **your** views
you may not like my views [but it's important that **we** respect each other =
B: [That's right
A: = as he said as students you know
B: That's right
A: **We** don't necessarily have to be friends but I think to keep the peace

and just you know to maintain a stable environment
it's important for **us** to respect each other

In the situated context of this extract, A and B are participants talking to one another about the documentary, racism, and related matters. As conversationalists, A and B's utterances are recipient designed for each other's understanding. Having just watched the documentary together, A can move to quote it by the indicator, "like one of the students said" (line 4), and B's assessment, "Yeah," (line 6) displays recognition of the quoted segment. While A's reported speech is recipient designed for B as a copresent interlocutor, it simultaneously addresses Whites as an absent, generalized other as indicated by the indexical terms "you" and "we." Clearly the indexical "you" in Excerpt 5 is not addressing or referring to the interlocutor, B. Analytically the addressee of the utterance needs to be distinguished from its recipient (Levinson, 1988).[1]

This use of the second-person address term, 'you,' is evident in all the respect reported speech excerpts (see excerpts 3–5), and the "you" in each can be heard as addressed to Whites. In all but one instance, the addressee is Whites as generalized other. The exception is excerpt 5 in which the speaker addresses a specific White individual by "you" as evident by her description of this White person's hair and clothing style (lines 3–4).

Prima facie it seems odd to address an absent other. But such an assessment takes speech too narrowly (Goffman, 1974). Just as speakers can draw on multiple voices from those not present, so also the addressees of such speech need not be present. While the addressee is absent, the reported speech is nonetheless coherent and appreciated as displayed by the recipients' responses (more on this later). Indeed, a significant element in the performative power of this respect-reported speech is due to the fact that Whites are the addressee.

Recipient's Uptake and Response to Reported Speech

Reported speech is commonly used within a larger discourse structure, such as narratives or claim-evidence sequences. The reporting speaker, not only reports speech, but also "editorializes" on that speech—assesses it as favorable or unfavorable, frames it as serious or ironic. What, then, does reported speech sequentially implicate or project? What, if anything, does the recipient do in response to reported speech?

In the following two extracts, after the initial utterance of "respect" in reported speech, the recipient immediately agrees.

Excerpt 6. From Excerpt 2: Two African-American females

4 A: like one of the students said
5 You don't have to like me but you know we do have to respect [each other =
6 B: [Yeah ←

Excerpt 7. From Excerpt 4: African-American males and female)

1 M: And I was sayin it's all about respect yo[u don't have to like what I d[o::
2 F: [Exactly [Exactly ←

A recipient can respond in other ways such as by attempting to complete the speaker's reported speech.

Excerpt 8. Two African-American females
(Continuation of Excerpt 3.)

13 A: I think because we're all college students
14 because we all came here for a purpose to get an education
15 and we all kno[w
16 B: [Everyone should respect each other on that basis= ←
17 A: =Yeah and just the struggle of being a student and tryin'- you know (.)
18 to get ahead to get resumes to get this and that
19 that's at least something we all have in common

As discussed earlier for excerpt 3, A marks the notion of respect as being from the documentary. As A continues in this excerpt 8, B apparently hears her as quoting another segment from the documentary on being college students as a basis for mutual respect (compare excerpt 1, lines 10–13). B displays recognition and agreement with this documentary segment by completing A's utterance as reported speech and thereby participating in the call for respect. B is able to complete the third part of this reported speech sequence that A began at line 13. A, in turn, responds with an acknowledgment token, "yeah," and continues with her point about the commonality of being college students (lines 17–19).

Other recipients respond by extending the notion of respect in other directions. In the following, the recipient, B, agrees with A's account of respect, but adds the explanation or attribution of Whites "that the lack of respect comes from ignorance" (lines 15–16).

Excerpt 9. Four Latino females

(Continuation of Excerpt 5.)

10 A: but you must understand that it's a matter of respect,
11 I respect your views and please respect me mine,
12 I don't ask anything other- we can sit down and have a whole
13 ( ) political argument and I would respect all your views
14 °I just don't have to (like) them° and ([ )
15 B: [I- I- I agree with you
16 but you have to agree (.) that the lack of respect comes from ignorance
17 A: Right right

In Excerpt 10, the recipient extends the notion of respect by claim-evidence sequences which draw on various forms of reported speech.

Excerpt 10.

(Continuation of Excerpt 2.)

17 it's important for us [to respect each other
18 B: [It would be much different if Blacks were the majority
19 because then Whites would be (complaining) that
20 we need to unify you know what I'm say[ing
21 A: [Right exactly
22 B: it would be much different because right now they're at the point like
23 well why do I have to respect you?
24 you know what I'm saying
25 you go your way and I'll go mi:ne:
26 but if the tables were completely turned the White people would be like

27 well we have to respect each other we gotta do this we gotta do that

28 and that's the way it would be

B's response envisions the possibility of African Americans being the majority and Whites the minority, to contrast what Whites would say as a minority versus what they do say now as the majority. B gives voice to Whites by using a prototypical quote to articulate Whites' current position: "well why do I have to respect you?" (line 23) and "you go your way and I'll go mi:ne:" (line 25). If Whites were the minority, though, they would be saying "well we have to respect each other we gotta do this we gotta do that" (line 27) or "we need to unify" (line 20). These voices or quotes attributed to Whites reflect what Whites would say if they were the minority. Here B draws on the conversational resource of hypothetical quotes (Mayes, 1990), what a speaker *would*, *could*, *should*, or *may* say. Even though such quotes are fictitious, or contrary to fact, they are interesting for understanding interracial meanings, in that they are how B gives voice to Whites.

Discussion of Study 1

None of the White participants drew on this discourse of respect in our data. Given that eleven African Americans and four Latinos discussed the respect segment, we do not attempt to compare these two groups. Their discursive positioning on respect in interracial contact seemed quite similar.

It is not simply the propositional content of these utterances about respect (as important as this may be), but the way the demand for respect is articulated that displays authority. So we need to attend to the performative aspects of reported speech as a conversational practice. Even though the participants' direct quotes convey little of the exact wording of the original, their reported speech does bearably capture its spirit. This is because the structural features of the original are captured: (a) the repetition of "respect," (b) the liking-respect-contrast sequence: (c) which is addressed to Whites.

This discursive positioning on interracial contact—of not caring if you are liked, but demanding respect—resonates strongly among these participants as defiance, affect display, or empowering speech. This is evident not only in the performance of the reported speech, but in the interlocutors positive responses to it. Interlocutors respond to the respect-reported-speech by overlapping agreement tokens, utterance completions, or extensions of the notion of respect.

In quoting the respect-liking sequence from *Racism 101*, the speakers are not only reporting another's speech, they are also partaking in the power of another's words. Power in the sense of being able to formulate in an eloquent and succinct manner a compelling discursive position on interracial contact. As mentioned earlier, another person's speech can give insight or voice to one's own feelings.

Study 2

Rationale

From Study 1, the salience of respect for students of color is clearly reflected in the respect-reported-speech sequences. But more understanding of the meanings of respect is needed. For members of the speech community, "what respect is" may be obvious and can be taken for granted. But given that respect is said to be a source of conflict in dealings with Whites and other out-group members, it seems worthwhile to further investigate the notion of respect.

Subjects and Analytic Method

Four focus groups were conducted by an African-American interviewer with 20 African-American participants (13 females and 7 males). Participants included university students and adult members of the community. Volunteers were solicited by a snowball sampling procedure. The session began by showing the videotaped segment from *Racism 101* (transcribed as the epigram introducing this article) and asking participants to discuss the significance of respect in a cross-racial context. The focus-group interviews ranged in length from 30 minutes to over an hour.

The focus-group materials are treated as conversations about race matters (Mishler, 1986; Potter and Wetherell, 1995). These conversations were audiotaped. The tapes were listened to a number of times, and the relevant segments on respect were transcribed for analysis.

Narratives of Disrespect during Service Encounters

The focus-group discussions revealed various uses of respect. When participants were asked what they meant by "respect," their characterizations seemed rather straightforward. More interesting were the narratives participants offered about the perceived lack of respect in their contact with Whites in settings such as stores. Narratives offer a valuable form of data for understanding a notion like respect, since the particular events of the story present the phenomena in a more concrete manner. So our analytic strategy is to examine those narratives in which respect becomes problematic. Like the research on face (Goffman, 1967), the significance of respect may be most apparent in situations in which it is noticeably absent.

Reported speech is a common device used in narratives to dramatize events and make them more involving for their interlocutors. Reported speech seems to be used for reconstructing the most crucial actions within the story. The audience is shown, rather than told, what happened. Reported speech is interesting for how it is employed to represent racialized incidents. It is used as a communicative practice to reconstruct what was said and done so as to convey a version of events and the character of the neutral, disinterested activity. Reported speech allows narrators to draw on the voices of others, or themselves, in recounting what happened in a particular event. We are interested in reported speech in the participants' discursive constructions of race and interracial contact.

Twenty-five narratives of African-American experiences of disrespect were observed from the focus-group data. The majority of incidents occurred in public settings, mostly in stores during service encounters. The magnitude of the disrespectful acts ranged from the seemingly minor or subtle, such as the absence of normal courtesies or politeness formulas from White service workers, to more major incidents involving institutional authorities, such as the police. We select instances of disrespect in stores, since they are more frequently cited in our narratives (also in Feagin's, 1991, and Bailey's, 1997, 2000 data). Such cases of disrespect are less well-known, at least to non-African-Americans, than the news-headline incidents of dealings with police. The mundane aspects of disrespect in stores accord well with Essed's (1991) notion of "everyday racism." These incidents are identified as disrespect by African-American participants due to their recognition of being treated in a way different than Whites or as deviating from general norms.

Many of the stories involved being in stores and receiving problematic treatment from service personnel. A common narrative involved the amount of attention or service that was received in stores. Some narratives told of receiving too much attention or not enough attention—not being served. The latter, not receiving timely service, is evident in the following narrative.

Excerpt 11.

1 F: I was at Home Depot and I waited about forty-minutes for this White lady,
2 she was taking care of this White couple
3 so I asked her a question and
4 after you're finished with them you know will you please help me out.
5 She messed around she messed around forty-minutes later she walks off
6 but then she comes back and she starts taking care of someone else
7 and I said to her excuse me I said I believe that I'm next
8 oh well you have to wait your turn
9 I said I do believe I waited my turn (and) somebody else
10 but I felt that because they were White and I was Black
11 she was like telling me
12 well you just have to wait till I get finished
13 and when I get finished with them I'll take care of you
14 and I started to ah started to get very angry (.)
15 started to ah blow my ( )- blow my head
((skip two lines))
16 but I felt very bad about it because I mean I was a customer just like they were
17 and after waiting for such a period of time =
18 I: Uhm
19 F: = and she knew that I was waiting for her

The complication in this story arises when F describes having to wait, while a White customer is given priority over her. This gives the events a racialized significance, rather than just bad service. Having to wait is reflective of one's status—the lower one's status, the more one has to wait (Hall, 1983: Henley, 1977). Waiting also suggests the invisibility thesis of African Americans in public.

Often the most important events in narratives are portrayed through reported speech, particularly direct quotations. In excerpt 11 we see the reported speech as a dialogue of the narrator confronting the service worker for being slighted (lines 7–9). Reported speech can be used for other purposes than reporting what was said. In this case we see the narrator moving from the reported dialogue to what the service worker is "really saying." In other words, we have a text (the reported dialogue, lines 7–9) and a subtext (lines 10–13) of what the service worker means.

(Excerpt from Excerpt 11.)

10 but I felt that because they were White and I was Black

11 she was like telling me

12 well you just have to wait till I get finished

13 and when I get finished with them I'll take care of you

Notice how the narrator gives voice to what is being implicated by the White service worker (lines 12–13). Reported speech works as a conversational resource to express the disrespectful subtext of this encounter. Indeed, this difference between text and subtext, between what is said and what is implicated, or between appearance and reality is a discursive structure evident throughout these narratives by African Americans in dealings with Whites.

Narratives and reported speech do not simply report what happened, they also evaluate these events. One way to evaluate events is to tell how they affected you. In this case we see the narrator avow that she became "very angry" (lines 14–15) and "felt very bad" (line 16). These may be seen as the emotional costs of being disrespected due to race during a service encounter. As will be seen, the emotional impact of being disrespected occurs in other narratives.

This narrative is a complaint story that focuses on a complication which lacks an adequate resolution (Van Dijk, 1987, 1993b). F tells of confronting the service worker once she starts to give precedence to White customers. F does not get her way, but she does stand up for herself. The lack of an adequate resolution to this disrespect, or everyday racism, makes her negative affect understandable.

Some narratives involved the other extreme, receiving too much attention in stores. Receiving too much attention indicated to African-American customers that their actions were being overly monitored by the White workers.

Excerpt 12.

1 M: so we all walk into the store you know basically

2 and I mean everything could be fine in the store

3 the saleslady could be writing something down, White people
4 but all of a sudden when you come in the store all of a sudden
5 she's fixing a coat by where you're looking at the clothes
6 or just questions like oh can I help you with anything?
7 or sometimes they get as bold as to say you know
8 that's very expensi[ve so things like that =
9 ?? [Yeah
10 M: = I mean when you see stuff like that I mean- I don't know
11 it hurts you so deep inside that you really just- that's why
12 I see so much negative stuff going on today because
13 people can hurt you with just the use of language like
14 you know how they talking to you? you just get so frustrated

The narrative portrays the service worker's actions as deviating from ordinary norms of shopping. The narrator readily sees through the service workers' strategies for scrutinizing the African-American's actions in the store. Again we see the narrator drawing on the disjunct between appearances and reality. In telling his narrative, M offers a three-part list of the service worker's problematic actions (lines 5–8), the last two of which are conveyed through reported speech. The first reported action ("fixing a coat") is familiar service worker activity, but it is framed as suspicious by "all of a sudden when you come in the store all of a sudden . . ." (line 4). In the second reported action, the narrator mimics the prototypical, White saleslady's voice, "oh can I help you with anything" (line 6), suggesting a subtext to this offer—surveillance. By quoting such a familiar service routine, the narrator calls attention to it as really being about something else. What appears to be friendly service is marked in this account as a monitoring activity. The third action, the reported speech, "that's very expensive" (line 6), is heard for its condescending implications.[2] The White service workers' reacting to the entrance of African-American customers clearly has negative implications, not only as to their being welcome, but more basically to their dignity and status as full-fledged members of society. The narrator not only recounts what happened, the events and reported speech, but also evaluates the significance of what happened. After listing the actions, M describes the feelings of being treated in such a way as being "hurt . . . with just the use of language" (line 13) and "frustrated" (line 14). Other participants also gave accounts of the negative emotions associated with being the recipient of disrespect: feeling "humiliated," feeling "bad," "bombarded," or "crying" after leaving the scene, though more common were feelings of anger. Honneth (1992, p. 192) claims that experiences of disrespect are described with metaphors about the body in states of decay. Such descriptions of negative feelings, or affect, work as a shorthand means to capture the tellers' critical evaluation for those events.

The following narrative conveys an instance of disrespect through the absence of normal courtesies during a service encounter.

Excerpt 13.

E: my White friends they used to think I was tripping about people
until I started pulling out instances when they happened
for example we bought tickets for a concert,
one of my White friends goes through
and the woman takes it and says thank you enjoy the concert,
I come through she's just going to snatch my ticket and give it back to me
and the other White friend comes back and she's all nice and jolly
I said now did you see that
I didn't do anything different than you did to that woman
but she treated me differently

This narrative of the absence of a ticket taker's politeness routine may seem to be a minuscule event, but given that it contrasts to how her White friends were treated immediately beforehand and afterwards, demonstrates that the event has a racialized significance. In brief, race is made relevant when it would not be ordinarily. The noticeable difference between the treatment received by the narrator's White friends and herself makes her race the only plausible explanation for how she was treated during this encounter.

The narrator uses reported speech to illustrate how she conveyed this incident to her White friends (lines 8–10). E mentions how her White friends did not believe her about being the recipient of disrespect in various situations. This accords with the notion of everyday racism, which people of color experience regularly but

Whites deny seeing or claim is exaggerated. Her narrative is a "proof story" (Essed, 1991) by showing the contrast in service given to her and to her White friends.

These narratives can be seen as portraying various racist incidents that are glossed by the participants as disrespect. The incident in the story makes relevant a response from the victim to resolve the breach and restore moral order. Given the fact that these racist incidents are presented as unsatisfactorily resolved means that these are problem stories. In the following we see another such incident. In particular, note the different voices D invokes to tell what happened, could have happened, or recurrently happens.

Excerpt 14.

D: Well I know what's important to me when I go inside a store I don't expect a
Caucasian person to hold on to their purs:e (.) or what have you,
I mean I had one particular incident where here I am at CVS
I'm stan- I'm at the cash register and I'm standing next to this woman
like any other person would (.)
but since I happened to be behind her she's talking to the desk clerk
could you please call somebody else to take care of him
I don't want to have him behind me (.)
and then when I addressed her point
and said to her why can't you explain this to me =
= if you feel uncomfortable how come you can't talk to me about this
why- how come you have to be sneaky and you know (.) behind my ba:ck?
and she- she was so upset about it,
and at the same time I surprised her because I didn't go to her level you know
I- I didn't raise my voice to the point of (.)
oh yeah let's call the police and >get this guy out of here<
but yeah she did call me a trouble maker,
I'm a trouble maker because I wanted to correct the situation (.)
and that's something I feel all Black people have said

well we can't go into the store we can't go into the store without being looked at?
we all want to be treated- we all want to have equal treatment or equal share
we want to be treated as equally as somebody else who's not Black

In this narrative, it is interesting how D uses different voices or forms of reported speech to tell his story. Reported speech as conversational practice is drawn on to reconstruct actions of the narrative, especially the most crucial actions. In his story, having set the context of being in line at a store, D switches footings to the overheard voice of "this (White) woman('s)" addressing the desk clerk (lines 7–8). What is disrespectful about this is not explicitly identified, but is readily apparent to the other African-American participants in the focus group. The disrespect is implicated through the White woman's expressed desire to keep a physical and social distance from an African American as well as a display of White fears of a young African-American male, e.g. clutching a purse; requesting to open another line.

The narrator shows how he responded through the direct speech of addressing this White woman (lines 9–12). In challenging this instance of racism, D explains how he purposefully refrained from raising his voice so as not to give anyone grounds for calling the police. Reported speech generally is used to tell of what *did happen*, what *was said*, but it also can be employed to tell of what *could* or would *happen*, so-called hypothetical speech (Mayes, 1990). As we see in this excerpt, D envisions what could have happened if he raised his voice in confronting the racist incident in the store: he draws on the service worker's voice, "oh yeah let's call the police and >get this guy out of here<" (line 16).[3] So hypothetical speech provides a resource to give voice to counterfactual conditions—what could, or might, or should have been said.

Reported speech can be used to give voice to what an *individual* said or to what an *aggregate* or *group* said or says. Reporting the speech of an individual—the service worker or the narrator—is the most common type in these narratives. In assessing what happened, D frames the events, not as an incident that happened uniquely to him, but as part of a larger pattern of disrespect that African Americans have come to expect. As D explains by drawing on the voice of African Americans as an aggregate, "that's something I feel all Black people have said well we can't go into the store without being looked at? we all want to be treated we all want to have equal treatment or equal share we want to be treated as equally as somebody else who's not Black" (lines 19–22). This segment fits with the theme of the emotional costs of being disrespected in predominantly White settings such as stores: being looked at and not being treated the same as other people.

Discussion and Conclusion

During a radio interview in the aftermath of the O. J. Simpson trial, the Irish journalist Connor O'Clarey commented on how he was surprised when he first came to the US to see a White man shining the shoes of an African American at the airport. From this he surmised that relations between the races in this country are primarily governed by economic considerations. While generally this may be the case, business transactions cannot be reduced to simply monetary exchange for goods and services. As our findings from the narratives in Study 2 indicate, the social interaction during service encounters is the primary area of African-American complaint about disrespect. Service encounters can be seen for both their instrumental and symbolic dimensions.

The troubling findings of these investigations is that the ordinary symbols of respect remain problematic for African Americans during service encounters with Whites. African Americans report the recurring experiences of racist incidents and disrespect, particularly in predominantly White, public settings. This may not be news to African-Americans but, we conjecture, will be news to many Whites.

These narratives of disrespect from Study 2 converge with Feagin's (1991) data of African Americans being the recipient of acts of discrimination in public places. Our narratives chronicle instances of disrespect that involves demeaning acts of both omission and commission. From these narratives, we may characterize disrespect as a moral ascription that glosses a derogatory act(s) based on race which reflects on how the recipient is being treated. These incidents may not be prosecutable as illegal acts of discrimination, but these acts are seen as disrespectful, negatively affecting the recipient's emotions, and can be seen as threats to negative face. The emotional costs of being disrespected were mentioned by participants. Having a mundane event transformed into a racialized incident can be a troublesome burden, especially so when it is recurring (Feagin, 1991).

Participants used reported speech in their narratives as evidence to document instances of deviation from norms or to note different service than that given to Whites. This documenting the incidents accords with Essed's (1991) study of the reasoning in inferring racism: Black women's accounts focused on how the act(s) in question were a deviation from ordinary norms or contrasted with how Whites were treated. This is similar to our data from Study 2. The reported speech worked to vividly construct instances of disrespect within narratives, and in some instances, what the narrator said in response. Some narrators used reported speech and a text-subtext device, where the subtext revealed what the service worker was "really" saying or doing. Reporting the speech of the service worker aids in objectifying and accounting for these incidents such that they can be more readily criticized by fellow participants.

The aims of these studies have been to examine reported speech as a conversational practice in talking race and to understand discursive positions on respect/disrespect in interracial contact. Reported speech emerged as a phenomenon of interest due to the fact that the respect-liking segment from *Racism 101* was the most frequently quoted portion of this documentary by African-American and Latino viewers in Study 1. A way to talk about the highly charged and troubling issues of racism is to draw on the speech of another, particularly speech that is powerful and compelling. Drawing on another's words and making them one's own through giving voice to them, can help articulate the reporting speaker's own position.

The news from Study 1 is that we need to attend to the performative aspects in reporting speech. While little of the exact wording was reproduced, the structural features of repetition, the contrast of liking to respect, and addressing Whites allowed the reported speech to capture something like the spirit of the original. The reporting speakers can be heard as strongly agreeing with the respect-liking segment to which they have given voice. This positive evaluation is displayed through paralinguistic or prosodic cues in performing the reported speech as well as by verbal assessments. The performative aspects frame the reported speech as favorable or unfavorable, serious or ironic (Goffman, 1974). Other studies have examined the performative aspects that frame the reported speech through negative evaluation, such as mocking or parodying the original speaker (Macaulay, 1987; Mitchell-Kernan, 1986). In Study 1, the performative aspects of doing the respect reported speech displays a strong affect (Kochman, 1981) or defiance (Orbe, 1994) for the participants. There seems to be a performative power (Álvarez-Cáccamo, 1996) in giving voice to this speaker's words of strength and resistance.

Drawing on the reported speech of demanding respect and not caring if liked by Whites displays a discursive positioning that reflects a growing confidence and willingness to speak out among today's African-American college students (Asante & Al-Seen, 1984; Houston, 1994). The notion of a discursive construction of race fits well with racial formation theory (Omi & Winant, 1994; Winant, 1994). Race is not reducible to underlying structures such as genetic differences or social class, but is itself a discursive construction involving multiple discourses in the process of being defined and redefined. For instance, compare this demand-for-respect discourse to the integrationist discourse of the 1960s (Omi & Winant, 1994). It is through people talking race that social realities such as interracial contact become defined and understood. The project here has been to examine one such conversational practice in which people draw on while talking race (e.g. reported speech) and the various discursive constructions that people align themselves with (e.g. respect as problematic in dealings with Whites; not caring if you're liked but demanding respect).

6

Discursive Constructions of Racial Boundaries and Self-Segregation on Campus

> Thirty years ago . . . black and white Americans . . . and members of many ethnic groups tended to lead, culturally and socially, largely segregated lives. Today they do so, for the most part, only as a matter of choice. Down on the ground,though, there is a lot of friction, since persons who never worked side-by-side before are finding themselves in situations of professional intimacy unimaginable . . . a generation ago (Menand, 1994, p. 21).

Today's institutions of higher learning in the USA are more diverse than ever before, but at the same time, there are reports of a climate of separateness—a "new segregation" (Asante & Al-Seen, 1984; Duster, 1992; Gitlin, 1995; Steele, 1996). On university campuses it is not uncommon to see different groups socially clustering among themselves, e.g., sitting in the cafeteria, at social events such as dances, or joining separate Greek organizations. In the student gym, I once observed three pick-up basketball games running concurrently—one with Whites only, one with African Americans only, and one with Asians only. There are different views about this self-segregation. One is the social support model: Students of color are numerical minorities on most university campuses, so in social life they need the support of their own cultural groups and organizations to succeed in higher education. Another approach is the integrationist model: It involves the supposition that if children of different backgrounds could grow up and be educated together, they would get to know one another and not develop the prejudices and stereotypes of their elders. Ultimately these models may not be conflicting, though rhetorically they have been used to point in different directions. These models provide a rationale for the present investigation, which examines how today's university students make sense of the discourses of separateness, boundaries, and difference on campus, in particular, between Whites and African Americans.

Perspectives on Boundaries

In public and work life society is increasingly integrated, yet in the private or social realm Whites and African Americans lead largely separate lives (Hacker, 1992).[1] It is not surprising then that university campuses would reflect society's broader patterns of residential and social segregation. A 1992 Columbia University study confirmed this pattern and revealed some mixed feelings about current intergroup conditions on campus.

> Students tend to see the campus as quite fragmented in general, and they perceive different groups as more or less isolated. . . . Of all respondents, 65 percent think spending a lot of time on campus with people of one's own racial or religious-group is a "natural thing to do," but 61 percent feel that it reduces the quality of the Columbia experience and 50 percent think it encourages antagonism among groups. At least half of the undergraduates are ambivalent about separatism (quoted in Cose, 1997, p. 88).

Intergroup relations theory claims the greater the perceived dissimilarity, the greater the subjective intergroup distance (Tzeng et al., 1986). Out-group members may be perceived as "too different" to motivate one to communicate with them. Perceived difference may result in increased levels of uncertainty and anxiety, which leads individuals to avoid contact with out-group members (Gudykunst, 1995). Groups with a history of conflict will be less likely to be motivated to converge in their communication with out-group members (Gallois et al., 1995). Communication accommodation theory points out that convergence across group boundaries can have rewards and costs—the latter, the potential loss of social identity (Giles & Coupland, 1992). Minority group members with a strong sense of group solidarity and dependence will perceive communication boundaries as stronger. Diverging in communication can underscore group differences and assert group identity.

Even when there is contact, if the communication is not of sufficient quality and depth, then it may not disconfirm existing stereotypes of out-group members (Rose, 1992). That is, the quality of communication needs to be interpersonal rather than intergroup so interlocutors can get to know each other as individuals rather than according to social or cultural-level categories (Gudykunst, 1995).

Groups that have little history of face-to-face contact will be more likely to misread each other's cultural communication style (Kochman, 1981), contextualization cues—paralingual markers such as volume, speech rate, intonation (Gumperz, 1982), and engage in a different interaction order (Rawls, 2000). For instance, Whites perceive African Americans to have the communicative traits: augmentative, aggressive, defiant, and hostile, while African Americans see Whites as: evasive, boastful, aggressive, and arrogant (Rich, 1974 cited in Pennington, 1979). The resulting "difficult dialogues" (Houston, 1994) and communication failures arising from misreadings of "the Other" increase levels of anxiety and uncertainty (Gudykunst, 1995), decrease levels of communication satisfaction (Martin, Hecht, & Larkey, 1994), and reinforce existing stereotypes (Chick, 1990). So it is not surprising that "avoidance" is the most frequently used strategy among Whites and African Americans (Martin et al., 1994). The orientation toward separation may be distinguished in various ways: (a) nonassertive, e.g., avoidance, (b) assertive, e.g., expressing the self, or (c) aggressive, e.g., criticizing assimilation or accommodation (Orbe, 1998).

Many have theorized about the continuing significance of race in North America (Frankenberg, 1993; West, 1994). At the same time, the idea of race as a scientific category largely has been debunked (Miles, 1989; Sanjek, 1994). Yet race continues to have social significance, as part of our "racial commonsense." While there have been historic changes in North America over the last 40 years, racism in different forms still persists. Even middle-class African Americans report on the commonplace occurrence of subtle forms of racism in public places, such as not receiving service in stores and restaurants, receiving excessive surveillance while shopping, or being treated less well than Whites during service encounters (Feagin, 1991; Cose, 1993).

As previously segregated groups increasingly come into contact at schools and the workplace, there has been a change in the face of racism—to a so-called "new racism" (Miles, 1989) or "symbolic racism" (Sears, 1988). Unlike the "old racism," expressed in explicit racist ideologies, the new racism is less transparent. This new racism gets articulated in code words, symbols, and the dominant group's resentment and resistance towards policies that benefit minorities

(Southern, 1987, pp. 287–288). The new racism invokes a more subtle discourse that justifies current systems of inequities (Wetherell & Potter, 1992) and even denies being racist (Billig et al., 1988; Van Dijk, 1992).

The interest is in the participants' discursive constructions of racial boundaries, separateness, and difference—in how participants talk about race matters and thereby discursively construct interracial realities through their accounts. Accounts also display participants' positioning—their understanding, evaluation, or alignment with other interlocutors. In addition to participants' accounts and positions, we are also interested how participants interactionally engage in this talk. What conversational practices are used to do talk about race matters? The research questions are: *What are students' discursive constructions of separateness, boundaries, and difference? How do Whites and African Americans account for these constructions?*

This is the third study from the data described in chapter 4. The first examines the use of reported speech in discursively constructing a portrait of interracial contact (chapter 4); the second looks at the African-American discourse of respect (chapter 5). In chapter 4 the materials under "intergroup distance" suggest the need for more study in this area, which we pursue here. The present investigation examines the discursive and rhetorical constructions of racial boundaries, separateness, and difference on campus by examining previously unanalyzed excerpts from the tapes and transcripts.

When notions of racial boundaries or separateness enter students' conversations, generally they are not mentioned in a neutral way. Such divisions are evaluated as either problematical and deserving some criticism, or as justified and readily explained. Here we examine how participants *discursively construct racial boundaries* and how they *position themselves*.

Accounts of Voluntary Segregation

Throughout the transcripts one finds mention of voluntary segregation among groups on campus. None of the participants explicitly disagreed with the fact of such separation, but they account for it in different ways and take different positions towards it. For instance, in the following transcript we see a student bemoaning voluntary segregation but her interlocutor justifying it.

Excerpt 1. Two African Americans

A: you know I feel a lot of time I feel campuses and especially at U campus that we practice voluntary segregation

B: Yeah

A: Just think about when you're sitting in the classroom Blacks will be sitting in one area Whites will be sitting in another area you know maybe on one side of the room and you don't mingle you don't interact with each other

B: Like that girl was saying before I don't think that has a lot to do with race I think it just has to do with the whole different mentality that we have like I'm here I really don't have much in common with the White people here=I mean I have some and I talk- but as far as really- like mus:ic and just general intere[st (it's all) different

A: [That's true too that's true too because outside of Black and White you do have Greeks that sit with each other

B: Yeah

A: Athletes who sit with each other but it is voluntary segregation

A's assertion of voluntary segregation on campus and her instance of it reflected in seating patterns in classrooms can be heard as criticizing such separateness. The terms A uses in describing class seating implicates her critical evaluation, "you don't mingle you don't interact with each other." The criticism arises from the noticeable absence of what is expected from the membership category of fellow students, i.e., "mingling" and "interacting." So the very mentioning of these seating patterns as conflicting category predicates can be heard as both an example and a criticism.

B takes A's utterance, not as a mere description or detached social observation, but as a criticism of campus racial relations. This recognition is displayed in B's account. B disagrees with the racial aspects of A's criticism, where 'racial' involves racist intent. B questions that the separation is a matter of "race," but rather is due to a "different mentality"—a not having "much in common with the White people here." B begins her response by invoking what "that girl" from the documentary had just said.[2] B's summary reported speech is used within her account to justify voluntary segregation as due to differences. The social distance is not due to racism, but due to cultural difference. These interactional patterns are normative because people sit by and talk to those with whom they have more in common.

A seems to find B's account convincing as she cites other groups (e.g., Greeks, athletes) who congregate and sit together. But A does reassert the label of "voluntary segregation," which seems to carry for her some implicit criticism of current intergroup patterns.

Whites also notice the group separateness on campus. In the following we see a similar explanation to excerpt 1, that people "feel more comfortable" with those whom they have more "in common."

Excerpt 2. Three Whites

A: Do you think people are separating themselves by choice or the separation is more forced

B: Well first of all I think it's by choice I mean I think people (.) feel more comfortable with people who they have a lot in common with ya know people (   ) cultural values ya know

==> what you call separation or segregation I mean I think a lot of it's by choice when it comes to the social (arena) and there's nothing wrong with that I don't feel like ah Black people are being prejudiced by choosing to hang around with other Black people (.) to a degree I think it might be forced to the degree that Black people come to the campus they're such a small minority that it's kind of intimidating and so they gravitate towards people who they have a common experience with

It is interesting how A formulates separation in his question as being "by choice" or "more forced." While A does not specify in what sense separation is "forced," he may be drawing on an episode from the documentary in which an African American who joined a White fraternity is interviewed and tells of the criticisms he received from other African Americans—"you are forgetting a part of who you are," becoming "an oreo" (*Racism 101* transcript, pp. 21–22).

B's answer offers the familiar having-more-in-common explanation for separateness. Further, he challenges the implicit criticism that African Americans are "prejudiced" for exclusively socializing only with other African Americans. B picks up A's term, "forced," but uses it in a different, broader sense—as African Americans being a numerical minority on a predominately White campus and turning to others with "a common experience." So "forced," in this sense, does not convey the acrimony suggested by A's prior usage.

B's sensitivity to word choice also is reflected in his hesitancy to adopt A's description, "what you call separation or segregation" (see arrow). The vocabulary used to describe a state-of-affairs can color how we evaluate it. B does not offer another term, but simply uses the indexical term "it."

Ascribing Responsibility for Separateness

In the first two excerpts, racial separateness is posed as a problematic condition by the initial speaker, and the interlocutor responds by justifying separation with an account of association based on commonalties. In the following excerpt we see the discursive construction of voluntary segregation taken in a different direction. These Whites perceive voluntary segregation as originating from the African-American community and being problematic.

Excerpt 3. Two Whites

A: Yeah ironically enough I think it's funny? like one of the students on TV said- on the video said something about how (.) how- about this segregation thing how that you know he said I'll probably get heck for sayin' this or whatever but I think there's some voluntary segregation on the part of the African-American community? I think that's true? not necessarily that I blame them =

B: Right

A: = but I definitely think that's true an::d: in the beginning of the video it was almost like UMass had these racial incidents therefore we should increase the minority population which I don't know necessarily in my experience and with talking with other people increasing the minority population would just increase the number of people who would segregate themselves

B: Right

Here we see A introducing the topic of voluntary segregation by reporting the speech of a White student from the documentary who attributed it to the African-American community.[3] It is a common conversational practice to broach a delicate topic by citing what another has said thereby giving oneself the option to align or not with the quoted position. A agrees with this reported speech from the documentary, but qualifies it as not a "blame."

A initiates her turn by framing her ascription of voluntary segregation as "ironically enough I think it's funny?" While what is "funny" here is not spelled out, the implication seems to be that it is ironic that African Americans would self-segregate given the historical legacy of imposed segregation.

A may not "blame" African Americans for segregating themselves, but she does take it as problematic. Having asserted the existence of voluntary segregation, A goes on to formulate a claim from "the beginning of the video" that more recruitment of minorities is needed. A rebuts this by arguing that it would only lead to more unwanted segregation.

It is interesting how A remembers the documentary. In looking at the documentary transcript, the segment that contains the call for increased African-American enrollment came in response to racist jokes on the student radio station at the University of Michigan (*Racism 101* transcript, pp. 6–7). Presumably a larger critical mass would improve conditions for minority students on campus. The aim here is not to portray A as a "judgmental dope" (Garfinkel, 1967), but to show how participants can use the documentary to form accounts for their own positions.

In the following excerpt, we see an African-American student formulate a perception held by Whites on voluntary segregation (arrow 1) and then challenges it and offers a counter-explanation and criticism (arrow 2).

Excerpt 4. Three African Americans

A: it's like the Black people are very aware of all the racial issues that go on and the White people just have this tendency to think that nothing's wrong that everybody's happy-go-lucky and
1==> that we as Black people are separating ourselves from them,
2==> but they don't realize that they are the ones who because
2==> of their ignorance basically that they are separating themselves from us. I'm not saying that every Black person necessarily wants to be friends with a White person because it's not true

A uses the rhetorical device of an appearance-reality distinction in her account: racial realities appear fine to Whites, but really they are problematic. Also, African Americans appear to be the source of segregation, but really it is due to the Whites.

A's ascription of "ignorance" (arrow 2) to Whites seems to be a central account in African-American discursive constructions of Whites. "Ignorance" in the sense of Whites' myopia to racial problems on campus. This ascription of ignorance is consistent with the finding that Whites deny seeing racism in their everyday experience, while Blacks encounter it regularly (Essed, 1991). Given that

Whites generally take racism as individual prejudice or discrimination, from an African-American perspective, Whites failure to see institutional aspects of racism may be glossed as “ignorance” (Blauner, 1989).

Difference as Boundary

In the transcripts examined thus far, participants have offered various generalizations or recurring patterns from their everyday experience to account for racial separateness. In the following case, we turn to a participant recounting a narrative of going to White fraternity parties. Narratives offer many particulars and concrete details of interracial events as well as the narrator’s evaluation of them.

Excerpt 5. Three African Americans

A: . . . so I guess it’s never going to change if you have that attitude
C: Do you think it’s because of what they do socially?
A: I mean that’s one reason because we don’t have like-
I don’t have the same interests as them =
B: = Do you think it’s a matter of color or just a matter [of
A: [I don’t know
lik[e
C: [I think it’s a matter of soc- I mean ( ) my freshman
and sophomore year I went to a lot of White fraternity parties up here
and had a ball::
B: I know I think White people know how to have more fun than Black
people we tend to just argue amongst each other
C: It was definitely different but it was never a problem of goin’ up in there
you know that’s because they don’t play the right type of music and =
B: Right
C: = everything else now we’re not into the same music I won’t be around
I mean I couldn’t see going out with you if you listening to rock

C questions A's critical upshot statement by suggesting an account of social differences (line 10). C initially suggests this account to A, then comes back to assert it before A can venture in a different direction (lines 14–16). This, of course, is a familiar conversational strategy—ask another a question about a topic you wish to discuss. C cuts her general assertion short and moves to tell a narrative about going to "a lot of White fraternity parties" and favorably assesses that experience as "had a ball" (line 16–18). C continues by claiming that there was no problem of going to White fraternity parties but for the fact that "they don't play the right type of music" to which B immediately concurs (line 21–23).

In addition to the music problem, she adds "and everything else" (lines 22–24)—an etceteras clause (Garfinkel, 1967) for all the other racial difficulties. C articulates the upshot of these differences by switching footings and assuming the voice of addressing the White male from her past, "now we're not into the same music I won't be around I mean I couldn't see going out with you if you listening to rock" (lines 24–25). In this story, C's reported speech of explaining to a White male why she would not go out with him can be heard as an explanation of a boundary—an explanation both to the White male and her current interlocutors.

Such sociocultural differences are mentioned at various points by African-American participants and are discursively used to warrant social distance. This mention of music signifies a readily identifiable popular culture difference.

Identity and Difference

Throughout the transcripts there seems to be competing discourses on identity, between a discourse of group identities and a discourse of personal identities. People can draw upon multiple identities in positioning themselves in interaction with others. How do participants discursively construct these different identities? In the following excerpt, we see B offering a storied account for her not being involved in Jewish organizations and peer groups, and instead taking a more individualistic approach.

Excerpt 6. Two Whites

B: . . . I mean the only thing I can kind of compare it to is being Jewish
but at U all the Jewish people pretty much stuck together and

integrated themselves a little bit I think and then there were stragglers
who pretty much did their own thing and didn't worry about it
but there was ((fraternity name)) which was an obviously Jewish fraternity
and friends of mine would often say you're Jewish but you don't hang out
with anyone who's Jewish and friends of mine who were Black
who didn't necessarily go with- who we're part of ALS and
part of all the Black on-campus organizations so they got a lot of the
same reactions from their friends like
why aren't you hanging out with all the Black people =
A: Um huh
B: = and stuff like that, and it's sort of a weird feeling but I've never hung out with
a lot of Jewish people so why would I have done that when I went to college
ya know it was never anything I thought about is this person Jewish or Black
or whatever I just hang with someone if I like hanging out with 'em
A: Um huh
B: But if someone comes up to me and says I'm White and proud to be White and
everyone should proud to be White I'm like who the hell is this freak get outta my
face ya kn[ow so if a Black person comes up and says that to me I'm Black =
A: [Hhhh
B: = I'm proud to be Black whatever I'm going to be like yeah whatever ya know
if a Black person comes up and hey let's go get a beer or something
I'm like cool that's fine ya know Hhhhh
it just turns me off when people are in your face about what they feel

B contrasts being group-identified versus being individualistic, and also contrasts being Jewish and being African American. B tells of receiving questions from others about why she does not socialize with other Jews (lines 16–17) and also of her African-American friends receiving parallel kinds of questions (lines 17–21). B accounts for this lack of within-group association by mentioning that she never did it in the past so why now; she does not consider a person's group membership, but rather "I just hang with someone if I like hanging out with 'em" (lines 23–26). B draws on a color-blind rhetoric to support her account of interpersonal relationships.

To illustrate her point, she imagines a hypothetical situation of two ethnically identified people, one White and one Black, talking to her and expressing White and Black pride respectively, and her negative reported thought in response to each in turn (lines 28–32). By contrast, if an African American approaches her as an individual, she would be receptive to that (line 33–34). As B says in her evaluation of this hypothetical scenario, "it just turns me off when people are in your face about what they feel" (line 35). In other words, she does not like ethnically identified others who express nationalistic sentiments. B's account can be interpreted as reflecting a kind of White privilege (Frankenberg, 1993) in that she as a White has more degrees of freedom in whether or not to make relevant her group membership.

B's hypothetical encounter is interesting for what it leaves out. The membership categories of comparison are ethnically identified and nonethnically identified, and African American and White. B imagines responding to three of the four categories of person, but does not consider a nonethnic White approaching her. Presumably this case is too obvious; it is taken for granted that she would be receptive to such a person. According to her practical reasoning, what shows her color-blindness is her receptivity to a nonethnic, African American and her dislike of an ethnically identified White.

A rather different positioning on group identity is evident in the following excerpt. M accounts for his avowal that he is going to send his kids to "a predominately Black institution." M recounts a dialogue from a movie and then compares it to his own background in terms of being an African American growing up in a White environment.

Excerpt 7 (Two African Americans)

M: . . . I'm probably gonna send my kids to a predominately Black institution

F: So you're planning on sending your kids to a predominately Black institution

M: For their undergraduate studies yeah

(.)

F: I don't agree with that

M: Hhhh see I always think of that movie Holl- not Hollywood Shuffle, I'm Gonna Get You Sucker you know that dude that does the interview? I don't know if you remember that movie but there this one part where they interview the big black hair in the neighborhood and the guy: from the TV station interviews him and after the interview is over and the hero says something you know blah blah ya know what I mean brother? then he goes ((with cleansed media sounding voice)) ha ha actually I don't know what you mean my mother was a lawyer my father was a doctor[all my friends were =

F: [Okay I get it

M: = White[hhhhh =

F: [I get it

M: = I went to Harvard you know

F: Shut up I get it stop teasing me (.) okay now =

M: = I mean my life was like that my life was like that?

F: Right

M: I moved from a predominately Black neighborhood in New York City in the South Bronx what's considered the South Bronx now to S. ((suburban, Virginia)) nothing but White kids I came down wanting to play basketball and they was all about playing soccer it was a completely different mind-set for me I grew up in a completely White neighborhood and a predominately White environment all through my high school and up until I went to college

In the *Racism 101* documentary, one of the African-American students talks about the psychological costs of attending a predominately White university and says that he will send his kids to a traditionally Black college.[4] While it is not specifically marked as such, this may be the backdrop for M's initial statement of sending his kids to a predominately Black institution. After F expresses disagreement, M attempts to justify his position by recounting a movie in which one of the characters is comically portrayed as "acting White" and lacking African-American cultural traits. This reported exchange from the movie echoes the cautionary tale of "forgetting who you are." The cost of social mobility may be losing your ethnic identity.

F takes the evaluative point of this recounting of the movie as "teasing" her, presumably for associating with Whites too much or not being "Black enough." M does not pursue this line but continues with his account by telling the story of moving from "a predominately Black neighborhood" to a "completely White neighborhood" and attending a White high school. As he evaluates it, "it was a completely different mind-set" to underscore the cultural differences. He gives the example of each area playing different kinds of sports: the implication of basketball as an African-American identified game and soccer as White. Differences in popular culture, such as basketball versus soccer, or listening to different music (excerpt 8) may not seem like major cultural boundaries, but they are readily identifiable by young adults. These popular culture differences appear to be further taken as emblematic of more profound cultural differences.

Dilemmas in Accounting for Boundaries

In the prior section, we saw participants offering accounts negotiating responsibility for the self-segregation and separateness on campus. Participants positioned themselves in various ways by criticizing, justifying, or explaining such boundaries. Conflicting accounts are held, not only between groups (Whites and African Americans), but also within these groups. In this section, we see that conflicting accounts are avowed by the same individuals. For instance, some participants say that voluntary segregation is only natural, but that racial separation is problematic. These seemingly conflicting views reflect, not only the complex and contested character of these issues, but also participants trying out and working through various discursive positions. As seen in the following excerpt, seemingly conflicting accounts are avowed by A.

Excerpt 8. Two African Americans

A: if you see someone hanging around with all these White people you feel like oh they lost their identity =

B: Yeah

A: = they're not Black enough and stuff like that I personally don't hang around with White people except in my classes I mean- I guess I'm to the point which is bad I'm not making any efforts- I'm not bending over backwards to make strong relationships or bonds with White people and they're not doing the same to me but I don't feel that I'm prejudiced, I feel that I have more interaction with Whites than other Black people that I know I can't explain it it's just like I really never felt the need to establish those relationships although I say- I know a lot of White people and I consider them acquaintances but we don't call each other up on the phone and stuff like that

In this excerpt, A displays ambivalent feelings about race relations. On the one hand, A reports her critical thoughts in the hypothetical situation of seeing an African American associating with Whites, "you feel like oh they lost their identity." On the other hand, she notes that she has no White friends, only acquaintances, no one she would call up on the phone. A assesses her motivation as "bad" in the sense that "I'm not making any efforts- I'm not bending over backwards to make strong relationships or bonds with White people." But she explains this lack of White friends as not due to prejudice—she has "more interaction with Whites than other Black people that I know."

A discursively portrays her own interracial relationships as conflicted while at the same time claiming some limited success in crossing racial boundaries. Her reported situation can be heard as a kind of dilemma (Billig et al., 1988) in that she reports being unable to form friendships with Whites, even though she would like to, to a certain degree, and even though she has more interracial contact than most. The dilemma seems to reflect a gap between an imagined ideal and her everyday reality. No resolution is offered for this interracial dilemma.

Other accounts reveal similar kinds of dilemmas: participants would like more interracial contact but there is some barrier that prevents it. In the following we see an account of the problem of crossing racial boundaries and a complaint reconsidered.

Excerpt 9. Two Whites

B: in some sense I'd like more integration on campus and
I'd like more equality but I get really intimidated and
I get really turned off:: if I'm going to have ya know-
if integration and equality means I'm going to have to go to Black rallies
where Black people are arguing about how angry they are,
to me you know that's not what I think of as integration
that's not how I think of equality
but it's hard for me to even judge because I don't know
what they've been through, ya know I'm sitting here talking about it
but I- I have absolutely no idea what they're going through

Continuing with the above-mentioned notion of accounting dilemmas, we see B expressing a desire for more "integration" and "equality" on campus, but not finding these at "Black rallies" (lines 1–7). B avows a kind of disappointment in her complaint about attending a "Black rally." B contrasts "integration and equality" with "Black rallies" and Black anger (lines 4–7). It is interesting to note what B makes relevant in her characterization of the Black rally. Kochman's (1981) description of cultural differences in conflict style and affect display could inform B's account. Also, the expectation of achieving some interracial solidarity at a political rally, given the historical legacy of grievances, may be somewhat naive.

In both excerpts 8 and 9, the speaker's account displays a kind of dilemma in that they would like more meaningful interracial contact but seem at a loss to know how to achieve it. Again, the gap between an imagined ideal and the real seems to work as a gloss for these accounts.

Many accounts complain of being unable to change, in some sense of being stuck in a larger pattern of intergroup distance. In the following excerpt we see an account of this intergroup distance and her interlocutor suggesting a differing account for it.

Excerpt 10. Three African Americans

A: It's like a rule when you come here you hang out with Black people
White people hang out with White people and there's no exceptions
to the rule you know so I guess I fit into that little circle because
I'm following right along with everybody else not that I don't want to
but like everything I do everywhere I go:: is predominately Black people
like I'm never in a White surrounding I never go to a party with a whole
bunch of White people so I never had the opportunity to interact with them
unless it's in the classroom and I'm content with it that way
so I guess it's never going to change if you have that attitude
C: Do you think it's because of what they do socially?
A: I mean that's one reason because we don't have like-
I don't have the same interests as them

A's initial account may be heard as betraying a certain ambivalence toward the current state-of-affairs of racial separateness. A's description implicates a reflexive self-criticism: having formulated a "rule" of racial separation, A describes her own actions, "I guess I fit into that little circle because I'm following right along with everybody else." A's word choice of "fit into that little circle" and "following right along with everybody else" are clearly critical ways of accounting for her actions—a kind of self-deprecatory admission of group conformity. A complains of the problems of in-group association resulting in the absence of social contact with Whites. In her complaint, A uses extreme-case formulations (Pomerantz, 1986) to make her case—the use of "everything" and "everywhere" (line 5) and the repetition of "never" (lines 6–7 and 9). These extreme-case ways of describing work towards portraying the problematic circumstances on campus.

In response to A's problematic description, C suggests an account for this separateness as due to social differences. A seems to readily concur with this as she formulates an explanation as not having "the same interests." A moment ago A had offered an explanation of conformity, which is clearly more critical than this different-interests account. Instead of charging A with inconsistency or changing her mind, we need to consider the communicative situation: in discussing such contested issues as race relations, participants try out different accounts to see what works and stands up to scrutiny from interlocutors. Indeed, over such complex issues, some participants display ambivalent feelings and offer completing accounts. Examining these accounts as arising in conversation, as responses to interlocutors, make their conflicting character more understandable.

Discussion

At the end of the day, what have we learned about the discourses of racial boundaries, separation, and difference? First of all, none of the student participants disagreed with the existence of racial boundaries or voluntary segregation, though not everyone actually used these labels. There was a range of accounts and discursive constructions. Some explicitly criticized voluntary segregation, while others implicitly took such separation as problematic, as evidenced by the way they characterized the phenomena, e.g., "you don't mingle you don't interact" (excerpt 1). Some participants disagreed with their interlocutor's criticism and offered justifications to normalize self-segregation. A discourse of cultural difference—music, sports, or general interest—was drawn on to account for voluntary segregation. Others justified separation, not by appeal to difference, but to commonalties, by citing the norm that people socialize with those they have more in common with. Broadly speaking, these divergent accounts can be heard as criticizing or ascribing responsibility for racial separation, or as defending it as normative.

Perhaps the most interesting finding is that some participants hold seemingly conflicting accounts; they are ambivalent about self-segregation. This is consistent with the above-mentioned 1992 Columbia University study. Students can voice conflicting accounts that reflect the multiple discourses on race (Omi & Winant, 1994; Winant, 1994). Some talk of separation as problematic, but when challenged by interlocutors, they avow that it as understandable. Or, some participants would like to have more interracial contact, while at the same time, they seem unable to know how to achieve it. These conflicting accounts fit Billig et al.'s (1988) notion of "ideological dilemmas"; various and even opposing accounts can be avowed by participants to make sense of their circumstances. Recall excerpt 10, where an African-American student criticizes her own seeming conformity in racial separation, and then in response to her interlocutor's suggestion, offers a justificatory account for such separation as due to different interests from Whites. This dilemma, articulated through participants' conflicting accounts, adds needed contextual understanding to the psychological, anxiety/uncertainty management explanation (Gudykunst, 1995) for interracial avoidance.

The project here has been to approach the discursive constructions of boundaries from, as it were, the bottom up (participants' talk), rather than from the top down (macrolevel categories of race, class, history). Such macrolevel approaches render talk into epiphenomena of causal structures, or at best, treat talk as ideology. But by looking at talking race, we can examine the communicative practices participants engage in making sense of and evaluating interracial relations. Participants' discourse is much more varied, nuanced, and contextual than suggested by traditional macrolevel approaches (Singelis, 1996). The intergroup relations thesis of in-group favoritism and out-group hostility (Tzeng et al., 1986) is not born out in these transcripts. The picture is more complicated; while in-group favoritism and out-group hostility persists, some participants are critical of their own group, or are understanding of out-group positions, while others are ambivalent and avow conflicting views.

The notion of ideology comes closer to the present project to the extent that ideology can be taken as a preexisting discourse that participants formulate in their terms, try out, assess, and take positions on. The social accountability model used here takes students as engaged in the normative enterprise of accounting for and making judgments about contested matters of race. These accounts are not simply a verbalization of participants' cognitive contents, e.g., attitudes (Wetherell & Potter, 1992), but rather a partaking in a discourse so as to try to articulate, explore, or criticize different positions on race. In offering accounts, participants are attempting to make more explicit their understandings, evaluations, and positions on these matters, which in turn allows interlocutors to align or diverge with the emerging discursive constructions.

Documentaries, film, or other mass-media productions would seem to be a way to raise issues of race relations and racism, and make viewers more empathetic about the other group's experiences. As we have seen, viewers can take oppositional positions or resist the dominant reading of the documentary. Participants' positions get examined in the postviewing discussions with peers. Having to account for a racial position moves one to formulate reasons, stories, and other discursive means to flesh out one's emerging views. The many conflicting accounts suggest that students' racial thinking is still fluid and that they are trying out different discourses from a variety of sources.

How participants use the documentary in their accounts could be a study in itself. Of the excerpts presented here, there are three points in which *Racism 101* is explicitly referenced, though all of the excerpts discuss issues that were shown in the documentary. Looking at the three explicit references (excerpt 1 and two references from excerpt 3), participants report what someone said in the documentary and then agree or disagree with it and elaborate. Other participants reported dialogue from a popular movie (excerpt 7), from their own past experiences (excerpt 5–6), or constructed hypothetical dialogue (excerpt 6). Reporting on another's speech allows the reporting speaker to raise a sensitive topic without having to embrace it as one's own view.

There are limitations to using volunteers for this study, since those most interested in the topic are most likely to volunteer. Another limitation is that participants' discussions followed their watching *Racism 101*, and these discussions occurred with a tape recorder running. However, it is difficult in the extreme to find naturally occurring discussions to record about race matters. Most of the prior discourse analyses of race employed an interview format. Given these limitations, the procedures used in the present study seemed successful in getting discussions going in the participants' own terms without the immediate presence of the researcher.

Many have observed how North Americans like quick solutions to problems, but over contested matters of race we do not seem able to achieve consensus. So we need to teach respect for differences (Scott, 1992) and also to see current tensions in a broader historical context. As one reviewer (Marwell, 1988) of *Racism 101* pointed out, improved institutional changes on university campuses provide the conditions for conflict; African-American students are more middle class than ever before, more of a critical mass on campus, and are willing to express grievances and demands.

7

Conclusion

In this work we have focused on the social accountability of talking problems. This project involved two primary pieces: the construction of problems and how participants position themselves and others, and secondly, how these constructions are achieved, the communicative practices used in talking problems. The main contribution of these studies lies in the situated descriptions of the practices, positions, and constructions of talking problems.

In this final chapter we will reexamine some of the principle findings of the different studies. In reexamining these findings we will consider the utility of the analytic perspectives used here. Looking at our perspectives and findings will allow us to weigh in on current controversies on ethnicity, gender, and power. We conclude with some conjectures on change and the ownership of problems.

Analytic Perspectives

To get at the social accountability of talking problems, we drew on the analytic perspectives of discursive constructionism and conversation analysis. As a general perspective, discursive constructionism captures persons' version(s) of the problem—what happened—the actions, events, or states-of-affairs made relevant in the problem telling. How the problem is formulated, what gets told, what is omitted, and how the actors are portrayed is crucial for social accountability. In telling problems certain interests are often at stake, so participants rhetorically design their version. In the course of constructing problems, who the interlocutors are in this exchange comes into focus. Positioning analysis throws into relief the relevant identities of participants and where they align themselves vis-à-vis one another. One of the principle features of positioning is the person's agency, responsibility, or accountability for the problem. Conversation analysis is useful in describing the various communicative practices in talking problems, that is, how these activities are interactionally accomplished. In examining these practices, we see them as conjointly constructed by participants. Here we consider these perspectives in terms of what they reveal about talking problems in our data.

Discursive Constructionism

Through various conversational practices, the social reality of the problem and person positionings become discursively constructed. A problem telling is designed for some recipients in the context of some interactional contingencies. For instance, BH's narrative of having to have the child and get married portrays his life changes by a discourse of necessity and constraint. Or African-American participants' narratives of being disrespected in public places frames events as troublesome—as an absence of ordinary norms of civility. Or the therapist's use of humorous exaggerated metaphors offers clients an alternative image of their relationships. The point here being that each of these is a version of actions, events, or states-of-affairs that are presented in particular circumstances to particular others. These versions could be retold by a different rhetoric resulting in a different sense of the problem, or even no problem at all.

A crucial aspect of talking problems is the person's relation to the problem in terms of responsibility, accountability, being affected by it, and the like. In talking problems, participants typically have a stake in how they are seen by others vis-à-vis aspects of agency and action. So persons position themselves in relation to the problem to be seen favorably or to minimize the discrediting implications of action. Positioning analysis focuses on how participants locate themselves—their stances—towards the problems and in relation to others.

Persons, also, may be positioned by others. In our studies, persons were frequently positioned by others as well as positioning themselves. For instance in the teen parent studies, we saw how each teen parent was positioned in a problematic way by interlocutors by the conflicting category predicates of being young and being a parent. In the four peers' transcript, BH avowed this problem and further positioned himself through his narratives as a reluctant father.

Just as the shape and evaluation of action and events are malleable and changeable, so is a person's positioning. Actions, events, and states-of-affairs on the one hand, and a person's positioning on the other, can be seen as opposite sides of the same coin. They are all discursively accomplished through talk-in-interaction. For instance, in the four peers transcripts BH interactionally repositions himself more favorably as a loving father and happy to have the child. This loving father avowal justifies BH's repositioning himself. In the school-family meeting transcript, the grandmother attempts to reposition her daughter's problem in the context of the family—the grandmother will watch the child, so her daughter can study thereby resolving some of the conflicting states. However, the codirector reasserts her original positioning of the teen mother by the conflicting predicates. So this attempted repositioning gets contested—at least in the eyes of the school.

Portraits of the other are inherently relational, so in offering an image of out-group members, an image of in-group members also is (implicitly) being discursively created. The reported speech of African Americans typically positions in-group member(s) as the unjustified recipient of racist actions, e.g., receiving racist notes or slurs, being negatively stereotyped, being treated differently in social relations. Most of the instances of reported speech in the studies were uttered by African Americans, which reflects their heightened awareness of racism and interracial contact. Being the victim of an injustice makes one more likely to recall and articulate such incidents. White students were positioned as being unaware of racism on campus or unwilling to admit it, while students of color positioned themselves as very cognizant of such racialized matters. Among Whites, reported speech constructs their deeds as ordinary, reasonable, or at worst, "stupid," but blown out of proportion by African Americans. Some Whites positioned students of color as overemphasizing their ethnicity, while positioning themselves by rhetoric of individuality rather than group identity. These findings are consistent with the asymmetry of perception of everyday racism between African Americans and Whites (Essed, 1991; Feagin, 1991; Hacker, 1992). These talking race studies add to the specificity of situated problematic events through which participants discursively construct interracial realities.

In looking at the discursive constructions of reported speech, we were also drawn to the Bakhtinian perspective of the "multivocality" of speech. Reported speech exhibits a "double-voiced quality" (Bakhtin, 1986) in the sense that the words of the original speaker are given voice by the reporting speaker. In giving voice to another's words, the current speaker uses those words by explicitly or implicitly assessing them. In assessing another's words, one takes up a footing in relation to it. The issue of the accuracy of the original version is bracketed, and reported speech is taken as serving the reporting speaker's own purposes. This using another's words for one's own purposes suggests a "dialogic relationship" between our speech and the speech of the other (Bakhtin, 1986). We draw on multiple voices that are juxtaposed—our voice and the voice of the other. This is another practice whereby problems are discursively constructed with others' voices.

Conversation Analysis

We have drawn on conversation analysis to describe the communicative practices through which problems get jointly constructed. Consider some of the practices in talking problems described here. In the therapy interview, the therapist retells some of the clients' problem tellings. The therapist cannot do this unilaterally; the retelling is conjointly achieved along with the clients. In articulating the therapeutic version, the therapist uses the practice of building off of what the clients had already said, but taking their tellings in a different direction. The therapist agreed with Jenny's version, but drew different implications from it. Instead of Larry not being open, as his partner Jenny claimed, his actions were glossed by the therapist as a different style, a style that complements Jenny's expressive style.

In doing this telling, the therapist cannot just offer the therapeutic version as a diagnosis; the therapist needs to engage the clients and their reaction to it. To engage the clients, the therapist pursues their evaluation of the therapeutic version through a post-positioned query or tag question. The client's response displays their understanding or assessment of the therapeutic version. Further, the client's response opens up a slot for the therapist to evaluate the client's answer or explain in more detail the therapeutic version. This practice of getting the clients' understanding or evaluation of the therapeutic retelling so as to project a possible further therapeutic explanation seems important in the therapist's pursuit of convincing the clients. While we gloss this practice as "the therapist retelling the clients' tellings," we can see how this retelling is jointly constructed as the therapist builds off of the clients' positions, responses, and assessments.

Therapy has been characterized as involving both the discourses of medicine and of morality (Bergmann, 1992). We may add to this characterization the art of rhetoric—for in and through words the therapist attempts to persuade clients of different ways to discursively construct their relationship. What is less understood—and to what this analysis attempts to contribute—is how the rhetoric of therapeutic reframings gets interactionally achieved through various conversational practices, such as telling clients about themselves and thirdturn evaluations of the clients' assessments of the therapeutic version.

Another conversational practice we have seen is ascribing conflicting category predicates of another to formulate a problem. The most explicit technique for doing this practice in our data was the codirector's listing conflicting category predicates of the teenage student-mother (chapter 1). We also saw this practice in the four peers' data. WH's muted "damn" in response to BH telling his age can be heard to implicate the problem through these conflicting predicates. That these conflicting predicates were heard as problems was seen through the recipients' responses. Recall how the grandmother offers a solution-account to the codirector's problem ascription. Or how BH moves into a narrative to explain his becoming a father.

This practice of conflicting category predicates can be heard at work in the therapy context when Jenny ascribes Larry as being private and their relationship as being like roommates. The obvious assumption being that an intimate partner should be open, and their relationship should be more than roommates. Interestingly, the therapist takes these conflicting category predicates and retells them as complementary, in a way that balances their relational system.

In talking about race, the practice of reporting another's or one's own speech seemed to be rich for investigating how the racial other or problematic racialized events are portrayed. Reporting speech is not simply a "reporting," it also involves making evaluations or assessments of what was said. Reported speech makes relevant an assessment from the teller or recipient. The teller's assessment component tells recipients how to interpret or frame the reported speech, that is, the assessment displays the teller's footing toward the reported speech, e.g., as critical, as frustrated, as supporting it. The assessment may be implicit, such as implicated in the intonational contour in reporting the speech. The teller's implicit assessment, then, allows the recipient to make the assessment explicit (Holt, 2000a). These assessments reveal the teller's positioning in talking race matters.

As we have seen there are various ways of doing reported speech. Direct reported speech involves (supposedly) quoting the speech of the original speaker. Another type we have examined is prototypical reported speech. This practice involves a teller summarizing a group's characteristic speech through a quote of a purported, prototypical group member. Prototypical quotes involve the speech apparently of a hypothetical individual speaker, but at the same time this speech is purported to be typical of the group of which the individual is a member. Using this practice of prototypical reported speech allows one to epitomize the group through their characteristic utterances, e.g., in chapter 4, excerpt 2, C draws on the prototypical voice of "the White students" in saying "well I didn't put it out" (line 8). These instances of prototypical speech of the racial other typically are preceded or followed by the teller's voice to respond to or to assess the prototypical other. This is consistent with the finding that reported speech involves not only a reporting but also an editorializing. Much of the reported speech of the racial other is portrayed as deficient or extreme. This commenting on or assessing the voice of the other reflects the teller's presumed position of being normative. A similar use of prototypical reported speech was found among White New Zealanders in portraying the Maori as the racial other (Buttny, in press).

The conversational practices reviewed here (e.g., prototypical reported speech, reported speech and assessment, conflicting category predicates, and retelling a prior telling) are *general* practices. That is, they are not unique to these particular individuals, but are ways of speaking available to other competent communicators for talking problems. We have seen these practices used by a variety of participants in different contexts. Also, we saw these practices used in talking problems, but we surmise they can be found in nonproblem talk as well. The discursive constructions of actions, events, or persons are more topic *specific*; they are constructions of teen parenthood, of interpersonal relationships, and of racism and interracial contact. These constructions are not limited to the particular individuals speaking, but are part of the available discourses for making sense of these respective problems.

Issues, Controversies, and Alternate Readings

It goes without saying that there can be more than one interpretation of data or reading of a transcript. Different analysts can interpret the data in terms of their perspectives and analytical vocabulary. Currently there are a number of approaches that use tape-recorded data and transcripts in doing research. The approach adopted here is social accountability in talking problems. Drawing on conversation analysis, the project is not so much for the analyst to give a reading of a text as much as to ascertain how the interlocutors interpret each other through talk-in-interaction. The focus is on the participants' displayed understandings, orientations, and communicative practices. Another tenant is the centrality of action and interaction: what persons do, or are attempting to do, and what this action projects, and how this is seen and taken by recipients. Given these ways of working, traditional categories of the person (e.g., race, class, gender) and features of the context (e.g., ordinary or institutional settings) can be recast in terms of participants' interpretations and action to be deemed relevant in a particular situation for these participants. To see person categories and contexts displayed in participants' orientations or actions allows us to make a stronger case for what is going on. It allows us to move from an a priori starting point to empirical evidence for claims.

Ethnicity

To illustrate some of these issues and controversies, consider alternate interpretations of our data. In the school-family meeting (chapter 1) the school representatives were observably White, while the family members were observably Latino. The ethnic categories of the participants did not become part of the analysis, since they did not appear to be relevant to the participants in this encounter. These categories were omitted from the analysis because there was no participant orientation to or display of these categories in the data. Other person categories, however, were relevant, as we have seen: gender, age, parenthood, student, codirector. From my initial viewing of the videotape and noting the apparent ethnic differences between the school and family members, I was especially keen on looking for how these ethnic differences might be relevant for these participants. From my observations, none were found. Of course, a more astute observer may find something that was overlooked in the data.

In the therapy studies, the therapist is observably Latino, and the clients are observably White. Here we come to the same conclusion as the school-family meeting; ethnicity was not interactionally oriented to by the participants, so it was not brought into the analysis. The point here being that categories, such as ethnicity, need to be empirically available in some way for analysis, rather than assumed to be relevant to what is going on.

In the talking race studies, ethnicity does become oriented to and discussed by participants and becomes a central part of the analysis. For instance, some accounts on the separateness among various groups on campus involved discourses of social identity. This was most apparent in those accounts from students of color that argued for the need not to lose ethnic identity. Other accounts suggested a sense of a dilemma in both wanting more meaningful contact with Whites while expressing concern over maintaining ethnic identity or receiving criticism from other African Americans. Social identity issues were the most noticeable difference between students of color and White accounts. Identity was virtually not an issue for Whites, "the privilege" (Frankenberg, 1993) of being the dominant group. An exception was a Jewish student who told of how she as a Jew received questions from others for why she did not associate more with her own group (chapter 6; excerpt 9). Her account involved a discourse of personal identity in contrast to group identity. In this case, and in others, Whites drew on a so-called "color-blind rhetoric" to bolster their avowals of individuality.

Now an analysis could be put forward about the school-family meeting (chapter 1) of how it is that the school representatives happened to be White and the family members Latino (Holt, 2000b, p. 32). Such an analysis involves themes of schooling, poverty, hiring, migration, and the like. These are important issues, to be sure, and they provide part of the historical and contextual backdrop to this meeting. But the reason they were not included in our analysis is that we are looking at talking problems and how they are jointly constructed by these participants in this interaction—not at the historical or sociological conditions surrounding these problems. Once this historical and contextual backdrop story is told, there is no way to distinguish between this particular meeting and the next meeting, which may have similar demographic characteristics of the participants.

Gender

Another controversy involves issues of gender and sexism seemingly found in the therapy studies. One of the main speech activities of these chapters was the therapist retelling the clients' tellings. The primary problem teller was the woman partner, Jenny. Jenny's main complaint was that her partner, Larry, was not more open, and their relationship has degenerated to being like roommates. The therapist, Carlos Sluzki, a man, spends a good portion of the consultation offering his version of their relationship as balanced. Instead of Larry not being open, as his partner Jenny claimed, his actions were glossed by the therapist as a different style, a style that complements Jenny's expressive style such that they balance each other. From a critical perspective, the female partner's voice can be interpreted as being silenced by the male therapist and the problem recast into individualistic therapeutic terms (Davis, 1986).

But the therapist also disagrees with some of Larry's claims and retells them as well. Retelling and reframing of problems is one of the main speech activities of therapists. As mentioned above, the therapist cannot do this unilaterally; the therapist needs to engage the client(s) in this new way to frame things.

Gender and ethnicity are both person categories. The argument here turns on the issue of relevancy: show how, if at all, gender or ethnicity is relevant to this particular interaction for the participants. Billig (1999) has argued that even labeling the participants as "therapist" or "clients" introduces assumptions about how these participants are to be seen. The point is well taken in that we can all too easily lapse into familiar or stereotypical ways of thinking about participants and what they are up to. But we need to identify the participants in some way. In this therapy example, I could have called the participants by their first names or just referenced them as participants A, B, or C. I elected to identify them as therapist and clients (or the clients from the couple as Jenny and Larry) because the participants oriented to each other in this way. The analytic challenge is, not to rely on background knowledge about therapists and clients, but to ground our claims in the participants' orientations, displays, and actions.

Power

Another controversy involves how to handle issues of power. Power is a multifaceted concept. A case could be made that all communication involves power: who gets their way, who is heard, who is silenced, and the like. But power is at times invoked by some critical perspectives in such a way that it obscures analysis of more subtle aspects of talk-in-interaction. So instead of the critical tendency to focus on persons, institutions, and their power, look to power as an emergent feature of interaction—how power is done. Instead of explaining the talk by invoking power—the institution, such as the high school or the university, or the dominant voice of therapy or of White racism, we have tried to get a fresh look at power by focusing on conversational practices, positionings of persons, and discursive constructions.

One way that power can be seen in our data is in how matters get talked about, defined, and understood. The ability of speech to name, identify, and categorize events, or persons can be seen as one form of power. As we saw in the talking race studies, identifying certain events as "racist" or just "stupid" was contested. Clearly the latter is a milder kind of rebuke. In the therapy material, whether Larry was "afraid" or had a "lack of trust," or in the high school data, BH preferring not to have the baby versus his love for the child matters in terms of accountability. Which characterization, description, or evaluation holds is consequential for the actor's positioning, how others act towards the actor, and what is to be done as a remedy.

It is widely recognized that there can be multiple versions of events. In the therapy studies, it may be a fact that Larry is less open and expressive than his partner, but while Jenny takes this as problematic, the therapist takes it as part of their relational system and frames it as balancing Jenny's expressiveness. In the talking race studies, the fact of so-called voluntary segregation on campus was not challenged by any of the participants, but how it was assessed varied considerably. Some students oriented to this separateness as problematic, while others took it as understandable and justified. Interlocutors may agree on the facts, but they disagree as to the implications, evaluation, or consequences of these facts. Not all versions of events are equal; some versions carry more weight, are more authoritive than others.

Aspects of power may be evident in the conversations in more subtle ways. In the talking race on campus studies, students complained of a sense of powerlessness in the sense of being unable to affect change or improve conditions on campus. Much of the reported speech by students of color is used to tell experiences of being the recipient of racism, stereotyping, or being a minority on a predominately White campus. For instance, a student comments on his lack of control, "they look at you like that and unfortunately there's very little I can do about that, because I am the only Black in almost all of my classes I'm the only Black person in there" (chapter 4, excerpt 8). Even the Whites' speech reflects a sense of powerlessness. The Whites' powerlessness is not nearly as pervasive; it is more a sense of a frustration in communicating with African Americans, e.g., "one of the biggest problems that people have- that White people have relating to Black people on campus is how to deal with the issue of race" (chapter 4, excerpt 11). From a communication satisfaction perspective (Martin et al., 1994) this implicit sense of powerlessness would be a way of explaining the avoidance of interracial contact on campus.

Through talking race and being a witness to the wrongs of everyday racism, participants can challenge current practices through narrating problematic events and holding others accountable (at least within the group). When we listen to students talking race, we can hear "the power of the spoken word."[1] Reported speech as a conversational practice allows one to draw on others', or one's own, words of strength and resistance. This was most apparent in the quoting of the respect-not-liking segment from *Racism 101.* Participants seemed drawn to respect as a ready solution. In addition, reported speech functions to make others' words visible as a way to reconstruct events and to criticize them. Reported speech can be seen to achieve a performative power for participants by building conversational alliances and counter-alliances (Álverez-Cáccano, 1996). Through discussing the troublesome features of racism and interracial contact we learn how to better recognize and criticize such problematic encounters.

The criticism gets made of discursive constructionism that "positions are empty shell or armour which people can, each in turn, borrow for themselves or others for presenting their action and their image in a positive light and in such a way that social order is maintained" (Törrönen, 2001, p. 318). What is missing, according to this critique, is attention "to the life history of individuals or . . . the larger social world" (p. 319). We have discussed the malleability of positionings that participants take up, e.g., BH as a reluctant father and as a loving father. What constrains or limits the positionings one can take up? Consider BH's response to the query, "Where's the ring?" and his assertion that it is being repaired. His interlocutors dismiss this response through teasing rebuffs. The point here is that positioning is an interactional construct—that which recipients will allow or accept from the person. This still leaves the question of *why* the interlocutors rebuffed BH's footing and implicated positioning. In looking at the data, NH responds by dismissing BH's answer as untruthful and what he heard last year from him. So "the life history of the individual" (e.g., "what you told me last year") or "the larger social world" (e.g., wearing a ring as a symbol of marital fidelity) may enter in, but they enter in because the participants bring them in and use them as conversational resources. Positioning of persons emerges through the talk-in-interaction and is coconstructed between individuals. Contra Törrönen (2001), persons cannot just take on any shell or armour because interlocutors will question or dismiss them.

Final Conjectures

Change

In talking problems, change is a discursive construction that can have variable meanings and evaluations for participants.

Change can be seen as the consequence of talking problems. Change is often a possible solution to the problem. This is, of course, commonsense knowledge. We have seen the participants orient to change in various ways and even discuss it as such. In the four-peers conversation, WH after hearing BH's story of being present at the birth of his child, says "that shit must've changed your life completely" (chapter 1, excerpt 8). BH concurs and eventually formulates it as, "everything's changed=my whole life has changed" (line 6). In this situated use, change is both good and bad. Bad, or problematic, because of having to grow up sooner due to newly added responsibilities. But also good, as OW glosses it, as being "responsible" (line 10, 15). Earlier BH avowed his love for his child and was glad they had the baby. So BH appears ambivalent to the change: on the one hand loving his child, but on the other dealing with the growing pains of added responsibilities and loss of adolescent pleasures.

Change, as a discursive construction, can be about actual or possible changes. BH's actual changes are discussed in the four-peers conversation, while possible changes become the focus of the school-family meeting. As we have seen, the codirector formulates the possible problem of the student-mother not graduating and the possibility of changing to a school more designed for her circumstances. The grandmother orients to the codirector's problem formulations by mentioning changes in the family to accommodate her daughter's studying. So what change will be implemented becomes a central focus of the meeting. Change is taken as both a problem (the conflicting category predicates) and a possible solution.

Change also becomes discussed in the talking race studies. As one student claims, in assessing the troublesome state of race relations of campus, "things will never change." This utterance is an extreme case formulation. It works as a kind of idiomatic summary statement of the current interracial affairs. In this context, change is equated with progress on dealing with racism. In the talking race studies, change can be heard as implicated in practically all of the problem formulations. For instance, in the narratives of being disrespected in public places, the clear implication is that how African Americans are treated in service encounters should be changed.

In the therapy studies, the changes implicated by the problem formulation get more complicated in that there are competing versions of the problem. Which version of the relationship problems hold will implicate what is to be done, what change is in order. On Jenny's version, Larry needs to be more expressive and open with her, and going to therapy would be a good way to achieve this. For

Larry there is not much of a problem, other than Jenny's overinvolvement in therapy. Given their respective versions of the problem the implicated directions for change become transparent. The therapist's version attempts to retell or transform Jenny's and Larry's version of the problem. For the therapist, since Jenny's emotional expressiveness is balanced by Larry's cool cautiousness, there is little necessity for change. As the therapist put it, "very important to move slowly" (chapter 2, excerpt 14).

There is also the change of which participants are not aware, or at least, do not orient to in their conversations. Changes, such as, the historic changes in laws governing race relations in the USA, in perception of teenage parents, and in expectations for a relational partner. Given the limits of our methodology, if the participants did not orient to or display it, such change was not included in the analysis.

One way to invoke at least a momentary change is to move into humor. It perhaps should come as no surprise that in talking problems participants should draw on humor. Humor appears in various guises: as exaggerated metaphors (e.g., balloon and rock), facetiousness (e.g., "the way you tilt your glasses," when she is not wearing glasses), teasing (e.g., "where's the ring"), mocking (e.g., imitating sounding White), a smile voice, and do on. We saw humor used to raise a problem, to avoid a problem, and to dissolve a problem.

Humor in talking problems involves the notion of footing, the person's stance towards what they are saying or toward their coparticipants. Persons can exaggerate, allude to, ironize, mock, be figurative, and the like. They also can be literal or serious. The literal or serious way of putting things may be the default condition.[2] Changing footings from serious into humor can reveal a certain performative capacity or artfulness. Taking up a humorous footing towards problems can allow participants to laugh at, rather than bemoan, the situation.

Ownership of Problems

Once clients tell their problem to the therapist, the problem is, in some sense, no longer theirs. Problems are not simply the clients' subjective sentiments or inner cognitions, but become an object for examination through talk (Coulter, 1979). At issue is not the teller and his/her experiences, but the problem and its properties (Jefferson & Lee, 1981). Problems can be scrutinized, questioned, and even challenged, in short, they are open to public criteria as to how they are to be described and ultimately evaluated. Individuals are not the final authority for their own avowals or affect. Those who profess irrational fears or unwarranted alignments can be challenged or overruled by others for holding these positions. This telling others about themselves was most apparent in the therapy studies, but was also seen in the school-family meeting when the codirector formulates and ascribes the teen-mother's problem. Even the four-peers conversation, where no authority figure is present, interlocutors ascribe problems of the teen father. As far as ownership of the problem goes, the individual may be responsible for it, but s/he does not have privileged access to it. Once the particulars of the problem are known, others can formulate it, retell it, and ascribe it. It is an interesting feature of intersubjectivity that, at times, others can see our problem better than we can ourselves.

In listening to these participants talking problems, I am struck by both the commonality of problems and the uniqueness of problems. "Commonality" in the sense that we all share these difficulties given our common human condition. So the couple's complaint in therapy about their partner being more or less open and expressive seems to be a relational issue that couples must navigate through (Rawlins, 1983). Also, the presuppositon of respect for persons seems to be a general condition necessary for ethical human interactions. The contradictory positions in which we find ourselves, or the unwanted changes from one status to the next seem to be general structures of the discourse of problems.

This commonality of problems may be because we have abstracted away from the situated particulars of events. Looking at the participants talking in our data, we can also see much more the particular contingencies of their situated problems. As a researcher I was surprised to hear the descriptions by students of color of everyday racism on campus—I had expected more interracial harmony. I was most surprised, and dismayed, by the African-American narratives of disrespect during service encounters. These talking race studies made me aware of my own situatedness or positoning as a White, middle-aged academic.

In the end, talking problems does bring in persons' positionings because of social accountability. Given our moral and social orders, we need some code or standards by which to evaluate our own and others' actions. Even as an analyst, or stranger, listening to others talking problems, we can hear these problems as uniquely the participants' own as well as hear them as similar to our own. Much like being at the theater, we hear the actors giving voice to problems of their own and to problems seemingly part of our shared human condition.

Appendix

Transcription conventions

The following is the Jeffersonian transcription system adapted from Ochs, Schegloff, and Thompson (1996, pp. 461–465).

I. Temporal and sequential relationships.

[
[A. Overlapping or simultaneous talk is indicated by separate left square brackets, one above the other of two successive lines with utterances by different speakers, indicates a point of overlap onset, whether at the start of the utterance or later. So in the following, BH's "A year" overlaps with OW's "months."

OW: A month and two- a year and two m[onths

BH: [A year

and two months, °something like that°

= B. Equal signs come in pairs—one at the end of a line and another at the start of the next line. They are used to indicate two things:

1. If the two lines connected by the equal signs are by the same speaker, then there was a single, continuous utterance with no break or pause, which was broken up in order to accommodate the placement of the overlapping talk. For example, in the following, BH continues on from line 32 to 34 with NH's overlapping talk.

32 BH: °That's- that's one thing I::,° [↑I never imagined =

33 NH: [$And I remember you$

34 BH: = myself be[ing a father

2. If the lines connected by two equal signs are by different speakers, then the second followed the first with no discernable silence between them, or was "latched" to it, as in the following.

BH: But then:: we had to keep it.=

WH: = Why?

(0.5) C. Numbers in parentheses indicate silence, represented in tenths of a second. For instance, (0.8) indicates 0.8 seconds of silence. Silences may be marked either within an utterance [see excerpt (a)] or between different speakers' utterances [see excerpt (b)]:

(a) GM: The ( ) baby is going to stay with (.) me

in the room in the *bassinet*

(1.3)

so she could sleep.

(b) GM: when she comes out of school she'll go home,

do her homework,

then::: she'll be with *the baby*.

(1.7)

CD1 But she is trying to live two lives right?

(.) D. A dot in parentheses indicates a "micropause," ordinarily less than 0.2 of a second.

II. Aspects of speech delivery, including aspects of intonation

The punctuation marks are *not* used grammatically, but to indicate intonation.

. The period indicates a falling or final intonation contour, not necessarily the end of a sentence.

? A question mark indicates rising intonation, not necessarily a question.

, A comma indicates "continuing" intonation, not necessarily a clause boundary.

:: B. Colons are used to indicate the prolongation of stretching of the sound just preceding them. The more colons, the longer the stretching:

Ther: Um hum (.) .hhh ah lack of trust means ah:: (0.9)
the ways in: which: (0.5) you ah::: (2.4) ah:: worry

For instance, the "ah" in the second line is stretched more than the "in" in the second line.

– C. A hyphen after a word or part of a word indicates a cut-off or self-interruption. As in the following:

BH: But I- I didn't want to-

word D. Underlining is used to indicate some form of stress or emphasis, either by increased loudness or higher pitch. The more underlining, the greater the emphasis.

WOrd Especially loud talk may be indicated by upper case; the louder, the more letters in upper case. In extreme cases, upper case may be underlined.

°word° E. Talk between two degree signs is markedly quieter or softer than the talk around it:

Jenny: °Well: I don't know°

↑↓ F. The up and down arrows mark sharp rises or falls in pitch:

Ther: ↑I have the impression that ↓tha:t's
the way it looks a bit now↑

>word< G. The combination of "more than" and "less than" symbols indicates that the talk between them is compressed or rushed.

<word> Used in the reverse order, they indicate that a stretch of talk is markedly slowed or drawn out.

hhh H. Hearable aspiration, such as laughter, is shown where it occurs in the talk by the letter h—the more h's, the more aspiration. The aspiration may represent breathing, laughter, and the like. Sometimes laughter is represented by attempting to capture how it sounds, e.g., HA HA, heh heh heh, and the like.

.hh If the aspiration is an inhalation, it is shown with a dot before it.

$word$ I. Words in between the dollar signs are said with a "smile voice." A smile voice involves a markedly higher pitch and an intonational contour comparable to smiling or laughing during speaking but without any laughter tokens.

III. Other markings

(( )) A. Double parentheses are used to mark the transcriber's descriptions of events, for example: ((cough)), ((telephone rings)), ((whispered)), and the like.

(word) B. When a word or words are in parentheses, this indicates uncertainty on the transcriber's part, but it represents a likely possibility.

( ) C. Empty parentheses indicates that something is being said, but no hearing can be achieved.

Notes

Introduction

1. In doing a search at my university library there were 242 book titles in the collection that began with the word, "Talking." The one with the closest affinity to my own is: *Talking Voices: Repetition, Diaglogue, and Imagery in Conversational Discourse* (Tannen, 1989). At the risk of being trendy, I add another "talking" title to this list to indicate the constructive or formative aspect of talk.

Chapter 1

1. I want to acknowledge the help and discussions in the early stages of this project with Kelly Clark and Paula Bradshaw.

2. Interestingly, two journalistic summaries of the film describe segments from the four peers conversation that we analyze in this chapter:

> One student, 18, describes the birth of his son...The young man talks about how his new responsibility has changed his life, his friends respond with a mixture of curiosity and approval (Krupnick, 1995, p. 13).
>
> Although his friends kid him at first, they soon fall quiet, caught a bit off guard by the genuine tenderness that comes across as the teenager describes how much his wife and child mean to him, how they've changed his life" (Lurie, 1994).

While these appear adequate to the journalistic tasks at hand of previewing the film, they are of necessity glosses on a range of conversational practices and positionings that we attempt to detail. Of course, given the open-textured character of language, our version too is a gloss.

Chapter 2

1. The term 'therapy' is used here throughout, rather than psychotherapy, counseling, and the like, because that is the activity term employed by the therapist.

2. By way of contrast, other therapeutic perspectives, such as the Milan school, rely exclusively on questioning (see Peräkylä, 1995, for a conversation analytic approach to the Milan school therapy).

3. The therapist's referencing the discussion itself, rather than continuing "within" the discussion, is what Bateson (1972) called "metacommunication"—a moving to a so-called metalevel to comment on the discussion itself. Making the discussion itself relevant implicates an activity both clients partake in, and thereby, can be heard as an attempt to shift the talk away from the clients' prior individual blames and accounts.

4. Unfortunately the videotape does not capture Jenny's bodily response at this point; her nonverbal displays plus the marked silence may be what the therapist is responding to here.

5. There are different kinds of therapy, some of which use such tests or exams; for instance, see Mehan (1990) on the psychiatric outtake interview.

Chapter 3

1. I could not capture or translate this sound by the use of letters, so I offer the description of how it sounds as, "deep heavy sound," which fits the therapist's contrastive point about Jenny and Larry.

2. Excerpt 6 also fits this client-initiated sequence, which extends into a humor round (the entire sequence is not reproduced in the above transcript).

Chapter 5

1. This case of a speaker addressing a not-present other does not fit Levinson's (1988, p. 173) classification scheme. We need a category of talk designed for a participating recipient, which is addressed to an absent aggregate of others.

2. Other kinds of narratives of disrespectful service encounters involve African Americans receiving condescending treatment. Some participants commented on being shown the least expensive merchandise or what was on sale, rather than top-of-the-line products. Also, narratives related the perceptions that service workers would avoid discussing "the technical capabilities of the product, they assume . . . you're not going to understand

it, they just like underestimate your intelligence." As these instances suggest, participants are keenly aware of the implicated stereotypes of being poor or lacking intelligence.

3. Other participants made a similar observation when confronting an incident of disrespect—they strategically avoided getting loud.

Chapter 6

1. For an opposing view to Hacker's "two nations thesis," see Thernstrom & Thernstrom (1997).

2. The documentary segment A refers to is the following, "I don't think that blacks on this campus separate themselves from whites—exclude whites from any parties because they're white. They may exclude them because they're different, because they have different values, or because they are, you know, just basically different" (*Racism 101* transcript, p. 22).

3. The original documentary segment is, "And I think, and I might get raked over the coals for this by some people—but I don't know how much of the minority community wishes to expand their vision to include whites. And that's pretty disturbing" (*Racism 101* transcript, p.19).

4. The portion from the documentary M may be referencing is, "It would be wrong for me to send my children to white institutions especially for their undergraduate experience. I think I've seen enough, as a black student at a white institution, both undergraduate and in law school, to realize that there are too many negative trade-offs. It's supposed to be a building experience. And I think I'll send my kids to a black school so they would experience that reinforcement and that, that self-building" (*Racism 101* transcript, p. 23).

Chapter 7

1. Paul Fry (personal communication) attributed to Frank Dance.

2. Thanks to Bud Morris for this observation.

References

Álverez-Cáccamo, C. (1996). The power of reflexive language(s): Code displacement in reported speech. *Journal of Pragmatics, 25*, 33–59.

Anderson, E. (1990). *Streetwise*. Chicago: University of Chicago Press.

Anderson, H., & Goolishian, H. (1992). The client is the expert: A not-knowing approach to therapy. In S. McNamee & K. J. Gergen (Eds.), *Therapy as social construction* (pp. 25–39). London: Sage Publications.

Aronsson, K., & Cederborg, A. (1994). Conarration and voice in family therapy: Voicing, devoicing and orchestration. *Text, 14*, 345–369.

Asante, M. K., & Al-Seen, N. (1984). Social interaction of Black and White college students: A research report. *Journal of Black Studies, 14*, 507–516.

Bailey, B. (1997). Communication of respect in interethic service encounters. *Language in Society, 26*, 327–356.

Bailey, B. (2000). Communicative behavior and conflict between African-American customers and Korean immigrant retailer in Los Angeles. *Discourse & Society, 11*, 86–108.

Bakhtin, M. M. (1981). *The dialogic imagination* (M. Holquist, Ed., C. Emerson and M. Holquist, trans.). Austin: University of Texas Press.

Bakhtin, M. M. (1986). *Speech genres and other late essays* (V. W. McGee, trans., V. C. Emerson and M. Holquist, eds.). Austin: University of Texas Press.

Bamberg, M. (1997). Positioning between structure and performance. *Journal of Narrative and Life History*, 7, 335–342.

Bamberg, M. (n.d.). *We are young, responsible, and male: Forms and functions of 'slut-bashing' in the identity constructions in 15 year-old males.* Unpublished manuscript, Clark University, Worcester, MA.

Basso, K. (1979). *Portraits of "the Whiteman": Linguistic play and cultural symbols among the Western Apache*. Cambridge: Cambridge University Press.

Bateson, G. (1972). *Steps to an ecology of mind.* New York: Ballantine.

Bauman, R. (1986). *Story, performance, and event: Contextual studies of oral narrative.* Cambridge: Cambridge University Press.

Baynham, M. (1996). Direct speech: What's it doing in non-narrative discourse? *Journal of Pragmatics, 25,* 61–81.

Beach, W. A. (1990). Orienting to the phenomenon. In J. Anderson (Ed.), *Communication yearbook 13* (pp. 216–244). Beverly Hills, CA: Sage.

Becker, A. L. (1994). Repetition and otherness: An essay. In B. Johnstone (ed.) *Repetition in Discourse Vol. 2.* Norwood, NJ: Ablex.

Benson, T. C. (Ed.), (1985). *Speech communication in the 20th Century.* Carbondale: Southern Illinois University Press.

Bergmann, J. R. (1992). Veiled morality: Notes on discretion in psychiatry. In P. Drew & J. Heritage (Eds.), *Talk at work: Interaction in institutional settings.* Cambridge: Cambridge University Press.

Bergmann, J. R. (1998). Introduction: Morality in discourse. *Research on Language and Social Interaction, 31,* 279–294.

Besnier, N. (1993). Reported speech and affect on Nukulalae Atoll. In J. H. Hill & J. T. Irvine (Eds.), *Responsibility and evidence in oral discourse* (pp. 161–181). Cambridge: Cambridge University Press.

Billig, M. (1996). *Arguing and thinking: A rhetorical approach to social psychology* (Second Edition). Cambridge: Cambridge University Press.

Billig, M. (1999). Whose terms? Whose Ordinaries? Rhetoric and ideology in conversation analysis. *Discourse & Society, 10,* 543–558.

Billig, M., Condor, S., Edwards, D., Gane, M., Middleton, D., & Radley, A. (1988). *Ideological dilemmas.* London: Sage.

Bilmes, J. (1985). "Why that now?" Two kinds of conversational meaning. *Discourse Processes, 8,* 319–355.

Blauner, B. (1989). *Black lives, white lives: Three decades of race relations in America.* Berkeley: University of California Press.

Brenneis, D. (1996). Telling troubles: Narrative, conflict, and experience. In C. L. Briggs (Ed.), *Disorderly discourse: Narrative, conflict and inequality.* New York: Oxford University Press.

Brown, H. I. (1977). *Perception, theory, and commitment.* Chicago: University of Chicago Press.

Brown, P., & Levinson, S. C. (1987). *Politeness.* Cambridge: Cambridge University Press.

Buttny, R. (1990). Blame-accounts sequences in therapy: The negotiation of relational meanings. *Semiotica, 78,* 219–247.

Buttny, R. (1993). *Social accountability in communication*. London: Sage.

Buttny, R. (1996). Clients' and therapist's joint construction of the clients' problems. *Research on Language and Social Interaction*, *29*, 125–153.

Buttny, R. (1997). Reported speech in talking race on campus. *Human Communication Research*, *23*, 475–504.

Buttny, R. (1998). Putting prior talk into context: Reported speech and the reporting context. *Research on Language and Social Interaction*, *31*, 45–58.

Buttny, R. (1999). Discursive constructions of racial boundaries and self-segregation on campus. *Journal of Language and Social Psychology*, *18*, 247–268.

Buttny, R. (2001). Therapeutic humor in retelling the clients' tellings. *Text*, *21*, 303–326.

Buttny, R. (in press). Multiple voices in talking race: *Pakeha* reported speech in the discursive contructions of the racial other. In H. Van den Berg, M. Wetherall, & H. Houtkoop (Eds.), *Analysing interviews on racial issues*. Cambridge: Cambridge University Press.

Buttny, R., & Campbell, J. L. (1990). Discourse direction and power: Diverging strategies during a welfare interview. In S. Thomas & W. A. Evans (Eds.), *Culture and communication, Vol. 4* (pp. 69–82). Norwood, NJ: Ablex.

Buttny, R., & Cohen, J. R. (1991). The uses of goals in therapy. In K. Tracy (Ed.), *Understanding face-to-face interaction: Issues linking goals and discourse* (pp. 63–77). Hillsdale, NJ: Erlbaum Publications.

Buttny, R., & Jensen, A. D. (1995). Telling problems in an initial family therapy session: The hierarchical organization of problem-talk. In G. H. Morris & R. J. Chenial (Eds.), *The talk of the clinic: Explorations in the analysis of medical and therapeutic discourse* (pp.19–47). Hillsdale, NJ: Erlbaum Publications.

Card, J. J. (1999). Teen pregnancy prevention: Do any programs work? *Annual Review of Public Health*, *20*, 257–285.

Chenail, R. J., & Fortugno, L. (1995). Resourceful figures in therapeutic conversations. In G. H. Morris & R. J. Chenail (Eds.), *The talk of the clinic: Explorations in the analysis of medical and therapeutic discourse* (pp. 71–88). Hillsdale, NJ: Erlbaum.

Chick, C. (1990). The interactional accomplishment of discrimination. In D. Carbaugh (Ed.), *Cultural communication and intercultural contact* (pp. 225–252). Hillsdale, NJ: Erlbaum.

Clift, R. (1999). Irony in conversation. *Language in Society*, *28*, 523–553.

Collier, M. J. (1996) Communication competence problematics in ethnic friendships. *Communication Monographs, 63*: 314–36.

Cose, E. (1993). *The rage of a privileged class.* New York: HarperCollins.

Cose, E. (1997). *Color-blind: Seeing beyond race in a race-obsessed world.* New York: HarperCollins.

Coulmas, F. (1986). Reported speech: Some general issues. In F. Coulmas (Ed.), *Direct and indirect speech* (pp. 1–28). New York: Mouton de Gruyter.

Coulter, J. (1979). *The social construction of mind.* Totowa, NJ: Littlefield.

Cronen, V. E. (1995). Coordinated management of meaning: The consequentiality of communication and the recapturing of experience. In S. J. Sigman (Ed.), *The consequentiality of communication* (pp. 17–66). Hillsdale, NJ: Erlbaum.

Davies, B., & Harré, R. (1999). Positioning and personhood. In R. Harré & L. van Langenhove (Eds.), *Positioning theory* (pp. 32–52). Oxford: Blackwell

Davis, K. (1986). The process of problem (re)formulation in psychotherapy. *Sociology of Health and Illness, 8*, 44–74.

Dixon, J. A., Reicher, S., & Foster, D. H. (1997). Ideology, geography, racial exclusion: The squatter camp as "blot on the landscape." *Text, 17*, 317–348.

Drew, P. (1987). Po-faced receipts of teases. *Linguistics, 25*, 219–253.

Drew, P. (1998). Complaints about transgressions and misconduct. *Research on Language and Social Interaction, 31*, 295–325.

Drew, P., & Heritage, J. (1992). Analyzing talk at work: An introduction. In P. Drew, & J. Heritage (Eds.), *Talk at work: Interaction in institutional settings*, pp. 3–65. New York: Cambridge University Press.

Drew, P., & Holt, E. (1998). Figures of speech: Figurative expressions and the management of topic transition in conversation. *Language in Society, 27*, 495–522.

Duranti, A. (1992). Language in context and language as context: The Samoan respect vocabulary. In A. Duranti & C. Goodwin (Eds.), *Rethinking Context* (pp. 77–100). Cambridge: Cambridge University Press.

Duster, T. (1992). Beyond the myths. In P. Aufderheide (Ed.), *Beyond PC: Toward a politics of understanding* (pp. 182–184). St. Paul, MN: Greywolf Press.

Edwards, D. (1994). Script formulations: A study of event descriptions in conversation. *Journal of Language and Social Psychology, 13*, 211–247.

Edwards, D. (1995). Two to tango: Script formulations, dispositions and rhetorical symmetry in relationship counseling talk. *Research on Language and Social Interaction, 28*, 319–350.

Edwards, D. (1997). *Discourse and cognition*. London: Sage.

Edwards, D. (2000). Extreme case formulations: Softeners, investment, and doing nonliteral. *Research on Language and Social Interaction, 33*, 347–373.

Edwards, D., & Potter, J. (1992). *Discursive psychology*. London: Sage.

Edwards, D., Potter, J., & Wetherell, M. (1993). A model of discourse in action. *American Behavioral Scientist, 36*, 383–401.

Essed, P. (1988). Understanding verbal accounts of racism: Politics and heuristics of reality constructions. *Text, 8*, 5–40.

Essed, P. (1991). *Understanding everyday racism*. Newbury Park, CA: Sage.

Emerson, R. M., & Messinger, S.L. (1977). The micro-politics of trouble. *Social Problems, 25*, 121–134.

Falk, D. R., & Hill, C. E. (1992). Counselor interventions preceding client laughter in brief therapy. *Journal of Counseling Psychology, 39*, 39–45.

Feagin, J. R. (1991). The continuing significance of race: Anti-Black discrimination in public places. *American Sociological Review, 56*, 226–241.

Ferrara, K. W. (1994). *Therapeutic ways with words*. New York: Oxford University Press.

Finneran, R. J. (Ed.) (1996). *The collected poems of W. B. Yeats* (revised second edition). New York: Scribner.

Frankenberg, R. (1993). *White women, race matters: The social construction of whiteness*. Minneapolis: University of Minnesota Press.

Frankl, V. E. (1967). *The doctor and the soul*. New York: Bantam.

Fry, W. F., & Salameh, W. A. (Eds.),(1987). *Handbook of humor and psychotherapy*. Sarasota, FL: Professional Resource Center.

Gaik, F. (1992). Radio talk-show therapy and the pragmatics of possible worlds. In A. Duranti & C. Goodwin (Eds.), *Rethinking context: Language as an interactive phenomenon* (pp. 271–290). Cambridge: Cambridge University Press.

Gale, J. (1991). *Conversation analysis of therapeutic discourse: Pursuit of a therapeutic agenda*. Norwood, NJ: Ablex.

Gallois, C., Giles, H., Jones, E., Cargile, A. C., & Ota, H. (1995). Accommodating intercultural encounters: Elaborations and extensions. In R. L.

Wiseman (Ed.), *Intercultural communication theory* (pp. 115–147). Thousand Oaks, CA: Sage.

Garcia, W. (1996). *Respecto*: A Mexican base for interpersonal relationships. In W. B. Gundykunst, S. Ting-Toomey, and T. Nishida (eds.), *Communication in Personal Relationships across Cultures* (pp. 137–55). Thousand Oaks, CA: Sage.

Garfinkel, H. (1967). *Studies in ethnomethodology*. Englewoods Cliff, NJ: Prentice Hall.

Giles, H., & Coupland, N. (1992). *Language: Contexts and consequences*. Pacific Grove, CA: Brooks/Cole Publishing.

Gitlin, T. (1992). On the virtues of a loose canon. In P. Aufderheide (ed.), *Beyond PC: Toward a politics of understanding* (pp. 212–226). St. Paul, MN: Greywolf Press.

Gitlin, T. (1995). *The twilight of common dreams: Why America is wracked by culture wars*. New York: Henry Holt.

Goffman, E. (1967). On face-work. In *Interaction Ritual*. (pp. 5–46). New York: Pantheon.

Goffman, E. (1974). *Frame analysis*. New York: Harper & Row.

Goffman, E. (1981). Footing. In *Forms of talk*. (pp. 124–159). Philadelphia: University of Pennsylvania Press.

Goody E. (1972). "Greeting," "Begging," and the Presentation of Respect." In J. S. LaFontaine (ed.), *The Interpretation of Ritual* (pp. 39–71). London: Travistock.

Gudykunst, W. B. (1995) Anxiety/Uncertainty Management (AUM) Theory: Current Status. In R. L. Wiseman (ed.), *Intercultural Communication Theory*, pp. 8–58. Thousand Oaks, CA: Sage.

Gumperz, J. J. (1982). *Discourse strategies*. Cambridge: Cambridge University Press.

Hacker, A. (1992). *Two nations: Black and White, separate, hostile, unequal*. New York: Ballantine Books.

Hak, T., & De Boer, F. (1996). Formulations in first encounters. *Journal of Pragmatics*, *25*, 83–99.

Hall, E. T. (1983). *The Dance of Life*. New York: Anchor Books.

Harré, R. (1980). *Social Being*. Totowa, NJ: Littlefield, Adams & Co.

Heath, C. (1992). The delivery and reception of diagnosis in the general-practice consultation. In P. Drew & J. Heritage (Eds.), *Talk at work: Interaction in institutional settings* (pp. 235–267). Cambridge: Cambridge University Press.

Hecht, M. L., Collier, M. J., & Ribeau, S. (1993). *African-American Communication*. Newbury Park, CA: Sage.

Hecht, M. L., Ribeau, S., & Alberts, J. K. (1989). An Afro-American perspective on interethnic communication. *Communication Monographs, 56,* 385–410.

Henley, N. M. (1977). *Body politics: Power, sex, and nonverbal communication*. Englewood Cliffs, NJ: Prentice-Hall.

Heritage, J. (1984). *Garfinkel and ethnomethodology*. Cambridge: Polity.

Heritage, J., & Watson, D. R. (1979). Formulations as conversational objects. In G. Psathas (Ed.), *Everyday language: Studies in ethnomethodology* (pp. 123–62). New York: Irvington.

Hester, P. (1998). Describing 'deviance' in school: Recognizably educational psychological problems. In C. Antaki & S. Widdicome (Eds.), *Identities in talk* (pp. 133–150). London: Sage.

Hester, S., & Eglin, P. (1997). Membership categorization analysis: An introduction. In S. Hester & P. Eglin (Eds.), *Culture in action* (pp. 1–23). Washington, D.C.: University Press of America.

Hewstone, M., & Brown, R. (1986). Contact is not enough: An intergroup perspective on the 'contact hypothesis.' In M. Hewstone & R. Brown (Eds.), *Contact and conflict in intergroup encounters* (pp. 1–44). London: Basil Blackwell.

Hill, J. T., & Irvine, J. T. (1993). Introduction. In J. H. Hill & J. T. Irvine (Eds.), *Responsibility and evidence in oral discourse* (pp. 1–23). Cambridge: Cambridge University Press.

Hollway, W. (1984). Gender difference and production of subjectivity. In J. Henriques, W. Hollway, C. Urwin, L. Venn, & W. Walkerdine (Eds.), *Changing the subject: Psychology, social regulation and subjectivity*. London: Methuen.

Holmgren, A. (1999). Presentation at the Conference on Constructionism and Relational Practices, Durham, NH.

Holt, E. (1996). Reporting on talk: The use of direct reported speech in conversation, *Research on Language and Social Interaction, 29*: 219–45.

Holt, E. (2000a). Reporting and reacting: Concurrent responses to reported speech. *Research on Language and Social Interaction, 33*, 425–454.

Holt, T. C. (2000b). *The problem of race in the twenty-first century*. Cambridge, MA: Harvard University Press.

Honneth, A. (1992). Integrity and respect: Principles of a conception of morality based on a theory of recognition, *Political Theory, 20*, 187–201.

Hopper, R. (1995). Trajectory in conversational play. In T. ten Have & G. Psathas (Eds.), *Situated order* (pp. 57–71). Washington, D.C.: University Press of America.

Houston, M. (1994). When Black women talk with White women: Why dialogues are difficult. In A. Gonzalez, M. Houston, & V. Chen (eds.), *Our voices: Essays in culture, ethnicity, and communication* (pp. 133–139). Los Angeles: Roxbury.

Hutchby, I., & Wooffitt, R. (1998). *Conversation analysis*. Cambridge: Polity Press.

Irvine, J. T. (1996). Shadow conversations: The indeterminacy of participants roles. In M. Silverstein & G. Urban (Eds.), *Natural histories of discourse* (pp. 131–159). Chicago: University of Chicago Press.

Jackson, S. (1986). Building a case for claims about discourse structure. In D. G. Ellis & W. A. Donohue (Eds.), *Contemporary issues in language and discourse processes* (pp. 129–148). Hillsade, NJ: Erlbaum.

Jacobs, S. (1990). On the especially nice fit between qualitative analysis and the known properties of conversation. *Communication Monographs*, *57*, 241–249.

James, C. (July 6, 1994). 5 years later, Mr. Wiseman goes back to school. *The New York Times*.

Jefferson, G. (1979). A technique for inviting laughter and its subsequent acceptance/declination. In G. Psathas (Ed.), *Everyday language* (pp. 79–96). New York: Irvington.

Jefferson, G. (1980). On "trouble-premonitory" response to inquiry. *Sociological Inquiry*, *50*, 153–185.

Jefferson, G. (1987). On exposed and embedded correction in conversation. In G. Button & J. R. E. Lee (Eds.), *Talk and social organisation* (pp. 86–100). Philadelphia: Multilingual Matters.

Jefferson, G. (1988). On the sequential organization of troubles-talk in ordinary conversation. *Social Problems*, *35*, 418–441.

Jefferson, G., & Lee, J. R. E. (1981). The rejection of advice: Managing the problematic convegence of a "troubles teller" and a "service encounter." *Journal of Pragmatics*, 5, 399–422. Reprinted in Drew, P., & Heritage, J. (Eds.) (1992). *Talk at work: Interaction in institutional settings* (pp. 521–548). Cambridge: Cambridge University Press.

Jones, C. M., & Beach, W. A. (1995). Therapists' techniques for responding to unsolicited contributions by family members. In G. H. Morris & R. J. Chenail (Eds.), *The talk of the clinic: Explorations in the analysis of medical and therapeutic discourse* (pp. 49–70). Hillsdale, NJ: Erlbaum.

Kochman, T. (1981). *Black and White styles in conflict.* Chicago: University of Chicago Press.

Krupnick, C. G. (1995). *High School II: Film study guide.* Cambridge, MA: Zipporah Films Inc.

Labov, W. (1984). Intensity. In D. Schriffen (Ed.), *Meaning, form, and use in context.* Washington, D.C.: Georgetown University Press.

Labov, W., & Fanshel, D. (1977). *Therapeutic discourse: Psychotherapy as conversation.* New York: Academic Press.

LaGrande, S., & Milburn, T. (in press). "Keeping it real": Identity management strategies used by teens in conversation. *Communication Studies.*

Langenhove, L. van, & Harré, R. (1999). Introducing positioning theory. In R. Harré & L. van Langenhove (Eds.), *Positioning theory* (pp. 14–31). Oxford: Blackwell.

Lennon, T. (Producer) and Bagwell, O. (Coproducer and Director) (1988). *Racism 101* [Film]. (Available from WGBH-Boston, MA)

Levinson, S. C. (1983). *Pragmatics.* Cambridge: Cambridge University Press.

Levinson, S. C. (1988). Putting linguistics on a proper gooting: Explorations in Goffman's concepts of participation. In P. Drew and A. Wootton (eds.), *Erving Goffman: Exploring the interaction order.* Boston, MA: Northeastern University Press.

Li, C.N. (1986). Direct and indirect speech: A functional study. In F. Coulmas (Ed.), *Direct and indirect speech* (pp. 29–45). New York: Mouton de Gruyter.

Louw-Potgieter, J. (1989). Covert racism: An application of Essed's analysis in a South African context. *Journal of Language and Social Psychology, 8*, 307–319.

Lurie, T. (summer 1994). Turning on to the power of ideas: A new Frederick Wiseman film looks at a city school that works. *Ford Foundation Report.*

Macaulay, R. K. S. (1987). Polyphonic monologues: Quoted direct speech in oral narratives. *Papers in Pragmatics, 1/2*, 1–34.

Malone, M. J. (1995). How to do things with friends: Altercasting and recipient design. *Research on Language and Social Interaction, 28*, 147–170.

Mandelbaum, J. (1993). Assigning responsibility in conversational storytelling: The interactional construction of reality. *Text, 13*, 247–266.

Manicas, P. T. (1987). *A history and philosophy of the social sciences.* Oxford: Basil Blackwell.

Margalit, A. (1996). *The decent society.* (N. Goldblum, trans.). Cambridge, MA: Harvard University Press.

Martin, J. N., Hecht, M. L., & Larkey, L. K. (1994). Conversational improvement strategies for interethnic communication: African American and European American perspectives. *Communication Monographs, 61,* 236–255.

Marwell, G. (May 27, 1988). What "epidemic" of campus bigotry? *New York Times.*

Mayes, P. (1990). Quotation in spoken English. *Studies in Language 14,* 325–363.

Maynard, D. W. (1988). Language, interaction, and social problems. *Social Problems, 35,* 311–328.

Maynard, D. W. (1991a). Interaction and asymmetry in clinical discourse. *American Journal of Sociology,* 97, 448–495.

Maynard, D. W. (1991b). The perspective-display series and the delivery and receipt of diagnostic news. In D. Boden & D. H. Zimmerman (Eds.), *Talk and social structure* (pp. 164–192). Berkeley: University of California Press.

Maynard, D. W. (1992). On clinicians co-implicating recipients' perspective in the delivery of diagnostic news. In P. Drew & J. Heritage (Eds.), *Talk at work: Interaction in institutional settings* (pp. 331–358). Cambridge: Cambridge University Press.

Maynard, D. W., & Clayman, S. E. (1991). The diversity of ethnomethodology. *Annual Review of Sociology, 17,* 385–418.

Maynard, R. A. (1997). Paternalism, teenage pregnancy prevention, and teenage parent services. In L. M. Mead (Ed.), *The new paternalism: Supervisory approaches to poverty.* Washington, D.C.: Brookings Institution Press.

McHoul, A. (1978). The organization of turns at formal talk in the classroom. *Language in Society, 7,* 183–213.

McNamee, S., & Gergen, K. J. (Eds.). (1992). *Therapy as social construction.* London: Sage.

Mehan, H. (1990). Oracular reasoning in a psychiatric exam: The resolution of conflict in language. In A. D. Grimshaw (Ed.), *Conflict talk: Sociolinguistic investigations of arguments in conversations* (pp. 160–177). New York: Cambridge University Press.

Mellinger, W. M. (1995). Talk, power and professionals: Partial repeats as "challenge" in the psychiatric interview. In J. Siegfried (Ed.), *Therapeutic and everyday discourse as behavior change.* Norwood, NJ: Ablex.

Menand, L. (October 6, 1994). The culture wars. *The New York Review of Books, 41*, 16–21.

Miles, R. (1989). *Racism.* New York: Routledge.

Miller, S. M. (1993) The politics of respect. *Social Policy 23*: 44–51.

Mishler, E. (1986). *Research interviewing: Context and narrative.* Cambridge, MA: Harvard University Press.

Mitchell-Kernan, C. (1986). Signifying and marking: Two Afro-American speech acts. In J. J. Gumperz & D. Hymes (Eds.), *Directions in sociolinguistics: The ethnography of communication* (pp. 161–179). New York: Basil Blackwell.

Mondada, L. (1998). Therapy interactions: Specific genre or "blown up" version of ordinary conversational practices? *Pragmatics, 8*, 155–165.

Morris, W. (1975). *The American Heritage dictionary of the English language.* Boston: Houghton Mifflin.

Mulkay, M. (1988). *On humor.* New York. Basil Blackwell.

Myrdal, G. (1944). *An American dilemma.* New York: Harper & Brothers.

Norrick, N. R. (1993). *Conversational joking.* Bloomington: Indiana University Press.

Ochs, E., Schegloff, E. A., & Thompson, S. A. (Eds.) (1996). *Interaction and grammar.* Cambridge: Cambridge University Press.

Omi, M., & Winant, H. (1994) *Racial formation in the United States: From the 1960s to the 1990s* (2nd edn.). New York: Routledge & Kegan Paul.

Orbe, M. P. (1994). "Remember, it's always Whites' ball": Descriptions of African American male communication. *Communication Quarterly, 42*, 287–300.

Orbe, M. P. (1998). From the standpoint(s) of traditionally muted groups: Explicating a co-cultural communication theoretical model. *Communication Theory*, 8, 1–26.

Payne, M. E. (n.d.). Spoken quotation: An analysis of quoted talk in conversation. Unpublished manuscript. Department of Communication, SUNY-Albany.

Penman, R. (1990). Facework and politeness: Multiple goals in courtroom discourse. *Journal of Language and Social Psychology 9*: 15–37.

Pennington, D. L. (1979). Black-White communication: An assessment of research. In M. K. Asante, E. Newmark, & C. A. Blake (Eds.), *Handbook of intercultural communication* (pp. 383–402). Beverly Hills, CA: Sage.

Peräkylä, A. (1993). Invoking a hostile world: Discussing the patient's future in AIDS counseling. *Text, 13*, 291–316.

Peräkylä, A. (1995). *AIDS counseling: Institutional interaction and clinical practice*. Cambridge: Cambridge University Press.

Peräkylä, A., & Silverman, D. (1991). Owning experience: Describing the experience of other persons. *Text, 11*, 441–480.

Peyrot, M. (1987). Circumspection in psycho-therapy: Structures and strategies of client-counselor interaction. *Semiotica, 65*, 249–268.

Philipsen, G. (1990/91). Situated meaning, ethnography, and conversation analysis: Person-reference in "High School." *Research on Language and Social Interaction, 24*, 225–240.

Pierce, R. A. (1994). Practice considerations: Use and abuse of laughter in psychotherapy. In H. S. Strean (Ed.), *The use of humor in psychotherapy* (pp. 105–112). Northvale, NJ: Jason Aronson.

Pinderhughes, E. (1989). *Understanding race, ethnicity, and power*. New York: Free Press.

Pomerantz, A. (1980). Telling my side: "Limited access" as a "fishing" device. *Sociological Inquiry, 50*, 186–198.

Pomerantz, A. (1984). Giving a source or basis: The practice in conversation of telling 'how I know.' *Journal of Pragmatics, 8*, 607–625.

Pomerantz, A. (1986). Extreme case formulations: A way of legitimizing claims. *Human Studies, 9*, 219–230.

Potter, J. (1996). *Representing reality: Discourse, rhetoric and social construction*. London: Sage Publications.

Potter, J., & Edwards, D. (2001). Discursive social psychology. In W. P. Robinson, & H. Giles (Eds.) *The new handbook of language and social psychology* (pp. 103–118). New York: Wiley.

Potter, J., & Wetherell, M. (1995). Discourse Analysis. In J. A. Smith, R. Harré and L. van Langenhove (eds.), *Rethinking methods in psychology*, pp. 80–92. London: Sage.

Psathas, G. (1990). Introduction: Methodological issues and recent developments in the study of naturally occurring interaction. In G. Psathas (Ed.), *Interaction competence* (pp. 1–29). Washington, D.C.: University Press of America.

Psathas, G. (1999). Studying the organization in action: Membership categorization and interaction analysis. *Human Studies, 22*, 139–162.

Racism 101 (1988). *Transcript*. Frontline #612: WGBH Educational Foundation.

Ravotas, D., & Berkenkotter, C. (1998). Voices in the text: The uses of reported speech in a psychotherapist's notes and initial assessments. *Text*, *18*, 211–239.

Rawlins, P. (1983). Openness as problematic in ongoing friendships: Two conversational dilemmas. *Communication Monographs*, *50*, 1–13.

Rawls, A. W. (2000). "Race" as an interaction order phenomenon: W. E. B. DuBois's "double consciousness" thesis revisited. *Sociological Theory*, *18*, 241–274.

Reddy, M. J. (1979). The conduit metaphor—a case of frame conflict in our language about language. In A. Ortony (Ed.), *Metaphor and thought* (pp. 284–324). Cambridge: Cambridge University Press.

Rich, A. L. (1974). *Interracial communication*. New York: Harper & Row.

Richman, J. (1996). Points of correspondence between humor and psychotherapy. *Psychotherapy*, *33*, 560–566.

Rose, T. L. (1992). The quality of interracial interactions. In W. B. Gudykunst, & Y. Y. Kim (Eds.), *Readings on communicating with strangers* (pp. 308–318). New York: McGraw-Hill.

Sacks, H. (1987). On the preference for agreement and contiguity in sequences in conversation. In G. Button & J. R. E. Lee (Eds.), *Talk and social organisation* (pp. 54–69). Clevedon, England: Multilingual Matters.

Sacks, H. (1992). *Lectures on conversation* (G. Jefferson, ed.). Oxford: Blackwell.

Salameh, W. A. (1987). Humor in integrative short-term therapy (ISTP). In W. F. Fry & W. A. Salameh (Eds.), *Handbook of humor and psychotherapy* (pp. 195–240). Sarasota, FL: Professional Resource Exchange.

Sanders, R. E. (1995). A neo-rhetorical perspective: The enactment of role-identities as interactive and strategic. In S. J. Sigman (Ed.), *The consequentiality of communication* (pp. 67–120). Hillsdale, NJ: Erlbaum.

Sanjek, R. (1994). The enduring inequalities of race. In S. Gregory & R. Sanjek (Eds.), *Race* (pp. 1–17). New Brunswick, NJ: Rutgers University Press.

Sarbin, T. R. (1986). The narrative as root metaphor for psychology. In T. R. Sarbin (Ed.), *Narrative psychology: The storified nature of human conduct* (pp. 3–21). New York: Praeger.

Scheff, T. J. (1968). The negotiation of reality. *Social Problems*, *3*, 3–17.

Scheff, T. J. (1990). *Microsociology: Discourse, emotion, and social structure*. Chicago: University of Chicago Press.

Schegloff, E. A. (1980). Preliminaries to preliminaries: "Can I ask you a question?" *Sociological Inquiry*, *50*, 104–152.

Schegloff, E. A. (1982). Discourse as an interactional achievement: Some uses of "uh huh" and other things that come between sentences. In D. Tannen (Ed.), *Analyzing discourse: Text and talk* (pp. 71–93). Washington, D.C.: Georgetown University Press.

Schegloff, E. A. (1984). On some questions and ambiguities in conversation. In J. Attkinson & J. Heritage (Eds.), *Structures of social action: Studies in conversation analysis* (pp. 28–52). Cambridge: Cambridge University Press.

Schegloff, E. A. (1988). Goffman and the analysis of conversation. In P. Drew & A. Wootton (eds.), *Erving Goffman: Exploring the interaction order* (pp. 89–135). Boston: Northeastern University Press.

Schegloff, E. A. (1991). Reflections on talk and social structure. In D. Boden & D. H. Zimmerman (Eds.), *Talk and social structure* (pp. 44–70). Berkeley: University of California Press.

Schegloff, E. A. (1996). Turn organization: One intersection of grammar and interaction. In E. Ochs, E. A. Schegloff, & S. A. Thompson (Eds.), *Interaction and grammar* (52–133). Cambridge: Cambridge University Press.

Scott, J. W. (1992). Campus communities beyond consensus. In P. Aufderheide (ed.), *Beyond PC: Toward a politics of understanding* (pp. 212–226). St. Paul, MN: Greywolf Press.

Sears, D. O. (1988). Symbolic racism. In P. A. Katz & D. A. Taylor (Eds.), *Eliminating racism* (pp. 53–84). New York: Plenum Press.

Shotter, J. (1981). Telling and reporting: Prospective and retrospective uses of self-ascription. In C. Antaki (Ed.), *The psychology of ordinary explanations of human behaviour*. New York: Academic Press.

Sidel, R. (1994). *Battling bias: The struggle for identity and community on college campuses*. New York: Viking.

Simpson, J. A., & Weiner, E. S. C. (1991). *The compact Oxford English dictionary* (2nd edn.). Oxford: Clarendon Press.

Singelis, T. M. (1996). The context of intergroup communication. *Journal of Language and Social Psychology*, *15*, 360–371.

Sluzki, C. (1990). Therapeutic conversations: Systemic blueprints of a couple's interview. In R. Chasin (Ed.), *Couple therapy: Many approaches to one case* (pp. 106–125). New York: Guilford.

Southern, D. W. (1987). *Gunnar Myrdal and Black-White relations: The use and abuse of an American dilemma 1944–1969*. Baton Rouge: Louisiana State University Press.

Steele, S. (1996). Self-segregation should be condemned. In P. A. Winters (Ed.), *Race relations: Opposing viewpoints* (pp. 209–215). San Diego: Greenhaven Press.

Sternberg, M. (1982). Proteus in quotation-land: mimesis and the forms of reported discourse, *Poetics Today* 3: 107–56.

Stewart, J. (1995). *Language as articulate contact: Toward a post-semiotic philosophy of communication*. Albany: State University of New York Press.

Strean, H. S. (Ed.) (1994). *The use of humor in psychotherapy*. Northvale, NJ: Aronson.

Suchman, A. (1993). "Get outa my face: Entitlement and authoritative discourse. In J. H. Hill & J. T. Irvine (Eds.), *Responsibility and evidence in oral discourse* (pp. 135–160). Cambridge: Cambridge University Press.

Tannen, D. (1989). *Talking voices: Repetition, dialogue, and imagery in conversational discourse*. New York: Cambridge University Press.

Thernstrom, S., & Thernstrom, A. (1997). *America in Black and White*. New York: Simon & Schuster.

Törrönen, J. (2001). The concept of subject position in empirical social research. *Journal for the Theory of Social Behaviour*, *31*, 312–329.

Tracy, K. (2002). *Every talk: Building and reflecting identities*. New York: Guilford Press.

Tracy, K., & Muller, H. (2001). Diagnosing a school board's interactional trouble: Theorizing problem formulating. *Communication Theory*, *11*, 84–104.

Tzeng, O. C. S., Duvell, C. J., Ware, R., Neel, R., & Fortier, R. (1986). Subjective intergroup distances of Blacks and Whites. In Y. Y. Kim (ed.), *Interethnic communication* (pp. 60–74). Newbury Park, CA: Sage Publications.

Van Dijk, T. A. (1987). *Communicating racism: Ethnic prejudice in thought and talk*. London: Sage Publications.

Van Dijk, T.A. (1992). Discourse and the denial of racism. *Discourse & Society*, *3*, 87–118.

Van Dijk, T.A. (1993a). *Elite discourse and racism*. London: Sage Publications.

Van Dijk, T. A. (1993b). Sories and racism. In D. K. Mumby (Ed.), *Narrative and social control* (pp. 121–142). Newbury Park, CA: Sage Publications.

Verkuytem, M., Jong, W. de. & Masson, C. N. (1995). The construction of ethnic categories: Discourses of ethnicity in The Netherlands. *Ethnic and Racial Studies*, *18*, 251–276.

Volosinov, V. N. (1971). Reported speech. In L. Matejka and K. Pomorska (eds), *Readings in Russian poetics*. Cambridge, MA: MIT Press.

Volosinov, V. N. (1973). *Marxism and the philosophy of language*. L. Matejka & I. R. Titunik, trans. New York: Seminar Press.

Watson, R. (1978). Categorization, authorization and blame-negotiation in conversation. *Sociology*, *12*, 105–113.

Watson, R. (1987). Interdisciplinary considerations in the analysis of pro-terms. In G. Button & J. R. E. Lee (Eds.), *Talk and social organisation* (pp. 261–289). Philadelphia: Multilingual Matters.

Watson, R. (1995). Some potentialities and pitfalls in the analysis of process and personal change in counseling and therapeutic interaction. In J. Siegfried (Ed.), *Therapeutic and everyday discourse as behavior change* (pp. 301–339). Norwood, NJ: Ablex.

Watson, R. (1997). Some general reflections on 'categorization' and 'sequence' in the analysis of conversation. In S. Hester & P. Eglin (Eds.), *Culture in action* (pp. 49–75). Washington, D.C.: University Press of America.

West, C. (1994). *Race matters*. New York: Vintage Books.

Wetherell, M., & Potter, J. (1992). *Mapping the language of racism: Discourse and the legitimation of exploitation*. New York: Columbia University Press.

Winant, H. (1994). *Racial conditions*. Minneapolis: University of Minnesota Press.

Wiseman, F. (Director) (1994). *High School II* [Film]. (Available from Zipporah Films, Cambridge, MA).

Wittgenstein, L. (1953). *Philosophical investigations* (G. E. M. Anscombe, Trans.). New York: Macmillan.

Wodak, R. (1981). How do I put my problem? Problem presentation in therapy and interview. *Text*, *1*, 191–213.

Name Index

Alberts, J.K., 100
Al-Seen, N., 100, 147, 149
Álverez-Cáccamo, C., 100, 113, 146, 179
Anderson, E., 124
Anderson, H., 44
Aronsson, K., 67
Asante, M.K., 100, 147, 149

Bagwell, O., 123
Bailey, B., 125, 138
Bakhtin, M.M., 96, 98, 121, 131, 171, 172
Bamberg, M., 7
Basso, K., 96, 102, 113, 121
Bateson, G., 190
Baumann, R. 97
Baynham, M., 120
Beach, W.A., 11, 67, 72
Becker, A.L., 131
Benson, T.C., 2
Bergmann, J.R., 4, 45, 46, 47, 76, 69, 84, 172
Berkenkotter, C., 45
Besnier, N., 113
Billig, M., 5, 101, 109, 126, 152, 163, 166, 177
Bilmes, J., 57
Blauner, B., 101, 157
Brenneis, D., 2
Brown, H. I., 10
Brown, P., 125
Brown, R., 100
Buttny, R., 4, 20, 44, 73, 92, 100,120, 174

Campbell, J.L., 20
Card, J.J., 20
Cargile, A.C., 150
Cederborg, A., 67
Chenail, R. J., 44
Chick, C., 151
Clayman, S.E., 8
Clift, R., 71, 92
Cohen, J.R., 44
Collier, M.J., 124
Condor, S., 101, 109, 126, 152, 163, 166
Cose, E., 124, 151
Coulmas, F., 97
Coulter, J., 70, 182
Coupland, N., 150
Cronen, V.E., 1

Davies, B., 6, 19, 41, 98
Davis, K., 44, 45, 69, 72, 177
De Boer, F., 25
Drew, P., 4, 45, 79, 80, 84, 92
Duranti, A., 125
Duster, T.,149
Duvell, C.J., 100, 122, 150, 166

Edwards, D., 1, 5, 33, 44, 54, 68, 101, 109, 126, 152, 163, 166
Eglin, P., 22
Emerson, R.M., 2

Essed, P., 101, 102, 126, 138, 143, 146, 156, 171

Falk, D.R., 72
Fanshel, D., 44, 59
Feagin, J.R., 126, 138, 145, 151, 171
Ferrara, K.W., 71, 92
Fortier, R., 100, 122, 150, 166
Fortugno, L., 44
Foster, D.H., 101
Frankenberg, R., 151, 160, 176
Frankl, V.E., 71
Fry, W. F., 71

Gale, J., 44, 71
Gallois, C., 150
Gane, M., 101, 109, 126, 152, 163, 166
Gaik, F., 48
Garcia, W., 125
Garfinkel, H., 3, 156, 158
Gergen, K. J., 67
Giles, H., 150
Gitlin, T., 100, 149
Goffman, E., 7, 71, 74, 90, 91, 113, 120, 133, 138, 146
Goolishian, H., 44
Goody E., 125
Gudykunst, W.B., 125, 150, 151, 166
Gumperz, J.J., 151

Hacker, A., 96, 125, 150, 171
Hak, T., 25
Hall, E.T., 139
Harré, R., 1, 6, 19, 41, 98, 125
Heath, C., 68
Hecht, M.L., 100, 101, 151, 179 124
Henley, N., 139
Heritage, J., 42, 45, 59, 62, 69, 82, 84
Hester, P., 7, 8, 22
Hewstone, M., 100
Hill, C.E., 72
Hill, J.T., 95, 120
Hollway, W., 120
Holmgren, A., 13, 45, 72
Holt, E., 79, 98, 120, 173
Holt, T. C., 176
Honneth, A., 124, 142
Hopper, R., 79
Houston, M., 100, 147, 151
Hutchby, I., 11

Irvine, J.T., 98, 99, 120

Jackson, S., 11
Jacobs, S., 11
James, C., 20
Jefferson, G., 3, 79, 182
Jensen, A.D., 44
Jones, C. M., 67
Jones, E., 150
Jong, W. de, 101

Kochman, T., 100, 101, 146, 151, 164
Krupnick, C.G., 189

Labov, W., 27, 44, 59
LaGrande, S., 20, 201
Langenhove, L. van, 1, 6
Larkey, L.K., 100, 101, 151, 179
Lee, J. R. E., 3, 182
Lennon, T., 123
Levinson, S.C., 125, 133, 190
Li, C.N., 97, 120
Louw-Potgieter, J., 101
Lurie, T., 189

Macaulay, R.K.S., 113, 120, 121, 146
Malone, M. J., 53
Mandelbaum, J., 9
Manicas, P.T., 2
Margalit, A., 124
Martin, J.N., 100, 101, 151, 179
Marwell, G., 168
Masson, C.N., 101
Mayes, P., 74, 99, 105, 136, 144
Maynard, D.W., 2, 8, 50, 53, 68

Maynard, R.A., 20
McHoul, A., 69
McNamee, S., 67
Mehan, H., 20, 190
Mellinger, W. M., 67
Menand, L., 149
Messinger, S.L., 2
Middleton, D., 101, 109, 126, 152, 163, 166
Milburn, T., 20, 201
Miles, R., 96, 126, 151
Miller, S.M., 124
Mishler, E., 137
Mitchell-Kernan, C., 113, 121, 146
Mondada, L., 91
Morris, W., 2
Mulkay, M., 71, 90, 92
Muller, H., 3
Myrdal, G., 125, 126

Neel, R., 100, 122, 150, 166
Norrick, N.R., 71

Ochs, E., 185
Omi, M., 102, 126, 147, 166
Orbe, M.P., 100, 146, 151
Ota, H., 150

Payne, M.E., 99
Penman, R., 125
Pennington, D.L., 151
Peräkylä, A., 42, 45, 47, 48, 67, 68, 84, 190
Peyrot, M., 62
Philipsen, G., 20
Pierce, R.A., 71
Pinderhughes, E., 101, 126
Pomerantz, A., 33, 109, 115, 165
Potter, J., 5, 101, 102, 106, 126, 137
Psathas, G., 8

Radley, A., 101, 109, 126, 152, 163, 166
Ravotas, D., 45
Rawlins, P., 183
Rawls, A.W., 100, 151
Reddy, M.J., 1
Reicher, S., 101
Ribeau, S., 100, 124
Rich, A.L., 151
Richman, J., 71
Rose, T.L., 150

Sacks, H., 8, 54
Salameh, W.A., 71, 72
Sanders, R.E., 5, 20
Sanjek, R., 96, 151
Sarbin, T.R., 44
Scheff, T. J., 44, 67
Schegloff, E.A., 8, 9, 22, 185
Scott, J.W., 100, 168
Sears, D.O., 151
Shotter, J., 12
Sidel, R., 100
Silverman, D., 42, 45, 47, 67, 68, 84
Simpson, J. A., 2
Singelis, T.M., 166
Sluzki, C., 43, 46, 68, 73
Southern, D.W., 152
Steele, S., 149
Sternberg, M., 97, 120
Stewart, J., 1
Strean, H. S., 71
Suchman, A., 97

Tannen, D., 97, 120
Thernstrom, A., 191
Thernstrom, S., 191
Thompson, S.A., 185
Törrönen, J., 179, 180
Tracy, K., 3, 5, 6
Tzeng, O.C.S., 100, 122, 150, 166

Van Dijk, T.A., 28, 101, 102, 126, 140, 152
Verkuytem, M., 101
Volosinov, VN., 96

Ware, R., 100, 122, 150, 166
Watson, D.R., 7, 8, 62, 82

Weiner, E.S.C., 2
West, C., 126, 151
Wetherell, M., 101, 102, 126, 137
Winant, H., 102, 126, 147, 166
Wiseman, F., 20
Wittgenstein, L., 70
Wodak, R., 44
Wooffitt, R., 11

Subject Index

accountability, (social), 4, 5, 6, 24, 100, 166–167, 169, 170, 174, 178, 183
accounts, 1, 3, 4, 12, 13, 15, 27, 8, 30, 34, 39, 42, 43, 44, 46, 52, 56, 67, 68, 69, 95, 108, 152, 154, 155, 156, 158, 160, 162, 163, 164, 165, 166, 167
  acknowledged but not addressed, 39, 42
  jointly produced, 19, 32, 41, 57
    See also construction: coconstruction (joint construction)
African American(s), 14, 15, 96, 101–103, 106–111, 113–118, 121, 123–127, 132, 136, 137, 139–141, 144–147, 149–152, 154–156, 158–164, 166, 168, 170–171
alignment, 11, 12, 13, 82, 85, 90, 169
assessment, 14, 22, 26, 28, 44, 53, 57, 58, 114, 118, 120, 121, 124, 133, 146, 163, 171, 173
  implicated assessment, 22
  second assessment, 79, 121
  See also evaluation

blame, 3, 4, 44, 67
  implicit criticism, 53

change, 180–182
conflicting category predicates, 8, 13, 20, 22, 23, 26–29, 33–36, 41, 153, 170, 173
  See also positioning, contradictory
construction
  coconstruction (joint construction), 5, 9, 13, 32, 41, 43, 45, 72, 172, 176
  discursive construction, 5, 12, 96, 104, 118, 149–168, 174, 180
    See also race, as discursive construction
conversation analysis, 5, 8–9, 11, 169, 172–174

differences (cultural/social), 118, 150, 153, 157–162, 165
dilemma (ideological), 15, 101, 114, 116, 162–165, 166, 176
discursive constructionism, 5–8, 169–172, 179

ethnicity (ethnic), 116, 117, 160, 171, 175–176
evaluation, 15, 22, 28, 60, 92, 104, 108, 110, 111, 120, 140, 152, 153, 157, 160, 161, 172, 178
  third-turn evaluation, 13, 38, 42, 60, 67, 68, 69, 173
  See also assessment
exaggeration, 14, 71, 107, 108, 143
  metaphorical exaggeration, 73–74, 76
  playful exaggeration, 73, 92, 114
    See also humor, humorous exaggeration
eye roll, 34–35

facts, 5, 22, 41, 178
footing, 7, 22, 27, 30, 41, 50, 52, 82, 84, 87, 116, 131, 132, 144, 158, 171, 173, 182
frame (framing), 12, 76, 73, 91, 92, 121, 132, 133, 141, 144, 146, 155, 170
  reframe, 13, 14, 43, 44, 52, 54, 67, 69, 70, 71, 91, 173, 177, 178
function, 11, 64, 86, 91, 96, 98, 102, 120

gender, 176–177

High School II documentary, 20
humor, 14, 31, 114, 181–182
  as fallback option, 91
  as time out, 71, 74, 91
  display recognition of, 77–78, 85
  duality in, 14, 90, 92
  embedded, 87
  facetious, 27, 76, 80, 90
  humorous exaggeration, 73–74, 76, 80, 92, 116, 121, 170
    See also exaggeration
  hypothetical quotes, 74
    See also reported speech
  initiated by clients, 72, 79, 80, 87, 92
  initiated by therapist, 72, 87, 91, 92
  irony, 27, 71, 84, 90
  jokes (joking), 22, 96, 116
  mock (mocking), 80, 90, 113, 146
    See also mimic
  non-linguistic vocalizations, 74–76
  serious functions of, 14
  teasing, 27, 79, 80, 90, 161
  therapeutic humor, 13, 71–92
  unintended humor, 80

identity, 150, 158–162, 169, 171, 176
intergroup
  contact hypothesis, 100
  distance, 104, 114–118, 158, 164
  relations theory, 150, 166
interviews
  focus-group, 15, 137
  high school, 13
  therapeutic, 46

Jewish, 158, 176

knowledge
  limited, 84
  specialized, 40

Latino(s), 15, 32, 96, 102–104, 123, 126–127, 136, 146, 175, 176
laughter, 22, 27, 74–76, 79, 80, 84, 86
  laughter particles, 81, 114
  mutual laughter, 79, 90

membership categories, 7–8, 13, 22, 30, 37, 153, 160
  oriented to by participants, 21
metaphor, 73–76, 83, 87, 92, 142
methods, 9–12, 72, 102–104, 137, 167, 181
mimic, 112, 114, 141
  See also humor, mock (mocking)
morals (moral order), 4, 124, 143, 145, 183

narrative, 6, 14, 23–26, 28, 30, 95, 98, 101, 104, 107–109, 111, 112, 114, 119, 120, 133, 157–158, 161, 170
  formulating the point of, 30–31
  of disrespect, 15, 124, 137–147
  of incidents, 44
  problem (complaint) story, 28, 101, 140, 143
  proof story, 143
noticeably absent, 58, 83, 138, 142, 153
noticing, 22, 27, 36

other, the, 14, 102
  generalized, 133
  portrait of, 96, 102, 121–122, 171
  racial, 12, 174

phenomenon(a), 11, 43, 78, 146, 165
positioning, 1, 5, 6, 9, 11–13, 20, 24, 28, 42, 98, 100, 121, 136, 152, 169, 170, 179–180
contradictory (conflicting), 7, 8, 19, 22, 26, 37, 41
See also conflicting category predicates
other(s), 5, 7, 19, 26, 28, 34, 38, 41
repositioning, 7, 30, 170
self, 5, 7, 13, 19, 24, 26, 30, 32, 40 41
subject positioning, 6, 183
possibilities, 36, 38, 39, 42, 45, 47–49, 56, 64
power, 1, 100, 177–180
control, conversational, 67–68, 178
of another words, 15, 137
of the spoken word, 126, 179
performative, 129, 132, 133, 146, 179
powerlessness, 179
practices
communicative (conversational), 2, 5, 8, 9, 19, 45, 96, 102, 104, 119, 121, 127, 131, 136, 146, 155, 169–170, 172, 173
general, 174
therapeutic, 43, 46, 51, 55, 67
problems, 1–5, 9, 68, 73, 169
alternative description of, 43
ascription of, 13, 29, 30
coconstructed character of, 5, 68
codirector's version of, 39
contradictory positionings as, 7, 19
See also positioning, and conflicting category predicates
extreme case formulation of, 33, 109, 165, 181
formulations of, 1, 3, 7, 22, 32, 32, 33, 35, 36, 182
implicating a, 41
natural history of, 2
potential, 13, 37, 39, 40, 45
See also possibilities
reformulation of, 44–45
therapist's version of, 59
professional cautiousness, 45, 50, 56, 57, 84, 85
prosody, 27, 33, 77, 87, 146, 173
smile voice, 27, 80, 86, 87, 90
whisper voice, 90

queries, postpositioned, 58–59

recommendation(s), 40, 46, 51, 56, 57, 60, 61, 62, 72, 75, 80
race
as discursive construction, 96, 102, 121, 123, 138, 147, 166, 167
See also construction
race-class-gender, 9, 175
racial commonsense, 151
race matters, 15, 102, 152, 167
racial formation theory, 15, 102, 147
talking race, 14, 95–122, 147, 166
race relations (interracial relations), 9, 12, 117–118, 120, 121, 152, 153, 163, 165, 171
interracial contact, 14–15, 100, 124–126, 137, 147, 166
racial boundaries, 149–168
racialized events/incidents, 12, 14, 142, 145, 157
racism, 12, 14, 100, 101, 105, 106, 107, 112, 116, 120, 121, 133, 143, 144, 146, 151–153, 171, 178
everyday, 101, 104, 126, 138, 140, 142, 171, 183
individual, 101, 157
institutional, 101, 157
new, 151–152
old-style, 126, 151
symbolic, 151
Racism 101 documentary, 15, 102–103, 104, 109, 110, 114–115, 118, 120, 123, 127, 128, 131–134, 137, 146, 153–156, 161, 167, 168, 179

repetition, 15, 22, 27, 66, 67, 69, 75, 82, 116, 129, 165
reported speech, 14–15, 23, 25, 28, 95–122, 123, 126–128, 132–136, 138, 140–142, 144, 147, 155, 158, 167, 171, 173, 179
  direct speech (quotes), 23, 97–99, 108, 111, 112, 115, 116, 119, 120, 128, 129, 131, 136, 139, 144, 173
  double-voiced quality of, 96, 98
    See also voice
  hypothetical speech (quotes), 74, 144
  indirect speech, 97
  prototypical quotes, 99, 113, 119, 120, 136, 141, 173
  quotes, 96–98, 102, 104, 112, 123, 124, 127, 134
  reported action, 23, 24, 141
  reported exchange (dialogue), 111, 114, 119, 140, 161, 167
  reported thought, 97, 113, 117, 160
  summary reported speech (quotes), 99, 106, 107, 108, 111, 115, 119, 129, 153
    of an aggregate (group), 99, 117–119
    of an individual, 99
resource(s)
  conversational (interactional), 6, 13, 50, 56, 59120, 124, 140, 144, 180
  for humor, 74, 91
  prior speech as, 98
  response as, 59, 69
respect (disrespect), 14–15, 123–147, 170, 179
  Also see narratives, of disrespect
rhetoric, 5–6, 13, 67, 149, 152, 170, 172
  color-blind, 160, 176
  of individuality, 171
  of necessity, 25
  rhetorical aspects, 12, 169
  rhetorical device, 156
segregation, self/voluntary, 15, 100, 115, 117, 122, 149–168, 178
service encounters, 15, 124, 137–145
stake, 5, 6, 169, 170
stereotypes, 100, 104, 109–114, 149–151, 171, 177

talk, 1, 166
  formative function of, 1, 69
  institutional character of, 42
  talk-in-interaction, 8, 20, 170, 177
  therapeutic talk as mystifying, 62
teenage parenthood, 9, 12, 13, 19–42, 170
tellings, 12, 13, 24, 41, 43, 45, 46, 48, 51, 59, 68, 72
  information-eliciting tellings, 46
  retelling, 13, 44, 45, 72, 73, 77, 92, 172, 173, 177
therapist, the, 12–14, 43–70, 170
  as expert, 92
  professional competence of, 53, 68
  third turn of, 59, 69
therapy,12–14, 43–70
  as persuasion, 56, 67–69, 122
transcripts, 10, 103, 104, 185–188
troubles, 3, 44, 46
  troubles-telling sequence, 3

voice
  double-voiced, 96, 171
    Also see reported speech
  of the documentary, 128
  of others, 138, 172
  of self, 138, 158, 172
  of the therapist, 43

White(s), 14, 15, 32, 96, 101–103, 105–111, 113–118, 121, 126, 129, 132–146, 149–156, 160–163, 171, 175
  acting White, 161
  White privilege, 125, 160, 176